KW-329-960

POETICS OF THE MIGRANT

In loving memory of my dear father,
Craig M. Potter
1959–2018.

Thank you for the honour.

POETICS OF THE MIGRANT

Migrant Literature and the Politics of Motion

◆　◆　◆

KEVIN POTTER

EDINBURGH
University Press

Edinburgh University Press is one of the leading university presses in the UK. We publish academic books and journals in our selected subject areas across the humanities and social sciences, combining cutting-edge scholarship with high editorial and production values to produce academic works of lasting importance. For more information visit our website: edinburghuniversitypress.com

© Kevin Potter 2023

First epigraph in Introduction from *Death of a Discipline*, by Gayatri Chakravorty Spivak. Copyright © 2003 Gayatri Chakravorty Spivak. Reprinted with permission of Columbia University Press.

Second epigraph in Introduction from *Migritude*, by Shailja Patel. Copyright 2010, Kaya Press. Reprinted by permission of the publisher.

Epigraph in Chapter 3 from Sandro Mezzadra and Brett Neilson, 'In the Space of Temporal Borders,' in *Border as Method, or, the Multiplication of Labor*, pp. 131–66. Copyright 2013, Duke University Press. All rights reserved. Reprinted by permission of the publisher.www.dukeupress.edu

Edinburgh University Press Ltd
The Tun – Holyrood Road
12(2f) Jackson's Entry
Edinburgh EH8 8PJ

Typeset in 12/15 Adobe Sabon by
IDSUK (DataConnection) Ltd, and
printed and bound in Great Britain

A CIP record for this book is available from the British Library

ISBN 978 1 3995 2499 5 (hardback)
ISBN 978 1 3995 2501 5 (webready PDF)
ISBN 978 1 3995 2502 2 (epub)

The right of Kevin Potter to be identified as the author of this work has been asserted in accordance with the Copyright, Designs and Patents Act 1988, and the Copyright and Related Rights Regulations 2003 (SI No. 2498).

CONTENTS

ACKNOWLEDGEMENTS

Several pieces had to come together in order to make this book a reality, and an entire network of support made it possible. The support begins of course with Professor Sarah Heinz, who took a chance (perhaps even a risk) on my project, and who gave me the only job (so far) that I have held for more than a year. Professor Heinz has also been an exemplar of kind, motivating and committed guidance, and has imparted on me a sense of finding my own voice as an academic. I would also like to extend my deep gratitude to my fellow research team members, Tatiana Konrad and Lukas Klik, who have been not only supportive, but also intellectually-engaged, colleagues. I would like to thank Professor Thomas Nail, whose blessings to adapt and expand his theories when I first began has carried me through these years, and who has also shown me a model for what a kind, supportive and devoted scholar ought to be. Similarly, I am grateful to Professor Alexandra Ganser-Blumenau, who has been an early fan of my research, has demonstrated that it is possible to be a successful academic and a genuinely good person. I am also deeply honoured to have had the comments and feedback from Professor Birgit Kaiser, a scholar who has been so generous with her time, but who has also over the years helped me grow into a proper academic. I would like to thank Professor Sylvia

Mieszkowski for hiring me directly out of my Ph.D and being patient with my adjustment period.

I am deeply indebted to the many other doctoral and early-career researchers I met and encountered, all of whom have been sources of inspiration and solidarity. A special mention goes to Michi Pasterk and Helena Oberzaucher – both of whom are friends I will never forget, and who have helped me many times with settling some of the clutter inside of my brain. I would also like to thank my dear friend and brother, Matthew Leroy, who stuck his neck out for me and has shown me what friendship actually looks like. I would like to thank every single one of my students, past and present, who have given me that strange thing known as a sense of purpose. Finally, I would like to thank my extraordinary therapist, Francesca, without whom I simply would not have managed the many pains these years brought.

INTRODUCTION: TOWARD A MOVEMENT-ORIENTED POETICS

Whatever our view of what we do, we are made by the forces of people moving about the world.
—— Gayatri Chakravorty Spivak, *Death of a Discipline*

Art is a migrant – it travels from the vision of the artist to the eye, ear, mind and heart of the listener.
—— Shailja Patel, *Migritude*

Poetics and Politics

In January 2019, the far-right United Kingdom Independence Party (UKIP), released a pamphlet titled 'What We Stand For'. Divided into four main themes, plus an introduction and conclusion, the document articulates a unifying set of values, placing emphasis upon principles of 'Patriotism, National Democracy, Political Democracy, Economic Democracy, Liberalism and Traditionalism' (1). The most intriguing section of this document – for its political scope, stylistic ingenuity, and appeals to voter resentments – is its conclusion:

UKIP is a patriotic and democratic party that believes in Britain, its people, and its future as a great and positive power in the modern world. We want to keep the best of the past but look forward to using our traditional values to meet the challenges of the future. The first duty of any government is to *protect its people*. This includes not just military defence and policing but also having effective border controls and preventing invasive immigration. Our current political leaders are in gross dereliction of their duty. (4)

The first thing to consider here is the genre it falls under: a political pamphlet. As such, it creates a mobile and portable form of political propaganda. 'What We Stand For' distills UKIP's disturbing nationalistic message into small, digestible pieces that can be passed between hands in a fast-paced material space – presumably on a street-corner, outside of bodegas, or to commuters passing through underground stations. Within this medium, the message develops within an inflexible and limited regime of communication, constructing boundaries of inclusion and exclusion. When the UKIP pamphlet describes a party that 'believes in Britain, its people and its future', we rely upon a narrow discursive scope that the pamphlet creates to impart its meaning. Our attention, thoughts, and feelings are directed to other associated terms and phrases – that is, these phrases are meant to parallel the four 'principles' written in big, bold, purple letters on the front page (see Figure i.1). The pamphlet employs these particular turns of phrase and, from there – following a brief outline of their political programme – readers are meant to detect patterns and a strong ideological coherence. The conclusion paragraph brings their outlined platform to a close, drawing readers to accept the continuity between their ideas. Protect 'Britain' and 'its people', therefore, corresponds to patriotism and democracy; its 'future' corresponds to political democracy and economic democracy; and 'our ... values' corresponds to liberalism and traditionalism. Inducing (dis-)affecting relations of resentment and distrust against the political, elite establishment, the conclusion's last sentence inspires a call to action: abandon those who demonstrate 'gross dereliction in their duty.' As a final sentence, it is immensely powerful. Its terseness and abrupt ending produces unspoken, as-yet-unrealised implications, enabling readers to make our own assumptions going forward and construct our own relation to its meaning. In other words, the space after the sentence encourages readers' visceral reactions and disaffections to intensify in many directions. We are left to drift into an intensive space of meaning, searching for the source of alienation and the cause of social instability. In a crowded metro carriage or in the heavy foot traffic of a city sidewalk, we hold this pamphlet in our hand and develop a new orientation to the social assemblage. Combining material conditions of social and economic instability and uncertainty with anti-immigrant rhetoric and propaganda in the news media, UKIP's message acts as another vector within this constellation, changing and reconstructing our sensible and intensive horizon that forms what is thinkable and what is visible.

Another way of framing this analysis would be to say that this pamphlet enacts a poetics. Through its strategic use of linguistic patterns and discursive cues, the UKIP pamphlet reflects (or, imitates, in the sense of *mimesis*) the party's own political regime, while also strategically relegating or effacing references which might de-stabilise their political message. Understood in terms of its Greek origin, *poiesis*, meaning 'to make', the poetics of the UKIP pamphlet constructs their imagined political message into one coherent system of meaning, and, in turn, reconstructs our own cultural language, affections, and knowledge. 'Poetics', says Richard Kearny, 'is about hearing and feeling as well as crafting and shaping' (2014:xix); and as a text, the UKIP pamphlet produces, as Gilles Deleuze puts it, 'new ways of seeing and hearing' and 'new ways of feeling' ([1990]1995:165).

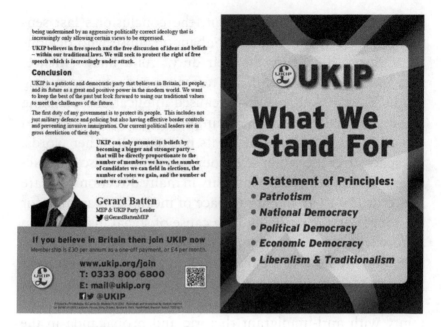

Figure i.1 UKIP 2019, 'What We Stand For'.
(Falls under parameters of Fair Dealing.)

The document constructs a regime of meaning, defining boundaries of what is thinkable and unthinkable, what is visible and invisible.

An interesting dimension within the system of meaning is the pamphlet's brief reference to 'invasive immigration.' Throughout the entire pamphlet, this is the only occasion in which immigration is mentioned at all, and its only association is alongside the qualifier 'invasive'. The reference to immigration in this manner has an important value for UKIP's overall political strategy. After all, the term 'invasive' conjures up associations with disease, violence, and war, further stoking voters' fears and justifying the ongoing effort to demonise immigrants. We can juxtapose this allusion alongside their easy-to-remember slogan, 'For the Nation', and recognise how this poetics bolsters the overarching theme of UKIP's platform: the idealisation of 'restoring' (so-called) political sovereignty.[1] Anthony Giddens describes the inter-connection between maintaining cultural homogenisation, on the one hand, and the glorification of political sovereignty, on the other:

> Nationalism is the cultural sensibility of sovereignty, the concomitant coordination of administrative power within the bounded nation-state. With the coming of the nation-state, states have an administrative and territorially ordered unity which they did not possess before. This unity cannot remain *purely* administrative however, because the very co-ordination of activities involved presumes elements of cultural homogeneity. (1985:219)

In analysing the political primacy and centrality of the nation-state, Nikos Papastergiadis argues that the project of building nation-states cannot be understood outside of the context of managed, regulated, and securitised human movement: 'Among the central aims of the project of nation-building was the unification of . . . diverse peoples under a common identity, and the regulation of movement across borders' (1999:2). However, Papastergiadis continues, 'the complex patterns of movement across national boundaries . . . have destabilised the foundations of the nation-state' (ibid.:2). This system of nation-building relies on coincid-ing and overlapping forces: 'diverse peoples' are unified 'under a common identity', creating a dominant ethnic iden-tity that maintains a veneer of diversity acceptable to the state's ruling power; but any movement or demographic change beyond these ideologically-constructed boundaries are seen as destabilising. This suggests, then, that 'diversity' is something controlled and managed, rather than one that can be reshaped by external forces. In other words, what counts as 'diverse' and what constitutes something 'desta-bilising' depends on the ideology and the constraints set by the capitalist hegemony (see also, Žižek 1997:46–47). This manner of conceiving sovereignty and the preservation of the nation-state, then, is consistent with the nationalistic ideologies that UKIP espouses – it operates as a necessary extension of the presumed centrality and primacy granted to national identity and borders. The hostility, furthermore, toward immigrants – represented as 'invasive' people – is a logical step from the legitimacy and authority UKIP cedes to The Nation. For, as a result of this place-based paradigm, a number of assumptions about migration emerge: (a) That movement and migration are marginal, secondary, and subordinate conditions relative to the primary status of borders and nation-states; (b) political representation is strictly permitted for people who are within pre-established legal, juridical and economic boundaries; and, (c) the migrant has a secondary, subaltern political status, and is thereby unrepresented by regimes of power.

Years after the release of this pamphlet, the consequences of such a paradigm have reached sinister proportions in the era of the COVID-19 pandemic. Nationalist parties and policy-makers around the globe weaponised their aggressive scare-mongering to agitate for stronger immigration enforcement and border controls. After all, politicians were able to score easy political points by blaming China for the Coronavirus outbreak, suggesting a subversive influence that that country might have over the rest of the world if immigration were allowed to continue. The political rhetoric has made it even clearer the extent to which immigration is identified with contagion, sickness, and instability. For example, Marian Kotleba, the leader of the Kotlebists – the People's Party Our Slovakia (well-established as a neo-Nazi party) – argued that, thanks to flexible immigration policies, 'Europe is full of illegal aliens of whose health conditions we don't know anything about' (qtd in Wondreys and Mudde 2022:88). In a similar vein, Ortega Smith, general secretary of Spain's

VOX wrote on Twitter that, after contracting COVID-19, his 'Spanish antibodies fight against the damn chinese virus' (ibid.). In broader terms, the pandemic has enabled far-right politicians to confirm their vociferous hostility toward migration and adherence to nationalism. Nigel Farage who, incidentally, previously headed UKIP, famously noted that 'we are all nationalists now' (qtd in Bieber 2022:13), and Laiura Huhtasaari from the right-wing Finns Party has suggested that 'the need for borders is being vindicated by the pandemic' (ibid.:19). In each of these statements, national identity, borders, and sovereignty are metaphorically tied to the body fighting off a foreign agent – an invasive entity that threatens to destabilise the body's autonomy and integrity. This discourse reflects what I might call a poetics of contagion, resonating with the paranoid poetics found in the UKIP pamphlet. The fact that COVID-19 has had such a devastating economic and social impact since its outbreak at the end of 2019 and the beginning of 2020 confirms the fascistic fears about a nation's retreat from traditional values.[2] According to those who idealise such a thing, the nation is a cultural body that has lost its vitality and strength thanks to a foreign invasion. By re-inscribing 'contagion' as both a figurative and biological force, chauvinism has now a new system of meaning that is articulated to the everyday experiences of living in a pandemic. These racist dogwhistles, therefore, have rich terrain upon which to appeal to and generate anxiety and panic.

The long-standing history of tying immigration to disease has been well-documented (Bieber 2022:19), and the moral panic surrounding sovereignty, borders, and isolation has only intensified in this current crisis. Far-right politicians therefore mobilise outrage against COVID policies and border controls; and through such a poetics, the 'invasive' nature of immigration is made more visible and thinkable. Moreover, the underlying ideologies of sovereignty and nationalism continue to provide discursive and affective support. The compatibility between this poetics of contagion and the poetics of sovereignty is such that the same metaphysical assumptions uphold both systems of meaning. That is, they both adhere to assumptions about stability and sovereignty that have long provided political and ideological backing for opposing immigration. I will devote the next section to touching briefly on this metaphysics.

Stepping Beyond the Poetics of Sovereignty

This tendency toward idealising sovereignty and nation-hood derives from a much deeper conceptual paradigm – what has been called a 'sedentarist metaphysics' (Malkki 1992:32; Cresswell 2006:26). Sedentarist metaphysics, says Tim Cresswell, invites a 'tendency to think of mobile people in ways that assume the moral and logical primacy of fixity in space and place' (ibid.:32). This paradigm though can be traced all the way back to Georg W. F. Hegel who, in his *Introduction to the Philosophy of History*, writes that '[i]n world history we are concerned only with those peoples that have formed states [because] all the value that human beings possess, all of their spiritual reality, they have through the State alone' ([1837]1988:41–2). This view of history has cast a long shadow over the ensuing centuries that followed Hegel, and has informed a large part of the discourses that privilege the primacy of fixity and place. To dramatise one example, Dimitris Papadopoulos and Vassilis Tsianos point out that 'the UNHCR [United Nations High Commissioner for Refugees] convention for asylum seekers protects the rights of refugees on arrival, but not when they are on the road' (2007:227). This example helps illustrate the legal and structural problems with a sedentarist metaphysics: namely, that the capacity to advocate for refugees requires having them settled in a fixed, circumscribable place.

To overcome the assumptions of this place-based paradigm, I will turn to, revise, and build upon a counter-history
of political and social formation – a perspective that recognises not only the ubiquity of movement, but its centrality
and primacy throughout social history: what Thomas Nail
calls (2015) 'kinopolitics', or a 'politics of movement' (from
the Greek *kinesis,* meaning 'to move'). This concept suggests
that 'regimes of social motion' (Nail 2015:4) have historically created the juridical, economic, and material conditions
for social and political formation (rather than the other way
around). The migrant here is, then, affirmed as the primary
constitutive figure of social history. The consequences of this
counter-history cannot be overstated: rather than the typical analyses which treat the migrant as a subject consigned
to the margins of history, relegated to a secondary political
status, kinopolitics reanalyses the migrant figure in terms of
their socio-historic primacy and active political power.

Because of the continuous expansion of globalised economic and industrial control, shifts in geopolitical borders and immigration policies, and the forced expulsion of
people due to deportation, colonisation, climate change,
land-grabbing, disenfranchisement, war, or violence, movement is thus understood as immanent to modernity and
social history. Rather than relying on a static, place-based
paradigm of territories and boundaries, kinopolitics produces a counter-history of movement and a counter-history
of the migrant. As the subject or figure of movement, the
migrant is the figure, according to Nail, who creates (and
is created by) diverse forms of expulsion and movement –
mechanisms which have governed the emergence of national
and social space (2015:24). As a result, this perspective
not only centres the migrant; it affirms the migrant as the
politically active, trans-historical force for political formation and social change. Viewed through this lens, therefore,
we unsettle and de-stabilise the presumed centrality granted

to nation-states and national purity, and rather envision a counter-history that recognises movement and migration as not only integral to, but constitutive of, social formation.

Kinopolitics offers a unique, affirmative counter-discourse and counter-history to the above-analysed place-based paradigm. Yet, this leads us back to the UKIP pamphlet from above, and particularly the *poetics* that it enacts. As stated previously, the party pamphlet's affective, epistemological and stylistic regime of meaning is unified within not only their ideology, but also broadly speaking within the discourse of political sovereignty. A renewed poetics, therefore, can also act as a discursive counterweight to the pervading ideologies of sovereignty, settlement and stasis – what I shall call a kinopoetics. Kinopoetics supplies an added layer to kinopolitics. While kinopolitics instantiates a counter-history of the migrant, a counter-poetics can similarly produce a regime of meaning that (re-)shapes and (re-)constitutes what is thinkable and visible.[3] Through the already well-established genre of migrant literature, one could start to recognise how these texts make (*poiesis*) migrancy and motion visible and thinkable. This view of 'poetics' is consistent, for example, with Jacques Rancière's idea of a 'distribution of the sensible' (2004:95), in which aesthetics and art produce 'modalities of what is visible and audible as well as what can be said, thought, made, or done' (ibid.:85). One can also connect this with Michel Foucault's conception of discourse – a system of communication invested with and reinforced through networks and regimes of productive power. Kinopoetics, in this sense, operates as both an object of study – the patterns of intensive movement produced in and from migrant literatures – and a methodology, extending politics into a *poetics* to reveal how these two modes of meaning mutually reinforce each other. In other words, kinopoetics operates in two ways. First, instead of categorising the migrant as merely a subject governed by forces of marginality, disenfranchisement and otherness (as we find more commonly in other analyses),[4] kin-opoetics reconsiders the migrant as a subject with their own affirmative, transformational potential. In this sense, migrant literatures can be seen as providing an index of movement, deterritorialisation, creative becoming, and pedetic force. Second, kinopoetics insists on what the migrant literary text does; that is, migrant literatures produce affective, relational and epistemological flows of intensive movement. From here, I will rely on a philosophical tradition associated with Gilles Deleuze and Félix Guattari, inheriting from them, first, a metaphysics of process and multiplicity; second, an emphasis on the politically-constitutive role of affect, intensity and relation; and, third, an ethics of joy and affirmation. The way that Deleuze and Guattari emphasise forms of becoming that exceed the bounds of representation offers a useful theoretical intervention for a poetics based on and in flows of movement.[5] By way of linguistic, affective and epistemological reorderings, migrant literatures are themselves regimes of motion – non-human entities that induce sensible and affective movements. Kinopoetics is then not just an analysis of how kinopolitics is shown or reflected in migrant literatures; it is also a critical appraisal of movement that literature itself enacts and makes. In other words, kinopoetics is not simply about movement; it makes movement, affectively and intensively. As affects and intensities move, so too do imaginative and epistemic capacities. In the pages that follow, my goal is to firmly establish kinopoetics, showing how it can best be used to open up possible readings of migrant literatures and, specifically, different forms of migrant literature.

The Migrant Turn in the late Twentieth Century

A tradition dating back several decades, migrant literature reflects upon the subjective and personal experience of moving from nation to nation, of being an outsider, and of operating in a language other than one's own. '[S]ince, roughly, the late 1980s,' writes Sten Pultz Moslund, 'we could speak of a "migrant turn" occurring shortly after the establishment of postcolonialism as an academic area of study' (2010:9). The study of anti-colonial literature and 'emerging national literatures of former colonies,' Moslund continues, 'gave way to the celebration of migration, bordercrossing and hybridity as central to the explanation of postcolonial experience' (ibid.). This was an era, therefore, of reshuffling and redrawing national, linguistic, ethnic, and cultural borders and boundaries, with the resulting impact of influencing and accelerating the movement of people around the world. The resulting literary impact was a canon of literatures meant to reflect upon this era of migratory movement. As Salman Rushdie (1992) puts it, '[m]igrants must, of necessity, make a new imaginative relationship with the world, because of the loss of familiar habitats' (125).

In the Anglophone context, migrant and diasporic authors emerge quite prominently throughout the second half of the twentieth century. In narrative prose, authors like Jean Rhys, George Lemming, Sam Selvon, V. S. Naipaul, Rushdie, Jamaica Kincaid, Edwidge Dandicat, Eva Hoffman, Dinaw Mengestu, Viet Thanh Nguyen, and Chimamanda Ngozi Adichie detail the experiences of migrant alienation and disempowerment, often (but not always) resulting from colonial and neo-colonial expulsion. Similarly, in the migrant poetry genre, authors like Derek Walcott, Kamau Brathwaite, Louise Bennett, Linton Kwesi Johnson, Claude McKay, David Dabydeen, M. NourbeSe Philip, as well as (more recently) Shailja Patel and D. S. Marriott use linguistic and formal techniques to dramatise the migrant experience. By playing with the syntactic and grammatical structure of language, migrant poets often make clever use of linguistic intermixing in order to demonstrate the instability of language and the hybridisation that occurs in transnational encounters (see Ramazani 2015). This canon of migrant literatures constructs a meaningful index of cultural hybridity and ambivalence, displacement, disenfranchisement, expulsion, and exclusion. Reread within the framework of kinopolitics, however, a kinopoetic interpretation enables me to reconsider migrant texts in a manner that emphasises the primacy of movement and the political centrality of the migrant. This critical perspective departs from previous analyses of migrant literatures and culture, whereby migrant, colonial, and diasporic identity are relegated to the subaltern, subordinated, or marginal space of incomprehensible difference (derived largely from a Hegelian-Marxist dialectic). As Stuart Hall puts it, in a posthumously published volume, '[t]he unequal relations of power, wealth and authority separated the colonised from the British. But colonizers and colonised were locked in struggle with each other in a re-enactment of Hegel's master/slave dialectic' (2017:177).[6] Kinopoetics, by contrast, repositions the figure of the migrant in the primary subject-position, and their difference here is understood as, and conceptualised through, an affirmative ontology of motion. Furthermore, instead of relying on a matrix of linguistic discourse and representation, kinopoetics makes use of movement-oriented language, activating *intensive movements* that disrupt affective and epistemological stabilities. The move from politics to poetics insists here on the capacity for literature to produce 'percepts' (Deleuze and Guattari 1994:175) that 'shock' (Massumi 2015:53) the regime of meaning into transformation; in other words, kinopoetics affirms movement as both extensive (in time and space) and intensive (change of internal, affective conditions), enabling the capacity to cross a sensible threshold, occupying a new relational and epistemological assemblage. This perspective relies on the supposition that literary texts are not disembodied or disconnected from the affective lives of readers;

rather the poetics of migrant literatures introduces alternative, destabilising registers that tear open our everyday
assumptions, ideally making the regime of kinopolitics
visible and recognisable (Rancière 2004:95).[7] The affects
generated from literary aesthetics reshape, challenge, and
undo our political opinions and sensibilities; and, the kinopoetics of migrant literature changes what is thinkable and
visible in the regime of migrancy and mobility.[8] This perspective involves, in the spirit of Arjun Appadurai, a theory
of rupture that takes politics and poetics as 'its two major,
and interconnected, diacritics', exploring their 'joint effect
on the work of the imagination as a constitutive feature of
modern subjectivity' (1997:3).

Kinopoetics (like kinopolitics) is multidirectional and
non-unitary. Kinopoetics is not a general theory of migrant literature, nor is it entirely meant to describe the compositional
principles of migrant texts. Rather, kinopoetics emphasises the
epistemological and affective forces embodied by and carried
out in different migrant literatures, and teases out the profound interconnection between cultural politics, movement,
and thought more generally. It opens up possible readings and
rereadings of migrant texts that can challenge the discursive
and ideological paradigms that undergird nationalism, xeno-
phobia, and racism. Throughout the *Poetics of the Migrant*, I
will outline the various directions and shapes kinopoetics can
take, while also developing its larger theoretical and political
implications. First, I shall detail the specific object of study for
this analysis: migrant literatures.

Migrant Literatures vs. Literatures of Migration

The invocation of migrant literatures here calls up a series of
adjacent genres: diasporic literatures and transnational literatures. While each of these genres often depict migrations
and detail the lives of different (im)migrants as such, I am

keen to strictly operate within the parameters of migrant literature as its own self-contained literary tradition. For, what
kinopoetics is attempting to enliven is the centrality of the
migrant as an affirmative and constitutive figure. As I will
show, some adjacent genres have a broad focus that I see as
being insufficient for a kinopoetics.

Diasporic literatures, for example, are literatures that
generally examine one trajectory of migration; that is, its
focus relies on a specified origin and specified destination of
a people (as a collective or as a family), thereby detailing a
conscious ethnic identity, heritage, or experience. 'Diasporic
narratives', argues Azade Seyhan, 'transmit a linguistic and
cultural heritage that is articulated through acts of personal
and collective memory' (2001:12). While diasporic literatures are unique in their depiction of collective experiences,
tensions, and traumas existing within diasporic enclaves,
particularly as they are connected through shared roots/
routes and histories, diasporic literature's distinct focus on
one shared cross-national trajectory would limit the scope
of kinopoetics. Similarly, so-called *transnational literatures* do not necessarily involve physical movement across
national and political boundaries, and are therefore not a
key focus for kinopoetics. Transnational texts are characterised as simply depicting instances of cross-cultural and
cross-linguistic exchange, often (but not always) within a
metropolitan, multi-cultural space. Again, while there are
overlaps between transnational literatures and migrant literatures – both depicting hybridised cultural contact, the
borrowing of cultural codes and customs, and the social
and political consequences of mobility and globalisation –
transnational literatures as such do not necessarily place
migrancy as a focal point.

Finally, I would like to suggest broadly that naming the
genre migrant literature, as opposed to migration literature or
literatures of migration, is a deliberate choice for the reasons

specified above – namely that the focus ought to rest upon the migrant as such. The speed, manner, direction, and intensity with which the migrant moves across boundaries, and the varying sites and junctions in which he or she arrives, provide the distinct forms of subjectivity and affects that kinopoetics is meant to highlight. These thematic features are often considered in migration literatures as well. As Søren Frank states explicitly, migration literature 'refers to all literary works that are written in an age of migration – or at least to those works that can be said to reflect upon migration' (2008:2). In terms of their thematic focus, migration literature also entails emphasising how 'characters cope with migration' and challenging 'questions of nation and nationalism' (ibid.:18). From these features alone, there is considerable thematic overlap between migration literature and migrant literatures, as I conceive of them.

Yet, significantly, 'migration literature' includes a much wider scope of concern. These texts move beyond one specific migrant figure, reflecting on related social problems: for example, the intergenerational effects that develop from a family's history of migration, without necessarily showing how immigration is experienced in the present, from the migrant's subjective point of view. In Zadie Smith's *White Teeth* (2001), for example, the narrative reflects upon the previous generation's movement, but does not actually describe the experience of migration solely from the migrant's standpoint. Migrant literature, thus, as my focus, has to do primarily with focalising the migrant *as such*, allowing their hybridised subjectivity and singular struggles guide the narrative; we are brought into a personal account (what Gérard Genette calls 'internal focalization' [1988:65]) of their (im)migrant experience. Dohra Ahmad, in her introduction for the 2019 anthology, *The Penguin Book of Migration Literature*, makes this distinction in spite of the book's actual title: 'It is the very complexity of the migrant experience that leads me to consider this an anthology of *migrant literature* rather than immigrant literature' (xv), as it is more 'holistic' (xvi). As a result, the texts reflect upon the power dynamics entailed in the process of settling in an arrival country and the formation of migrant subjectivity. In other words, the term 'migrant literature' asserts, again, the centrality of the migrant, whereby their thoughts, movements, perceptions, and words actively shape the complex political and social assemblage that they enter into. Much like with diasporic and transnational literatures, migration literature maintains features and dynamics useful for kinopoetics. However, with a consideration on the migrant's movement extending across national and geographical space, the migrant's actual physical movement, or their interior experiences of alienation, are the specific aspects most useful for kinopoetics. This focalisation affirms the migrant subject, just in the way that they are considered within the realm of kinopolitics.

The focalisation discussed here (and which I will detail more in the concluding section of Chapter 1) provides a dimension of my text selection criteria. The texts I have selected for analysis nearly all share the quality of internal focalisation – that is, that we gain access to the story through a character or protagonist's point of view. As a result of this I have narrowed my selection of texts to those which rely on this formal technique, producing that quality whereby the migrant really creates the spatial and intensive structure through which they pass. The only exception to this device arrives in Chapter 5 with Linton Kwesi Johnsons's poem, 'New Cross Massakah'. As I will show in that chapter, the innovative feature of that poem is the speaker's capacity to invent a space in which he is not a participant, and to use his passage in and out to identify with the victims of a horrific crime. The effect here is such that the poem moves readers through an imagined circumstance and creates the possibilities for what can be apprehended.

The other dimension of my selection criteria is sub-genres within migrant literature. To properly deploy kinopoetics, I have engaged a range of texts that differ in several thematic, formal, cultural, and linguistic ways. Yet, in each case, established sub-genres within migrant literature help provide settings and circumstances that map more directly onto different migrant subjectivities and figures I examine (I will say more about these sub-genres in the next section). Kinopoetics is not meant to give a comprehensive or general theory for all migrant literature. Rather I examine types of migrant literature which lend themselves to – or make possible – different forms of movement and migrancy. The texts I chose within these sub-genres simply act as test cases for this analysis to start with, but that could otherwise go in many directions.

Taking, therefore, sub-genres within migrant literature as my main object of study, I will now give a brief summary outline of the chapters that will follow, describing how this book is organised and the themes I plan to address.

Chapter Outline

To better conceptualise kinopoetics and what it entails, *Poetics of the Migrant* begins with the theoretical traditions that this concept inherits and builds upon. The first half of the book is divided into two chapters: in the first, I touch on the theoretical constellations that converge in and constitute kinopoetics; in the second, I summarise earlier traditions that have engaged migration and literature. The latter is where I expand and, sometimes, critique the theoretical scope. Developing an outline of critical traditions, including not only those which kinopoetics deploys, but also those from which this book departs, Part I provides a systematic and useful guide to enter into the rest of the book. Chapter 1 is, therefore, a thorough and extensive theoretical outline. It focuses, specifically, on the concepts upon which I rely the most: poetics, kinopolitics, and affect and sensation. Starting with the complicated and multi-layered concept of 'poetics,' I trace this concept to its very beginnings all the way back to Aristotle's *Poetics*. As I proceed, however, this section gives a diachronic overview of this concept and, particularly, the several shapes it has taken in more recent years. I argue that 'poetics' must to be understood as operating on two levels: first, as the formal compositional principles for creating a coherent literary text; and, second, as Linda Hutcheon puts it, 'an open, ever-changing theoretical structure by which to order both our cultural knowledge and our critical procedures' (1988:16). I show that these two dimensions of the term are inseparable from one another; and that they demonstrate a distinct continuity between literary poetics and 'cultural poetics' (Greenblatt 1997:471) as well as how methodology and theory reinforce each other. Showing how poetics came to have different meanings in the present nevertheless enables one to see that kinopoetics fits easily within this long history and legacy.

The political upshot, though, arrives with kinopolitics, the political counter-history of movement from which I inherit kinopoetics. The third section of Chapter 1 summarises extensively what kinopolitics is and how it provides an important paradigm for this book, while also emphasising the particular aspects that concern the move from politics to poetics.

To complement the theory of poetics, especially its epistemological dimensions, I turn to affect and sensation. Through this tradition, I stress the continuous relationship between affect, sensation, the body, and meaning, describing the intensive movement between states that changes knowledge and sense as they are connected to our relational (for example, spatial, linguistic and temporal-cultural) subjectivity. This section is crucial, as it presents the theoretical linchpin of this project, bringing politics into contact with

poetics, affect and movement (both extensive and intensive) –
all of which culminate in kinopoetics. Kinopoetics, as I
conceive of it, adds a layer to kinopolitics that enables this
counter-history of movement to be made legible. I then conclude Chapter 1, attempting to establish kinopoetics as its
own movement-oriented poetics, allowing me to describe
in detail how this concept can be used and shaped going
forward.

   Chapter 2 begins to engage the broad traditions of migrant
literature, Postcolonial Studies, and state-based metaphysics
that have, up to now, dominated the field of migrant literary studies. I begin by pursuing a thoroughgoing outline of
the ideological and discursive underpinnings of citizenship,
statehood, and sovereignty, addressing what I have already
referred to as a 'sedentarist metaphysics' (Malkki 1992:32;
Cresswell 2006:26). In turn, this section illuminates the dominant, state-based paradigm that informs the legal and political regime of migration-management. It is this paradigm, I
argue, with which theories of migration and kinopolitics are
in dialogue. Immediately following this opening section, I then
outline what I deem a poetics of migration, introducing some
ways in which poets and critics have attempted to challenge
the centrality of states and citizenship. In this section, I rely on
the more conventional discussion of poetics (in other words,
a concern for form in poetry), describing different types of
poetics that occur throughout the development of migrant
poetry. While this review is by no means comprehensive, it
will enable me to underscore the diversity within the migrant
literature tradition. This typology includes transnational poetics, poetics of relation, minor literature, and poetics of migritude. Each of these types of poetics will be accompanied by
examples of well-established, canonised texts in the literary
tradition. I also show the manner in which these poetic types
overlap, but also how migrant authors uniquely and strategically utilise these formal preoccupations to carry out or reflect

the particularities of (im)migrant experience. After engaging and expanding this tradition – one from which I derive considerable inspiration – I undertake an excursus into Postcolonial Theory, considering some famous concepts and theorists in Postcolonial Studies, showing how the major upshot of Postcolonial Theory is its ongoing challenge to sedentarism. I also suggest how kinopoetics adopts, but also modifies and exceeds, the theoretical constellations of Postcolonial Studies. The following sub-section re-evaluates the major thinkers[9] and concepts within Postcolonial Theory, recuperating and modifying them through the philosophy of movement. The overall aim of Chapter 2, therefore, is an attempt to give a fair hearing to previous theories and concepts I have worked with during the process of my research. While I do not rely as heavily on these fields, readers will notice an appreciation and admiration for this scholarship, and the manner in which a philosophy and politics of movement simply updates and enhances their theoretical work. Building on, yet moving perceivably beyond them, I elucidate the innovative quality of kinopoetics, showing how it pushes this field of migrant studies into new domains. Combining the two chapters that comprise Part I, this first half of *Poetics of the Migrant* helps readers gain a solid theoretical footing to enter into Part II.

The chapters that comprise Part II (Chapters 3 to 5) are where I participate in and enact kinopoetics, setting up therein a typology: 'destructive kinopoetics', 'wandering kinopoetics', and 'stuttering kinopoetics', all of which are articulated to sub-genres within the migrant literature tradition. In addition, and as I demonstrate, these types correspond to different migrant configurations upon which I will focus: the nomad, the vagabond, and the barbarian. Chapter 3 is the first close reading chapter in which I introduce the first type of kinopoetics – what I call a 'destructive kinopoetics', coinciding with the migrant figure of the nomad. This kinopoetics relates to the genre of Magic Realism, wherein authors destroy the experience of time and space, and displace the centrality of a unified, place-based social milieu to make way for a divergent, mobile, and decentered world. The resulting idea is to show a world that transcends the bounded limitations of the nation-state, and places a primacy or privilege on the convergence of two worlds into one field of vision – what Salman Rushdie calls a 'stereoscopic vision'. Here, the nomad's experience of the world that is otherwise contradictory or paradoxical is given credence in the text, showing us how the migrant often has to negotiate between two versions of reality. As Wendy Faris argues, Magic Realism 'provides a fictional ground in which to imagine alternative narrative visions of agency and history' (2004:136); and this is often done by empowering migrant subjects to liberate themselves from the constraints of time and space. Mohsin Hamid's *Exit West* (2017) and Chitra Banerjee Divakruni's *The Mistress of Spices* (1997) offer helpful test cases for this discussion.

Chapter 4 outlines what I call a 'wandering kinopoetics'. A wandering kinopoetics considers the historical figure of the vagabond and their position in certain postcolonial and migrant literatures. Crucially, the emphasis here is on narrative representations of urban spaces, thereby offering a unique, conflicting spatial experience: on the one hand, the migrant figure attempts to blend into a social milieu by not sticking out as an outsider; on the other, their outsider status leaves them criminalised and alienated to the very society into which they are trying to assimilate. This specific narrative setting has had a long history going back to the Victorian era. This section explores the movement of the vagabond who, as Zygmunt Bauman puts it, 'was the bane of early modernity, the bugbear that spurred the rulers and the philosophers into an ordering and legislating frenzy' (1996:28). The vagabond offers a distinct configuration of criminalised migrancy, as the wandering subject having to negotiate various sites of power, all while embodying a 'wayward' and 'erratic' subjectivity. The criminalisation, though, is not something crystallising in overt and coherent ways; it is not, in other words, shown in the explicit juridical and institutional realm of police arrest and criminal prosecution. Rather, this analysis assumes the becoming-vagabond moments developing with the imperceptible sensations of daily life, creating what we might call a 'micro-politics of suspicion' – noting for example the everyday paranoias, dismissals, surveillance patterns, and suspicions one encounters (often non-verbally) when existing as an immigrant. These are the sensations the migrant passes through but which also 'transpierce the body like arrows' (Deleuze and Guattari [1987]2014:415) – that confine and criminalise the migrant, making them pliable and obedient to a system of social discipline. Such a subject-position allows me to comment on the affective and internal experiences that come with moving and wandering through politicised spaces of modernity; yet, I valourise and affirm these erratic and wayward capacities as transformational, deterritorialising, and positive. Here Monica Ali's *Brick Lane* (2003) and Teju Cole's *Open City* (2012) provide the textual focus for this chapter.

Chapter 5 constitutes the third and final close reading chapter; and this time the focus lies specifically with non-standard uses of language, demonstrating what I consider a 'stuttering kinopoetics'. This section adopts Gilles Deleuze's insistence that '[c]reative stuttering is what makes language grow from the middle, like grass; it is . . . what puts language in perpetual disequilibrium' ([1993]1998:111). For Deleuze, this creative use of language 'make[s] language take flight' such that it 'bifurcates and varies, . . . following an incessant modulation' (ibid.:109). The implications here are significant in terms of migration and cross-cultural encounters within language. In particular, the barbarian – a figure conceived according to presumed political and linguistic inferiority – acts as the counter-historical migrant figure within this constellation. Authors within the migrant tradition will often employ playful, non-standard uses of English to demonstrate cultural difference, on the one hand, and challenge the ideologies of language and power, on the other. This, in turn, upsets and frustrates the typical reading experience, since it has to cope with changing rhythmic, grammatical, and syntactic structures. Putting language into 'disequilibrium' creates vibrations and shifts linguistic orderings, thereby breaking open the typical ordering of English grammatical structure, and moving our perception into a new epistemic and sensible regime. To support this kinopoetics, I examine the poetry of John Asgard and Linton Kwesi Johnson, and the manner in which they 'invent a minor use' (ibid.) of language in their poetry, but also produce new affective movements through experimentation.

The two parts of *Poetics of the Migrant* – differing in focus and analytical structure – solidify more thoroughly the complexities that I envision for kinopoetics, thereby leading me to the Conclusion chapter. From this point, I return to summarising the main points touched upon throughout this book. I offer some final words about the interconnection between literature and cultural politics, particularly through the realm of market systems and commodification. To do so, I invoke the laws of motion and value analysed within the Marxist tradition, to suggest that a migrant text is subject to patterns of valourisation, intensive and extensive movement, acting as an agential, kinetic cultural object. Rita Felski's notion of a 'post-critical reading' will further add to this, suggesting that there is an additional dimension of understanding the life of the text as something that acts upon our cultural sensibilities. As we enter this paradigm, though, we should always bear in mind, on the one hand, forces of movement and, on the other hand, of commodification (including how they interact).

I argue here that reading kinopoetically affirms the migrant literary text as a means of 'fashioning a sensibility, redirecting one's affections', thereby 're-contextualiz[ing] what we know' and reorienting our perceptions (Felski 2015:178–82). The life of the text, as it is disseminated throughout different contexts of material life, enables it to change, shape, and reorient our cultural knowledge and the varying regimes of inclusion and exclusion that exist within political life – doing precisely what a poetics ought to do.[10]

Notes

1. This is also stated explicitly on the UKIP Manifesto, under the category 'Brexit'.
2. Such a need to uphold and preserve traditional values has created a wedge-issue in many countries regarding lockdown rules and vaccination mandates. It is no accident, in my mind, that the parties who brand themselves on preserving such traditions have been most vocal opponents of lockdown policies (Skopeliti 2020).
3. A more detailed explanation of 'poetics' will be touched upon in the next chapter. (Chapter 1, sections headed Poetics: A Diachronic Study and Defining Poetics.)
4. See Chapter 2, sections headed Poetics of Migration: A Typology and Postcolonial Theory: Identity, Representation, and the 'Holy Trinity'.
5. More on this in Chapter 1, section headed Affect, Sensation, and Intensive Movement.
6. A more detailed outline of this Hegelian-Marxist tradition will be carried out in Chapter 2, section headed Sedentarism and Sovereignty: The Master Texts Behind the Nation.
7. As Deleuze and Guattari note in *What is Philosophy?*: 'It should be said of all art that, in relation to the percepts or visions they give us, artists are presenters of affects, the inventors and creators of affects. They not only create them in their work, they give them to us and make us become with them, they draw us into the compound' (175). Deleuze clarifies this

point in *Negotiations*, suggesting that 'percepts' are 'new ways of seeing and hearing', while 'affects' are 'new ways of feeling' (165).

8. I must be careful not to universalise about readers and their susceptibility to changing their perceptions. The disposition and social and material condition of the reader will have an important role to play in this regard. Nevertheless, affects are already usefully regarded as a means of generating shaping interests and activating relations among a people; and far-right demagogues rely on this capacity. In this way, I consider migrant literature to be a counter-force, a bulwark against disaffecting forces.

9. The so-called 'Holy Trinity' (Huddart 2011:60; Chrisman 2021:30) of Postcolonial Theory: Edward Said, Gayatri Spivak, and Homi Bhabha.

10. Parts of the chapter are adapted and modified from my article, 'Centrifugal Force and the Mouth of a Shark: Toward a Movement-Oriented Poetics', *ARIEL: A Review of International English Literature*, Vol. 50, no. 4 (October 2019): Pp. 51–77.

PART I

PART 1

CHAPTER 1

HOW KINOPOETICS WORKS

The concept of kinopoetics calls upon and ties together a range of theoretical constellations. The three I rely on most heavily are: poetics, kinopolitics and affect-sensation. In this section, I will give an overview and summary of these concepts, and the ways in which they supply useful analytical tools for kinopoetics. In particular, I will clarify how I will use these concepts throughout this book, sometimes in unconventional ways. Combined these concepts produce the internal theoretical system that kinopoetics enacts. Using poetics (*poiesis* – 'to make'), kinopolitics, and affect, kinopoetics truly makes the movement that its name suggests. As I will show below, both extensive and intensive movement converge into developing the concept, and poetics offers the dimension that creates a method and object of study for literary analysis.

As this chapter concludes, readers will see how these theories supply meaningful tools, not only theoretical, but lexical and discursive. This will also set up readers to discern how this project diverges from the traditions covered in Chapter 2, but also what kinds of concepts they can come to expect in Part II.

Poetics: A Diachronic Study

Invoking poetics in the concept kinopoetics opens up a series of concerns, questions, and discourses, all of which should be carefully addressed. Especially given its long history, going all the way back to Aristotle, and its meandering pathway through twentieth century literary theory, poetics is a term that is both theoretically fraught and unstable, but yet tends to be one that critics unreservedly lean upon. Although it may seem a quaint gesture to rescue the work of the literary (white, male) forefathers, I will begin conceptualising poetics by returning to Aristotle, in an attempt to excavate relevant features of *Poetics* that prove useful for our present time and for kinopoetics. For Aristotle, poetics refers to the compositional principles and strategies that poets rely upon when writing a poem (and, specifically for his time, epic poems). These are not only the formal and stylistic considerations (for example, plot structure), but also the moral and political ones: how and which characters are represented and in what manner, and how this reflects qualities of virtue and ethics shared by society at large.

In his translator's introduction to *Poetics*, Malcom Heath insists that Aristotle's text must first be understood in 'the broader context of his philosophical work' (1996:ix). 'Aristotle's interest', says Heath, 'is philosophical; that is, it is driven by his desire to understand' (ibid.:xi). For Aristotle, poetry derives broadly as a human activity that enables us to better grasp and understand the external world: 'The production of good poems is an activity that can be understood, and the *Poetics* is an attempt to lay that intelligibility open to inspection' (ibid:xi). The 'activity' of producing poetry is something Aristotle treats as a form of *tekhnê* (sometimes translated as craft or skill) that expresses the governing laws and rationales behind a poem. While we might recoil from phrases like 'laws' and 'rationales', we can still recognise the constructedness and creative 'making' (*poiesis*) built into the concept of poetics – aspects which we still retain well into the present and previous century.[1] Moreover, and finally, alongside visual art forms, Aristotle sees poetry as something rooted in the 'human desire for knowledge', and that 'both painting and poetry' operate as 'forms of *mimêsis*' (ibid.:xiii). Mimêsis (which Heath has translated as 'imitation') produces a significant feature of poetics for Aristotle, but also brings its cultural and political implications into focus (which I will detail more below). For Aristotle, '[i]mitation comes naturally to human beings from childhood . . .; so does the universal pleasure in imitations' ([c. 335 BCE]1996: 6). Poetry, then, for Aristotle, is placed alongside other human intellectual activities – ethics, politics, physics, and metaphysics – that satisfy the innate joy and satisfaction of understanding objects in the external world. The poet, through his or her skill (*tekhnê*) for elevated and rhythmic language, similarly assures that audiences can better grasp objects in their full completeness.[2] The capacity, then, to enact this mimetic quality is derived from the poet's *tekhnê* and inclination, broadly, to bring forth (*poiesis*) objects to be recognised.

In chapter five of Aristotle's *Poetics*, he valourises the poet's capacity to articulate universalities in contradistinction to historical particularity:

> It is clear . . . that the function of the poet is not to say what has happened, but to say the kind of thing that would happen, i.e. what is possible in accordance with probability or necessity. The historian and the poet are not distinguished by their use of verse or prose; it would be possible to turn the works of Herodotus into verse, and it would be a history in verse just as much as in prose. The distinction is this: the one says what has happened, the other the kind of thing that would happen. For this reason poetry is more philosophical and more serious than history. Poetry tends to express universals, and history particulars. The universal is the kind of speech or action which is consonant with a person of a given kind in accordance with probability or necessity; this is what poetry aims at, even though it applies individual names (1996:16).

Several parts of this passage express ideas and concepts which we, in literary studies, have long abandoned – specifically those which refer to 'universals'. Later in this section, and in Chapter 2, I will indicate some moments during which theory and critique departed from the idealisation of universality. Nevertheless, two key elements within this passage – one being that of the 'possible', and the other being the distinction between poetry and history – are those which establish some continuities between Aristotle's conception of poetics and kinopoetics, and connect them to broader cultural and political implications.

Historically speaking, the notion that poetry, on the one hand, instantiates universality and, on the other hand, says the kind of things 'that would happen' helps to clarify why poetics, from Aristotle onward, had wide-ranging political, cultural, and social implications. Particularly, if we combine this commentary with the concept of *mimesis*, we get a strong sense for the implications of Aristotle's *Poetics* and the long shadow it cast over the ensuing centuries in the Western world. B. M. Reed writes that, in general, classical, medieval, and early modern authors 'worry less about form and more about poetry's ability to educate readers, especially young people' (2012:1060). So, for the decades that followed Aristotle and the Classical Era, poetry was treated in relation to its moral, didactic qualities 'My advice to the skilled imitator [or, poet]', says Horace in his famous 'Ars Poetica', 'will be to keep his eye on the model of life and manners, and draw his speech from there' (Horace [10 BCE]2010:129). Even for Aristotle, poetry was meant to provide the ability to purge (*catharsis*) the bad emotions and appetites that humans have. In the Medieval Era, poetry was, of course, still understood to entail allegorical aspects that supplement literal, denotative meaning in language. So, during this period, there was an existing preoccupation with symbolism and metaphor; yet poetry's capacity to provide civic instruction and social

correctives was held to a higher esteem.[3] While the moralistic qualities of poetry held sway until well into the Early
Modern period and beyond, poets did begin to shift emphasis toward innovating style and form. Poets and dramatists,
for example, began departing from Aristotelian prescriptions
(most notably Shakespeare's changes to the Aristotelian tragedy), and contemporary critics, such as George Puttenham,
attended 'closely to sound, distinguishing Elizabethan stress-
based meters from classical quantitative prosody' (Reed
2012:1060). In 1595, Sir Philip Sydney, for example, noted
the two sorts of 'versifying' between Ancient verse and Modern verse: '[T]he ancient no doubt more fit for music . . .; the
latter likewise with his rhyme striketh a certain music to the
ear, and in fine, since it doth delight, though by another way,
it obtains the same purpose . . .' (Sidney [1595]2010: 281).
We can easily see that, while poetry was still assessed according to social utility, poets were still keen to change the means
by which this was achieved – either through vernacular language and literature, differing structures and subplots, and
stylistic innovations. Similarly, as the Early Modern period
began to wane, debates about poetry's role alongside other
art forms began to crystallise, continuing well into the twentieth century. Yet, attempts to locate the medium specificity
of poetry and therefore isolate art forms from one another
have since received heavy scrutiny within the study of poetics
(a point I will touch upon below).

A crucial switch, though, occurred in how society at large
viewed the social position of art as such. Toward the end
of the Early Modern period, critics, poets and philosophers
started to abandon the Aristotelian model of poetry, questioning the need to ascribe to it a moralistic, didactic quality.
Ushering in the era of Enlightenment aesthetics, Immanuel Kant's *Critique of Judgment (Kritik der Urteilskraft)*,
published in 1790, sought to separate moral and political
judgments from aesthetic ones. In particular, Kant insists

upon the presumed autonomy that art maintains, and the need for critique to remain 'disinterested' (*uninteressiert*).[4] Kant's injunction toward separating aesthetic judgment from 'interest' marked an important departure for the critic's relationship to art in general. Rather than evaluating art's capacity to demonstrate virtue, moral goodness, and civic instruction, art and literature upheld their own autonomy; and as a result, our assessment of them was to be unperturbed by moral considerations or the need to satisfy pleasure (Damon and Livingston 2009:6). For poetry, as well, it was no longer considered necessary to have a poem or narrative teach lessons about virtue or to provide insight; rather, our reading of it should simply consider the 'purposiveness' (*Zweckmäßigkeit*) that enables its form to cohere. As Ludwig Wittgenstein would later (1967) put it, 'Do not forget that a poem, although it is composed in the language of information, is not used in the language-game of giving information' (160). In other words, reading poetry is less about extracting information, lessons, or insights, and more about recognising the autonomy of the art as such. Kant's observations in *Critique of Judgment*, therefore, inaugurated over two centuries of literary theory and literary criticism, as several thinkers continue to revise and update his observations.

Concurrently and alongside Kant, poets of the Romantic tradition (namely, Shelley, Wordsworth and Coleridge) insisted upon investing poetry with sincerity, assuring that it accurately communicates 'a writer's innermost thoughts, feelings, experiences, fantasies, and dreams, especially as they touch on abstractions, spiritual matters, and historical causes that transcend the merely personal and arbitrary' (Reed 2012:1061). Such conceptions of poetry and mimesis are reflected in William Wordsworth's famous dictum in his Preface to *Lyrical Ballads*, that 'all good poetry is the spontaneous overflow of powerful emotions' ([1802]2009:22). From this standpoint, we have not only a new idea for how literature ought to be evaluated; but this also reconfigures poetry's mimetic quality. In this case, poetry is meant not necessarily to reflect human virtue or to enhance moral awareness. Rather, poetry from the Romantics onward was assessed according to its sincerity – sincerity toward emotional, subjective experiences (spiritual or otherwise). Kant, of course, provided a necessary influence upon these ideas, asserting as he did the relationship between aesthetics and 'the sublime' (*das Erhabene*).[5] As the encounter with art evokes powerful sensations, the reader's and artist's imaginations become equipped to accurately apprehend the totality of the world and of art itself. In turn, the phenomenology of the (internal and external) world is constituted in the subject's imagination.

The tradition of poetics often called 'expressive poetics' (Reed 2012:1061) that pervaded the remainder of the nineteenth century also supplies an important dimension to the concept of poetics as I will develop it in this chapter. In this instance, the aspect of 'making' (*poiesis*) is firmly built into both Kant's conception of aesthetics and the sublime, as well as the Romantic poets' adherence to the sincerity of expression. In both cases, thinkers and authors place a premium upon the active participation of the imagination in apprehending the totality of an object (for example, a painting, an architectural masterpiece, or elevated poetic style) and the complexities of internal subjective experience. Positioning the role of imagination and the subject's thinking capacity as constitutive of aesthetics, Kant and the Romantics inaugurated a conception of art and poetry that remains important for poetics today. Moreover, it is important to bear in mind a shift that emerged as a result of Kant's *Critique* – namely, turning the judgment of art and literature into its own, self-contained methodology, thereby paving the way for the institutionalisation of literary and art criticism. Toward the end of the century, Matthew Arnold, taking cues from Kant,

helped solidify literary criticism within the academy, noting
that the rule of criticism ought to be that of 'disinterestedness', 'refusing to lend itself to any of those ulterior, political, practical considerations about ideas . . . which criticism
has really nothing to do with' ([1875]2010:703). Criticism's
'business', continues Arnold, 'is simply to know the best that
is known and thought in the world, and by in its turn making
this known, to create a current of true and fresh ideas' (ibid.).
Positioning the role of the critic as someone actively involved
in the creation of 'true and fresh ideas', Arnold valourises the
task of the critic and what criticism as such ought to aspire
to. As a result, the explosion of literary theory throughout the
twentieth century introduced several theorists who revised
and reconfigured the nature of critique, mimesis, aesthetics
and poetics.

The early part of the twentieth century remains a hugely
important time not only for the study of literature in the
Western world – its theorisation and institutionalisation –
but also the revival of poetics as an object of study. In the
previous centuries, poetics was narrowly conceived first
along Aristotelian lines – the laws and rules for creating a
narrative, drama, or poem; then later, through the Medieval
and Early Modern era, poetics was recognised in terms of
poem's capacity to reflect morality and human virtue; and
then, finally, poetry was assessed according to the sincerity of
emotion and spiritual experience, perceptible to the reader's
or viewer's imagination. Yet, following Kant's and Arnold's
insistence on disinterestedness, the approach to literary
aesthetics took on a different approach, taking seriously the
presumed autonomy of literary art. Such an approach entailed
changing the critic's analysis of a text's meaning, specifically
in the relationship between *form* and *content*. Moreover,
following Arnold's insistence upon knowing 'the best that is
known and thought in the world', critics were keen to reflect
the political, scientific, and philosophical paradigms that

emerged, particularly those following Karl Marx, Charles
Darwin and Sigmund Freud, as well as the onset of Literary
Modernism.

In the late 1910s and early 1920s, the Russian Formalists emerged with an attempt at systematising the study of
literature and, in particular, literary form.[6] What was significant about such a project is the fact that it re-established
literature and form as being akin to Aristotle's formulation
of poetics. In other words, just as Aristotle positioned poetics as its own human intellectual activity and outlined the
compositional principles of poetry, epic, and tragedy, so the
Russian Formalists insisted that literature should be treated
with scientific, systematic seriousness, arising from its instrin-
sic 'literariness' (*literaturnost*). The Russian Formalists had
to speak, according to Viktor Shklovsky (1919), of 'the laws
of spending and economy in poetic language based on its
own workings, not on prosaic language' ([1919]2015:161).
In other words, according to Shklovksy, the function of
the language within its particular domain (whether prose
or poetry) must be spoken about on its own terms, not in
relation to other types of writing. Each text is assumed to
have a governing and specified law for how it is created and
the manner in which its language ought to function. So, for
the Russian Formalists, the formal arrangement of a given
text was uniquely suited for its own purposes, and it abides
by these principles in order to ensure its own literariness.
Moreover, though, for Shklovksy, Boris Eichenbaum and
others, literature instantiated these formal principles in order
to create a certain 'estrangement' (*ostrananie*).[7] Literature is
meant to uphold a certain 'distancing' effect, from which
the content or message cannot be so readily gleaned. Such a
distance confirms literature's literariness, and establishes literature as such as its own distinct object of study – an object
characterised by its uniquely estranging use of language (that
is, its poetics). Consequently, this shift redefines poetics in

such a way that emphasised its effect and its relationship to meaning – an aspect that remains an important dimension.

What followed the Russian Formalists was a related, yet broader field known as Structuralism – a field which inherited some of its foundational ideas from the Formalists as well as the linguistic theories of Ferdinand de Saussure.[8] However, one important distinction between the Structuralists and the Formalists was that the Structuralists did not necessarily see literature in isolation; rather, literary art (alongside several other domains) existed within a broader governing (or, structuring) system.[9] What the Structuralists and the Formalists shared in terms of their approach within literature is a distinct preoccupation with literary form and its unifying coherence, seeing each text as following an underlying compositional structure. In other words, the Structuralists, too, enabled poetics (in the Aristotelian sense) to gain purchase and prominence in Literary Studies. Tzvetan Todorov's *Introduction to Poetics*, first published in 1939, makes the forceful case for reintroducing Aristotle back into the twentieth century:

> [Aristotle's] *Poetics* breaks down the symmetry thus established between interpretation and science in the field of literary studies. In contradistinction to the interpretation of particular works, it does not seek to name meaning, but aims at a knowledge of the general laws that preside over the birth of each work . . . Poetics is therefore an approach to literature at once 'abstract' and 'internal'. ([1939]1981:6)

Todorov continues, locating the specific object of study suited for a study of poetics: 'It is not the literary work itself that is the object of poetics: what poetics questions are the properties of that particular discourse that is literary discourse' (1981:6). So, again, though he does not use the word *literariness* here, this emphasis on what makes literary discourse 'literary' is that quality unique to the medium itself, and what distinguishes it from other written discourses. As a Structuralist, Todorov's concern 'is not instances of meaning but the possibility of meaning: the ways in which the system allows meaning to be made' (Brooks 1981:xi). In several ways, the issue of the 'possibility of meaning' still persists in the present-day study of poetics; but the manner in which such qualities are uncovered are no longer strictly to do with style, form, and coherence.

A necessary reaction to the Structuralists emerged in the mid-to-late twentieth century, crystallising in the Post-structuralists. Taking some of the cues from Saussurian linguistics regarding the arbitrary relationship between the signifier and signified, the Post-structuralists reject nevertheless the idea of literature's governability by, or subjection to, larger structuring systems. Rather, for theorists like Jacques Derrida, Paul de Man, Julia Kristeva, and Roland Barthes, texts can work to actively deconstruct these structures. A text, according to Derrida,

> is neither causality by contagion, nor the simple accumulation of layers. Nor even the pure juxtaposition of borrowed pieces. And if a text always gives itself a certain representation of its own roots, those roots live only by that representation, by never touching the soil, so to speak . . . To say that one always interweaves roots endlessly . . . is to contradict at once the concept of system and the pattern of the root. (Derrida 1997:101–2)

The text itself, in order to resist causal linearity to a wider structuring system or essences, treat 'writing as the disappearance of natural presence' (ibid.:159), or the deconstruction of pre-established realities and origins. The consequences here for a study of poetics are quite significant. There is no longer a presumed mimetic quality of a text that corresponds to or imitates the essence of the external world. Rather, decon-struction aims at revealing to what extent there are disunities or discontinuities from the external world, bringing those breaks to the forefront. As Derrida puts it, a deconstructive reading 'attempts to make the not-seen accessible to light' (ibid.:163). So, here the Structuralist model of a literary text – with formal continuities, ideological coherence, or system of compositional principles – is subverted. The metaphysical presence given to mimesis as a reflection of or determined by a wider social structure is now abandoned, and replaced with an emphasis on incoherence and disunity.[10] The correspon-dences between, therefore, the written word and its meaning are rejected, making room for a multiplicity of meanings and textual possibilities.

So far, this history of poetics is contained within a hugely Eurocentric, patriarchal, and heteronormative hegemony: it is very white and very male. Luckily, the middle part of the twentieth century met several important critical and theo-retical upheavals, not least as a result of changing social and political concerns. The boom of feminist criticism, race theory, queer theory, and Postcolonial Studies gave way to a rich and multifaceted scholarly landscape, all seemingly operating coincidentally. While I feel it is beyond my abil-ity to give a comprehensive overview of these fields, a few important advancements are worth noting with respect to literary criticism and poetics. Elaine Showalter, for example, in 1979 advocated for what she calls 'gynocritics' (217). Showalter invites critics and scholars to reconsider the pre-mium given to male-centric theories and narratives, turning our attention away from such over-saturated representa-tion, and to question the centrality of men within the literary canon. As a result, critics are not only meant to question how we read one text in particular (as we should); we are also meant to question the literary canon as such whereby male authors and critics dominate the academic world and the publishing industry. Yet, within feminist criticism, of course, there is considerable diversity. For example, while Showalter is skeptical of the Post-structuralist and Marxist traditions, since for her they create a 'theoretical impasse in feminist criticism' ([1979]1997:219), Elizabeth Meese notes that Michel Foucault and other Post-structuralists speak 'directly to those functioning outside of the literary critical establishment' ([1985]1997:223). In other words, according to Meese, Foucault's reflections upon locating power's relation to truth and knowledge bear directly on feminist concerns, as they critique the discursive and institutional forces that establish male-centric narratives as the sole unit of reference for literary theory. By questioning the established knowledge, whereby literature is a solely male-coded preoccupation and the arbiters of literary quality, feminist critics can mark a radical departure from this system, while also deconstructing its foundational assumptions. In terms of a poetics, this also means judging particular formal elements not through masculinised norms, but rather highlighting systems of meaning that articulate uniquely female experiences.[11]

A similar preoccupation is taken up in Postcolonial Studies. Crystallising as a 'distinct category only in the 1990s' (Barry 2009:185), Postcolonial criticism nevertheless traces its origins to several decades prior, wherein theorists and authors began questioning the basis under which European world-historical discourse is treated as universally valid. Critics and theorists here demonstrate the extent to which white, European authors have established the canon for Great Literature, thereby causing those non-white, non-European authors to come under erasure. This tendency, of course, derives from the long-lasting legacy of colonialism, whereupon a European world order was imposed upon the rest of the world, expanding political, juridical and economic power through conquest and ongoing repression. As a consequence, this system continued to shape the literary world as well. From around the 1940s onward however, as processes of decolonisation were on the rise all over the world, literary authors, too, began to decolonise their own practices in terms of style and language, as well as historicity. Many attempted to create a productive engagement with a decolonised identity, divorced from a European metaphysics (cf. Glissant 1997:189). For example, in the French-language school of négritude, thinkers such as Aimé Césaire and Léopold Sédar Senghor have offered a theoretical framework that 'exists within a broad intellectual constellation including not only surrealist Modernism or Bergsonian vitalism but ethnological culturalism, Christian personalism, and Marxist humanism (as well as Jewish messianism and philosophical pragmatism)' (Wilder 2015:9). Envisioning a poetic engagement with decolonisation and its affective contours, Simone Bignall writes that '[t]he subjective style of Négritude correlates with intuitive reason and an image of thought as affective and creative' (2021:254). This philosophical and poetic commitment to a creative 'image of thought' and decolonisation offers a profound precursor to kinopoetics.[12] In other instances, authors confronted the historic traumas wrought by colonialism.

Consequently, several problems arise here in terms of a poetics, especially in the Anglophone world. In particular, literary theory and poetics has had to adjust its methods to accommodate a wider world beyond the Global North. After all, when it comes to the stylistic and formal elements unique to a particular text, what happens when those assessments are derived from tools fashioned within the institutions of the Anglo-American hegemony? In response to this question, Postcolonial critics and authors emerged in an effort to destabilise this hegemony, offering a counter-aesthetics or counter-poetics to the imposed practices within the Anglo-American canon. From such a standpoint, authors started questioning the necessity of complying with or conforming to the standards set up by canonised, Western authors – authors whose stylistic ingenuities and creative acumen were widely celebrated as being 'classics'.[13] Similarly, Postcolonial critics question the over-reliance on English (or French or German) as the only viable languages for Literature, realising that beyond the Western world there are languages and, even, dialects that have their own history and structures. Finally, due in large part to the history of colonialism, Postcolonial scholars offer interventions into the imposed historical orders established by the great colonial powers (Portugal, Spain, the UK, France, among others). The influence of Postcolonial Studies on poetics and, indeed, kinopoetics cannot be overstated, as a large part of the counter-discursive efforts taken up within Postcolonial Theory act as theoretical and conceptual precursors to kinopoetics.[14] Suffice it to say for now that much of the resistance to treating literature as strictly 'national', and placing a primacy on 'place' and 'identity' as the sole categories for existence are built into both Postcolonial Studies as well as kinopoetics.

To add to this overview of poetics, I shall now consider the wider constellations and applications of poetics – other forms of media beyond literature that can also be said to entail a poetics. To enter this terrain, I can first return to Derrida's *Of Grammatology* in which he famously offers a critique of 'logocentrism', or the centrality and primacy granted to writing and speech as being the only systems of language constitutive of meaning. 'For some time now,' writes Derrida, 'one says "language" for action, movement, thought, reflection, consciousness, unconsciousness, experience, affectivity, etc. Now we tend to say "writing" for all that and more: to designate not only the physical gestures of literal pictographic or ideographic inscription, but also the totality of what makes it possible' (1997:9). From here, an important feature of poetics needs to be retained: after

Derrida and the Post-structuralists, poetics is no longer strictly concerned with literary and poetic form. The critique of logocentrism enables scholars and critics to apply poetics to other media, as well as within the methods of certain critical traditions themselves. Poetics, from here onward, describes a much wider preoccupation the manner in which meaning is made (*poiesis*). Because different forms of media also require efforts to produce and invite co-participation in meaning (within and beyond the object itself), poetics can be seen as having resonance beyond simply literature. As a result of this departure, texts like Gaston Bachelard's *Poetics of Space* (1958), Gabriele Brandstetter's *Poetics of Dance* (1995), Linda Hutcheon's *Poetics of Postmodernism* (1988), Raul Ruiz's *Poetics of Cinema* (2006), and Birte Christ and Stefanie Mueller's 'Towards a Legal Poetics' (2017) arose to adopt a theoretical and critical framework to foreground the *constructedness* of meaning throughout these different forms of expression. Such assumptions have been well-established within and beyond literary studies, suggesting that there are high stakes regarding perspective, frame, and voice. As Mieke Bal insists, narrative voice, structure, mediation, and description form the capacities for fiction (whether through literature, film, or other arts) to function not as opposite from reality but as a 'special inflection of reality . . . enriched by the imagination' (2021:35). Furthermore, many thinkers began to issue metacommentaries on particular critical procedures, styles, and discourses within and toward these different media.

Given the complexity and dynamic shifts within this history, poetics seems almost unrecognisable from where it began all the way back in Aristotle.[15] Especially after Derrida and the Post-structuralists, it would seem counter-productive to still rely on a concept that insists upon literary form, unity, and coherence within a particular text. Yet, on the other hand, Derrida's questioning of logocentrism, along with these more recent iterations (Hutcheon 1988; Brandstetter 1995; Christ and Mueller 2017) within the realm of poetics permit critics to widen our scope of concern. In the next section, I will therefore provide a definition of poetics that retains some aspects from these previous traditions, while insisting that my use of the term enables me to connect movement, meaning, and politics as it is made (*poiesis*).

Defining Poetics

After this contentious history of literary theory and criticism wherein the approaches toward literature (as well as the literature itself) began to revolutionise dramatically, bringing poetics into the twenty-first century can provide a set of challenges. In hearing the term 'poetics', connotations are still conjured up either toward the specific devices within a poem as such – its form, or the particular metaphors utilised – or as something closer to the Structuralist idea of continuity and coherence. Without poetics meaning elevated style, ideological coherence, textual unity, or the specific compositional principles and genre-specific laws governing a particular poetic creation, what is left of poetics? I would like to return, first, to Aristotle's *Poetics*, in which he describes the function of the poet as being that which relates to 'what is possible' (1996:16). This aspect of poetics finds a similar invocation all the way into Derrida's *Of Grammatology*, in which he insists that 'writing' can entail 'the totality of what it makes possible' (1997:9). This connection suggests that one continuity between the Aristotelian model of poetics and the more recent strands of literary theory and criticism (such as deconstruction) is the distinction between history and poetics – that poetics offers a supplementary system of meaning that assures possibilities as well as particularities, distinguishable from (and even sometimes counter to) history.

Second, I would like to insist that the constructedness of meaning that poetics is meant to convey, given its root *poiesis*, remains an integral part of the concept. In other words, the deliberate manner in which meaning, information, and knowledge is arranged, structured, and delivered constitutes a poetics in itself. Even if that manner is deliberately disjointed or de-stabilising, poetics nevertheless foregrounds the disjointedness and unstable nature of the particular object (literary or not) to examine the manner in which it shapes the conveyance of meaning. Getting much closer to a viable definition of poetics, Stephen Greenblatt identifies what he calls a 'cultural poetics': 'the sum written discourses through which we apprehend and act upon the world and, more particularly, the discourses through which we distinguish between the imaginary and the real' (1997: 471). Following Greenblatt (who inherits this framework largely from Foucault), poetics is not necessarily restricted to the particularities of literary form, but rather a wider set of discourses and systems of meaning that impart cultural knowledge upon us. Such discourses enable a capacity to determine a regime of what is thinkable and unthinkable, or what is visible and invisible.

Finally, poetics here ought to not only be an object of study, but it should also entail a set of methodological and critical procedures. Recalling Showalter's push toward a 'gynocritics' as a critical tool for a feminist reading (or a 'feminist poetics', as the title of her essay suggests), here she considers the manner in which the critic approaches a text in order to apprehend or consider otherwise neglected or unrecognised aspects. This dimension of poetics, therefore, involves redirecting the critical focus in order to extract meaning from the text, and to bring specific discursive tools to participate in the construction of meaning. The critical consideration of a text and the interpretive, theoretical framework the critic operates in, therefore, also constitutes part of a poetics.

So, given all of these features, a viable definition of poetics should entail the complexities that arise given the long, contentious history of criticism and theory. For the remainder of this text, I will define poetics on two interrelated and interconnected levels:

- First, the formal and linguistic qualities within a text that produce a certain aesthetic effect;
- Second, the manner in which broad systems of meaning (that is, regimes that determine what is thinkable and unthinkable, visible and invisible) are connected and constructed throughout our cultural life.

The above definition refers broadly to what poetics is as an object of study: what we are looking at in a text. Given that my own critical focus is, in fact, within literature, it is important to retain part one of that definition, but to also assume that it cannot necessarily be separated from part two. Moreover, such a definition enables me to reflect upon the relationship that literature has as a constitutive part of social, cultural, and political knowledge, changing the field of what we can recognise, see, and comprehend. Finally, as I proceed through this project, I will show that poetics as a methodology works alongside and appraises this two-part definition, ensuring that these features are properly illuminated. The capacity to extract or detect the manner in which broad systems of meaning are connected and constructed depends entirely upon the critical procedures and language one decides to employ. The methodology provides the orientation toward the text, as well as the way I write about the text, that illuminates the object of study, as readers will note in Part II. Kinopoetics is an approach toward migrant literature that activates and affirms movement. It is a way of looking at and analysing the text that recognises the creative and productive role of the migrant in shaping the social, political, spatial, or linguistic world in which they enter. Furthermore, writing kinopoetically, means I arrive with a set of discursive and critical practices. Kinopoetics is not just what a text is, but it is what one does in staging the literary analysis. In this case, that system of staging relies upon movement-oriented language and discourse to better appraise the moving object of study.[16]

Kinopolitics: Expansion by Expulsion

In the present political climate, we are witnessing both the acceleration as well as securitisation of social movement, as resources and ideas circulate at faster and faster rates, and border policies become ever more restricted. At the same time, a social panic has set in, as alarmist news media and political leaders declare the existential threat of 'migrant invasions' and 'demographic changes'. It is within this context that Thomas Nail introduces (2015) and expands (2016) the notion of kinopolitics. In *The Figure of the Migrant*, Nail states that kinopolitics is the theory and counter-history of 'social motion': 'Instead of analysing societies as primarily static, spatial, or temporal, kinopolitics understands them primarily as "regimes of motion"'(2015:24). Established and formed social regimes are 'always in motion: directing people and objects, reproducing their social conditions (periodicity), and striving to expand their *territorial, political, juridical, and economic power through diverse forms of expulsion*' (ibid.). Social motion, however, is not a homogenous nor unidirectional process. Rather, there exist continuous social flows; and, indeed, a thorough-going study of human migration necessarily entails 'a study of flows': 'measuring the movement of human populations is more like measuring a continuous and variable process than a fixed social body' (ibid.:25). Therefore, from a demographic and statistical standpoint, the study of various population and diasporic flows provides a meaningful conceptual starting-point. A political analysis and philosophy of migration is 'precisely the analysis of social flows: flows across borders, flows into detention centers, counter-flows (strikes), and so on' (ibid.:26). By underscoring the pervasiveness of flows as such, we are able then to analyse 'bifurcations, redirections, vectors, or tendencies' (ibid.), rather than any perceived totalities or unities.

Indeed, as continuous flows sprawl out in diverse, non-linear, zig-zagging directions, they are often redirected back onto themselves, giving the perception of relative stasis. Nail calls this a 'junction' and, once flows arrive at a junction – that is, redirect back onto themselves in a position of momentary stasis – then societies find 'points of relative stability in a sea of turbulence': 'The house is a territorial junction, the city is a political junction, and the commodity is an economic junction, and so forth' (2015:27). The junction, in a sense, provides the bordered and bounded spatiality designed for stopping, managing and redirecting of social flows. These regimes thus achieve a perceived sense of stasis, offering them juridical, political, and economics means of inclusion/exclusion. 'Many kinds of political junctions,' says Nail, 'yoke and direct social motion' (2016:28).[17] Within these junctions, political power and citizenship can find stability and comfort, so long as the system is uncompromised by the bifurcations and counter-flows of migration. Thus, powerful juridical and political structures deploy all available disciplinary resources in order to secure this perceived stasis.

Finally, kinopolitics relies on an understanding of the constitutive role of circulation. Circulation, in the broadest, socio-political sense, involves transporting resources and people, managing the expansion and contraction of global markets, and moving and trading commodities (Nail 2015:30). Distinct from flows, circulation creates the 'regulation of flows into an ordered network of junctions' (ibid.:29). Several consequences of continuous circulation, though, exist at the economic and cultural level. Economically speaking, commodities, food supplies, financial debt, and labour is circulated across and throughout international boundaries in order to avert economic collapse and to manage equilibrium, creating more and more displacement and globalised trade dependence. Culturally speaking, increased human mobility and the transportation of ideas throughout the globe generate hybrid cultural assemblages and multiple relational possibilities, such that historical totalities, linguistic essence, and national homogeneity are deterritorialised, destabilised, and de-centred. 'Hybridity', says Nikos Papastergiadis, 'is both the assemblage that occurs whenever two elements meet, and the initiation of a process of change' (1999:170). In terms of imperial hegemony and authority, says Homi Bhabha, in *The Location of Culture*, hybridity 'unsettles the demand that figures at the centre of the originary myth of colonialist power' (1994:165); it is capable, in other words, of disrupting and disturbing 'presences of authority' (ibid.:162). Cultural contact and intermingling across national boundaries, resulting from intensive and extensive movement, ultimately expands the possibilities of social identity-formation and co-constructed forms of subjectivity.

In elucidating the multi-directional, overlapping forms of movement and mobility, Nail diagnoses different forms of 'kinopower', which operate according to a logic of 'expansion by expulsion'.[18] A precursor to this idea can be found in Karl Marx's analysis of 'primitive accumulation' ([1867]1990:873), referring to the capacity to accumulate capital and assets through forms of violent, racialised dis-possession and expropriation. Nail, though, radicalises the idea of primitive accumulation, describing rather a broader counter-history of circulation, expansion and expulsion. These forms of expansion and expulsion are also not necessarily uniform, and do not always follow the same typology and structure. Rather, there are four types of kinopower that have operated throughout social history. First, there is the 'centripetal force', or 'territorial kinopower' in which regimes of power accumulate territory by pulling from the periphery inward: 'It harnesses the flows of the earth in various junctions – it fences them in and stores their surplus in an ever-increasing series of vessels: pen vessels, house vessels, food vessels, burial vessels' (Nail 2015:43). Centripetal force in this sense creates 'the kinetic conditions for a social center' which can be created by 'accumulating from a heterogeneous periphery of individual farmers or even multiple territories' (ibid.). Territorial kinopower, therefore, redirects the movement of agriculture and land into a consolidated center, attracting them or pulling from the periphery, in a centripetal motion.

Second, there is 'political kinopower' that operates in the inverse manner; that is, it operates by way of 'centrifugal force'. Centrifugal force is the name for motion that is directed outward; by displacing people and assigning them a political position of inferiority and aterritoriality, centrifugal force thus sends people from the centre out to the periphery – creating a situation of permanent exile or refuge (Nail 2015:135). Through depoliticisation (in other words, the depriving of political representation or power) or deportation, regimes of power redirect people outward in order to secure or create a fortified system of inclusion/exclusion. Those who are simply deprived of property or belonging to the nation are subsequently expelled by way of various types of centrifugal force – war, discipline, famine, captured slavery. This is especially crucial when considering the refugee crises that arise from the Middle East and Africa as a result of military intervention and invasion, and, in particular, the political attitudes and perceptions toward these refugees.

Third, one also finds a 'tensional force', or 'juridical kinopower' (Nail 2015:60), which is capable of securing juridical linkages and enclosed boundaries that divide and assign various degrees of belonging within the *polis*. 'Enclosure laws', 'vagabond laws', and 'witch hunts', for example, operate in such a manner, criminalising movement and statelessness, while also instilling social fears and phobias of those who are beyond the national boundary. As Bhabha points out, the term territory itself is etymologically bound up with fear: 'Etymologically unsettled, "territory" derives from both *terra* (earth) and *terrēre* (to frighten) whence *territorium*, "a place from which people are frightened off"' (1994:142).

Finally, kinopolitical history has relied on 'elastic force', or 'economic kinopower' which is capable of redirecting social flows 'into a more flexible state of equilibrium' (Nail 2015: 81). This is precisely done in a manner of managing labour, expanding or contracting markets in order to ensure proper growth without restriction. Creating various levels of precarity among lower- or working-class people (proletariat) ensures a level of economic growth through the management of wages and the ultimately limitless capacity to generate and disperse capital. With each of these kinopolitical forces outlined, we thus have a sense for the conditions that determine migrancy throughout social history. Yet, indeed, each of these forms of kinopower not only create the migrant as such, but they create different *figures* of the migrant corresponding to each type of kinopower or kinopolitical force. Shared among these figures is their subjection to the logic of expansion by expulsion, but also the capacity to enact a pedetic social force, or a force of political pressure, autonomy, and resistance to which kinopower reacts. As a political strategy, therefore, regimes of social motion construct and invent migrant figures to legitimise dispossession and expulsion. Yet, when considered within the counter-history of kinopolitics, these figures compose a typology of active, affirmative figures of social transformation.

The first figure of the migrant is the nomad. Being the migrant figure of centripetal force, territorial power expands by sending the nomad into 'social and ecological expulsion'.[19] That is, in order to accumulate territory and agriculture, the nomad had to be expelled simply 'because there are not enough territorial flows left over for them and they are in the way' (Nail 2015:46). The nomad, then, is simply the figure left out of the territorial expansion – the one who was 'expelled from territorial sedentarism' and must therefore create 'a different way of life' (ibid.:47). The second figure of the migrant, associated with centrifugal force, is the barbarian. It is with this figure that the idea 'of natural political inferiority' was invented 'in the ancient world largely to conceptualise political slavery' (ibid.:52). In other words, centrifugal force operated by manufacturing political categories of inclusion and exclusion, enabling political regimes to expel those who are viewed as different from or simply unintelligible to the geographic or political center. This was the political use of the term *barbarian* – it was a phrase used to describe the stuttering and babbling sound of the foreigner who does not speak Greek. By applying such a category, the *civis* or *polis* – both words 'that applied to cities' and reflect a 'political center' (ibid.:53)– assigned the barbarian characteristics of natural or political inferiority, justifying the ambition to colonise, enslave, kidnap, or deport those who were deemed unrecognisable or unworthy of the political territory. The third figure of the migrant (and final one for this project) is the vagabond – the criminalised migrant figure associated with tensional force. We will recall that tensional force creates laws restricting the right to stay within a certain territory, but also, paradoxically, disciplines landlessness and aterritoriality.[20] The vagabond, like the barbarian, was a political category not necessarily of political inferiority, but of criminality and homelessness – an unstable and heretical migrant who must be expelled, penalised, and disciplined, for the sake of territorial expansion.

   The final figure of the migrant, produced through 'elastic force', is the proletariat. This may seem a strange designation since, as Nail points out, 'not all of the proletariat is always and in every case a figure of the migrant' (2015:85). For instance, 'if the proletariat is considered an actively employed and relatively stable class identity' (ibid.), then it is not necessarily considered a migrant, or considered to be stateless, moving, or beyond political territories. Yet, on the other hand, '[i]f the proletariat is considered according to its economic expulsion from the means of production,' (ibid.) then it intersects and overlaps with other figures of the migrant mentioned above. Thus, the proletariat is the figure of the migrant who is economically expelled, constituting either a 'floating unemployed' or acting as part of what Marx called the 'industrial reserve army' (1990:781). In both senses, they are, as Friedrich Engels says, those 'whose sole existence depends on the demand for labor' (Engels 1847). In terms of movement, the proletarian either has little access to private property or economic productive forces; or is in a precarious state of rootlessness, leaving their homes to seek out employment opportunities or to escape economic and environmental hardships. The proletariat is a migrant figure created by economic forces that require a transient, moveable, and expendable labour force who can be redistributed as 'surplus labor power' (Nail 2015: 222; Marx 1990:788).

With each figure of the migrant outlined above, it is important to recognise that these figures exist as a result of different forms of kinopolitical force or kinopower. Depending on the material conditions of each of these kinopolitical forces, a migrant figure was either created or relied upon in order to achieve territorial, political, or economic expansion. The hegemonic system, operating by a logic of 'expansion by expulsion', created the figures who were necessarily expelled from or left out of the political territory. These figures are defined by their movement; yet, the direction or conditions of their movement differ between social situations and historical moments (although they do overlap and intersect in a number of ways). In some cases – especially with the barbarian and vagabond – they were forced into a socially-defined, second-class citizenship status that enabled systems of political power to expel them or criminalise their movement. Being viewed as unworthy of legal or political accommodation or representation, they were viewed as 'failed citizens' (Nail 2015:3), thereby justifying the hostility, racism, aggression, and discipline that they received, while their statelessness or movement was managed and controlled by legal and political institutions. The remaining migrant figures – the nomad and the proletariat – were figures who were deprived of access to the agricultural resources or to the economic forces of production. Thus, the capacity for expansion required their mobility in order to ensure territorial growth and political power. All of these migrant figures are political and social figures of movement, and are thus outside of the stable junctions of national borders and political territories. Since our democratic and political systems operate according to a place-based logic, whereby political stability, sovereignty, and stasis are the governing principles of legitimacy and belonging, there is simply no room or accommodating system that can allow for those who are in constant motion. So, by sheer virtue of their mobility, migrants are politically unstable and exist beyond the scope of political recognition and representation. Yet, what is meant to be shown through kinopolitics is that these migratory figures are relied upon for social and political formation: their expulsion, movement, and displacement create the material, economic, and social conditions to secure political power and force.

However, it is important to recognise not only the conditions for political formation, but also the transformative capacity for political change. Here, too, the migrant operates as the constitutive figure, moving against or redirecting social motion in order to destabilise power and to push through the borders and territories of kinopower. In this way, all four figures of the migrant are each endowed with a positive, or affirmative capacity, empowered to create new social territories and new regimes of motion with their own active and transformative political power. This is what Nail calls 'pedetic motion':

> Pedetic motion is the force of the foot – to walk, to run, to leap, to dance. As a social form of motion, it is defined by its autonomy and self-motion. It is different from the social forces of centripetal, centrifugal, tensional, and elastic power because it has neither centre nor surplus. Instead, its movement is irregular and unpredictable. It is turbulent. It does not expand by social expulsion but by inclusive social transformation. (2015: 125)

In this sense, pedetic force is the force of autonomy that migrants enact as a way of forging their own motion and direction. Applying collective pressure against fortified territories of political power, operating to-and-fro through continuous oscillation, or creating a strong collective flux, or wave, into the *polis*, the migrant thus transforms, deterritorialises, and destabilises the assumed primacy of social stasis, creating motion and lines of flight of their own. As Deleuze and Guattari put it, the migrant 'enjoys an autonomy and direction all its own' ([1987]2014:443), operating according to 'singularities that are impossible to universalize' (ibid.:440). By enacting their pedetic motion and counter-movement against kinopower and the forces of expansion by expulsion, each figure of the migrant thus creates new possibilities for social formation, and rejects the coercive push of kinopower.

Of course, each figure of the migrant performs their own pedetic force, which is also never unitary nor one-directional. The nomad, for instance, enacts pedetic force by simply deserting or escaping from 'kinopolitical domination' (Nail 2015:130), and then perform a 'raid against territorial societies when their movement is blocked' (ibid.:134); the barbarian takes 'refuge' and acts in revolt against kinopolitical power, returning to his or her home after being forced out by depoliticisation and war (ibid.:136–7). The vagabond, as the lawless and landless figure, is rebellious heretic, exerting social pressure internally and externally: 'The vagabond heretic wanted a personal transformation, a release of his or her spirit from confinement' (ibid.:154). And, finally, by applying social pressure to the elastic force of economic kinopower, the proletariat operates against the forces of coercive capital mobility by, paradoxically, refusing to move, while yet also moving against 'the dominant form of social motion (territorial, political, juridical, or economic)' – in other words, through strikes and resistance (ibid.:171). For each of these figures – the nomad, the barbarian, the vagabond, and the proletariat – their unique pedetic motion gives them the means to create their own motion, and to resist the domination of kinopower. Furthermore, pedetic force is what constitutes the affirmative aspect and quality of the migrant. Understood in this light, the migrant exists as the transformative, revolutionary figure of social history, and is the figure through which political change and opposition occur. Rather than being simply relegated to a secondary, subaltern political status, the migrant is the primary force of difference and the creator of alternative histories and lines of flight. Throughout moments of history, the migrant has carried out new, counter-movements against the expulsions and expansions of kinopower.

Having outlined here a kinopolitical counter-history, now I move to poetics in a way that retains the connection with movement as a constitutive force. To do so, I turn to affect theory, outlining what I deem an 'affect-sensation continuum', to stress the continuities between relational power, redistributions of the sensible, and intensive movement. Such movement enables a qualitative shift in the regime of what is visible and thinkable, adding the capacity for migrant texts to make kinopolitical movement legible. To do so, a poetics therefore supplies intensive movement to the migrant's extensive movement, observed within the migrant text.

Affect, Sensation and Intensive Movement

Going all the way back to Aristotle, we remember that poetics is often preoccupied with knowledge. In *Poetics*, Aristotle claimed that the aim or motivation to make (*poiesis*) a poem that imitates (*mimesis*) the external world derives from an innate human desire to fully apprehend the world. In some ways, as we saw earlier in this chapter, this aspect of poetics has virtually remained up until today, although has slightly altered in emphasis (for example, we would no longer essentialise about an inherent human instinct to know and imitate the world, as Aristotle suggests). Similarly, there is a strong tradition in the realm of critique (going all the way back to Kant) which enables us to apply a rigorous form of analysis and account of the aesthetic object, creating a method or an approach that is deeply invested in knowledge. This is the epistemological dimension to poetics that remains a key feature: it induces or shapes what is thinkable and knowable, often making the sensible world cohere by artistic means. Today, literary critics continue to confirm literature's capacity to shape individual and cultural knowledge (Felski 2008; Kramnick 2018), and some have even gone as far as to explain the overlaps between literature, epistemology, and ethics (Attridge 2004; Spivak 2012). The challenge for kinopoetics, though, is to draw out the interconnection between literature, movement and knowledge. After all, kinopoetics should not merely focus on and analyse the migrant figure, aiming to draw out their historic and social primacy. Rather, kinopoetics, when thought of as the object of study, should also be a kind of moving poetics – a making (*poiesis*) of movement (*kinesis*) such that it makes migrancy legible and thinkable. Here, then, it would be helpful to turn to a theoretical tradition that connects movement with knowledge. In so doing, I will draw into relation the theoretical work on affect, knowledge, and movement, theorised within the realm of affect theory; and I will combine this with the work on aesthetics and the 'distribution of the sensible', theorised by Jacques Rancière, ensuring that poetics is directly linked with movement.

Affect, like poetics, is a concept with a complicated theoretical and philosophical history. Throughout the late twentieth century, critical theory and cultural studies began recognising what is now known as the 'affective turn' with theorists as wide-ranging as Antonio Negri, Sara Ahmed, Gilles Deleuze, Félix Guattari, Eve Sedgwick, Lauren Berlant, and Franco Berardi. 'When in the early to mid-1990s', Patricia T. Clough explains, 'critical theorists and cultural critics invited a turn to affect, they often did so in response to what they argued were limitations of post-structuralism and deconstruction' (2008:1). The turn toward affect inaugurated a 'substantive shift in that it returned critical theory and cultural criticism to bodily matter which had been treated in terms of various constructionisms under the influence of post-structuralism and deconstruction' (ibid.). As a result, theorists in this field insist on seeing affective capacities as constitutive forces in the phenomenology of meaning and political subjectivity, rather than being merely interpellated through performative linguistic signification. Furthermore, within affect studies, there is considerable diversity among theorists about what the term affect means. While some have insisted on affect as not being necessarily distinct from emotion (Ahmed 2014:207), others take an approach that insists on using affect to connect to a wider range of movements and connections that are not yet fully formed into recognisable categories. Gregory J. Seigworth and Melissa Gregg provide a starting point for approaching affect in all of its breadth in their introduction to *The Affect Theory Reader*:

> Affect, at its most anthropomorphic, is the name we give to those forces – visceral forces, beneath, alongside, or generally other than conscious knowing, vital forces insist-ing beyond emotion – that can serve to drive us toward movement, toward thought and extension, that can like-wise suspend us (as if in neutral) across a barely registering accretion of force-relations, or that can even leave us over-whelmed by the world's apparent intractability. Indeed, affect is persistent proof of a body's never less than ongo-ing immersion in and among the world's obstinacies and rhythms, its refusals and invitations. (2010:1)

This framing around affect creates a useful approach for examining the modes of relationality and potential that con-stitute our lives. In terms of political power, affect has been a basis for consideration going all the way back to Dutch phi-losopher Baruch Spinoza, whose philosophy has met a resur-gence in the works of Negri and Deleuze (Ruddick 2010:21). It is through Spinoza and neo-Spinozist approaches that we can locate a nexus of affect, knowledge, movement, and power; and we begin an analysis, as Spinoza famously stated, with understanding 'what the body can do' (Spinoza qtd in Seigworth and Gregg 2010:3). More specifically, it is in this tradition that theorists locate affect 'in the midst of things and relations (in immanence) and, then, in the com-plex assemblages that come to compose bodies and worlds simultaneously' (Seigworth and Gregg 2010:6). Affect, then, is something that moves and modulates in passing through the social assemblage, describing a social and political ontol-ogy that is in constant motion and change.

It is in the philosophy of Gilles Deleuze (and some of his collaborations with Félix Guattari) that affect connects politics, ethics, epistemology, and ontology; and it is from this basis that I will also move toward its relation to poetics. In *Spinoza: Practical Philosophy*, Deleuze instantiates not just an analysis of affect, but an 'ethology': 'Ethology is first of all the study of the relations of speed and slowness, of the capacities for affecting and being affected that characterise each thing' (1988:125). Another way of putting this would be to suggest that an analysis of social relations and material processes should be concerned with how different human and non-human forces are sped up or slowed down; and that the political project involves mapping out the complex composition of material relations and potentials that animate individual, as well as collective, power. For Deleuze, his Spinozist and vitalist ethics is based upon the capacity to accelerate or liberate one's *potentia* and achieve a joyous becoming.[21] Joy-through-affectivity, then, under this politics achieves a certain political and ethical primacy.[22] Politics and ethics, under this conception, are meant to determine, enhance and liberate the body's capacity for affecting and being affected. These bodily capacities produce relative degrees of freedom and power, and are shaped by a variety of material and intensive forces through which a body passes. So, then, the production of affects is affirmed as a form of political liberation and ethical valourisation; and by enhancing intensities and accelerating the body's *potentia*, we begin to empower a process of joyous becoming.

What makes this Spinozist understanding of affect useful for kinopoetics is that it is intertwined with knowledge. As the body passes through intensive states, it accumulates experiential understandings of where it can move and with what capacities. These ways of knowing are not necessarily conscious thoughts or categories, but rather a deep relational sense of one's position alongside human and non-human entities. 'Affects under Spinoza's definition,' writes Brian

Massumi in *Politics of Affect*, 'are basically ways of connecting, to others and to other situations' (2015:6). The more intense our affects, the stronger our 'sense of embeddedness in a larger field of life – a heightened sense of belonging, with other people and to other places' (ibid.). This enhanced sense of embeddedness creates an expanded political and ethical knowledge; one's relational potential, power, speed, and slowness assure, in turn, an active participation in the present – allowing the body to understand how the present augments or diminishes our affectivity. The more intensified affects create collective bonds, the more affectivity spreads from the molecular level across the social assemblage. As Deleuze and Guattari state later in *Anti-Oedipus*, *potentia*, or 'desire' is 'plugged into the existing social field as a source of energy' ([1983]2013:44). Knowledge then is created by these varying degrees of affectivity, allowing us to gain an adequate understanding of our material, social and collective circumstances. In Deleuze's *Difference and Repetition*, he outlines how someone comes to gain adequate ideas about the world through gestures of 'sensory-motivity':

> The movement of the swimmer does not resemble that of the wave, in particular, the movements of the swimming instructor which we reproduce on the sand bear no relation to the movements of the wave, which we learn to deal with only by grasping the former in practice as signs . . .We learn nothing from those who say: 'Do as I do.' Our only teachers are those who tell us to 'do with me,' and are able to emit signs to be developed in heterogeneity rather than propose gestures for us to reproduce. In other words, there is no ideo-motivity, only sensory-motivity. When a body combines some of its own distinctive points with those of a wave, it . . . involves difference, from one wave and one gesture to another . . . (1994:23)

For Deleuze, learning and knowledge are achieved through experimentations with the virtualities of the present – creatively using one's body to affect other bodies, assuring an active participation with 'what is happening and about to happen contemporaneuously (becoming)' (Seigworth 2010:185).[23] In *What is Philosophy?*, co-authored with Guattari, they write that '[t]o think is to experiment, but experimentation is always a process of coming about – the new, remarkable, and interesting' (Deleuze and Guattari 1994:111). By continuing a sensory experiment, our understanding of what our bodies 'can do', in the Spinozist sense, is heightened through affecting other bodies and, in turn, being affected ourselves. This virtuality exists at an almost imperceptible level but is the key, molecular relay-point at which one is capable of activating that which 'forces us to think' (Deleuze 1994:139). We learn our capacities and potential through sensory-motivity, opening ourselves up, actively, to being affected in the present. Susan Ruddick explains: 'The expansion of our capacity to act is at once relational, produced by mutually reinforcing collaborations, and the outcome of a complex interplay of affect and reason. It is through this interplay that we move from a passive experience of joy to an active understanding of the nature of the associations that empower' (Ruddick 2010:26).[24] Finding our relational power and 'sense of embeddedness in a larger field of life' (Massumi 2015:6) means realising how we move, connect, and collide with other human and non-human bodies. Such knowledge is developed through affect and intensive movement.

Before I discuss how affect and knowledge connect directly to poetics and literature, I will venture into another useful theory from philosopher Jacques Rancière. Rancière's theories, particularly those in *The Politics of Aesthetics*, supply a meaningful and important dimension to the ways in which migrant literatures (and art in general) reshape political regimes of legibility and visibility, especially bringing out what I see as an 'affect-sensation continuum'. That is, based on a combined framework from both of these thinkers, one can see how sense and affect join one another in shaping what is sensible and visible to us; and for both Rancière and Deleuze, art and literature have an important function to play.

Instead of using 'affect' Rancière insists on the 'distribution of the sensible', which is 'a system of self-evident facts of perception based on the set horizons and modalities of what is visible and audible as well as what can be said, thought, made, or done' (2004:85). Similar to Deleuze, Rancière suggests that there exists a perceptible ordering of the social and political world – its hierarchies as well as its 'forms of inclusion and forms of exclusion' (ibid.). Different organs of power within a society, too, confirm or enforce this distribution of the sensible, 'preclud[ing] the emergence of politics' (ibid.:93); meanwhile, dissent is achieved in the political subjects' capacity to intervene and redirect the phenomenological horizon of the visible and audible (ibid.:88–89). For Rancière, aesthetics and art have a specific role to play here in determining 'what can be apprehended by the senses' (ibid.:85); and, writing (as a form of art) produces a distribution of the sensible, disturbing the 'general law' that determines forms of inclusion and exclusion within a community (ibid.:89). A significant point here is that, for Rancière, art and literature can intervene in the distribution of the sensible, enabling us to apprehend or imagine a world in which the ordering of society – its hierarchies and borders – are reshaped and altered. Perhaps, too, a redistribution of the sensible can make perceptible a counter-history of migrancy and movement – where the migrant is not the exception, consigned to the margins, but rather upholds a political primacy.

Bringing Ránciere in connection with Deleuze and Guattari, all thinkers an understanding of how an epistemological reshaping is enabled through art and aesthetics. For Deleuze and Guattari, sensation and affect mutually reinforce one another in shaping this perceptible and sensible world.[25]

Crucially, for Deleuze and Guattari, art itself creates 'affects' and 'percepts'; that is to say, they produce 'bloc[s] of sensation' (1994:164) that 'surpass ordinary affections and perceptions' (ibid.:65). In doing so, writers and artists produce varying types of sensation, namely, 'vibrations, clinches, and openings' (ibid.:177) that rupture and tear open ('deterritorialise') our everyday opinions and expectations. Here one can see a useful connection to Rancière: for Deleuze and Guattari, affects and percepts are not only constitutive of the phenomenology of our material world; they also intervene and break open the dominant social and historical opinions, unleashing new possibilities and ways of relating to our embodied and material existence.[26] Much like the redistribution of the sensible that, according to Rancière, art and literature are capable of enacting – thereby making a different social and material arrangement visible and sensible – so, too, for Deleuze and Guattari, art and literature produce a sensible world, acting as a 'beam of light that draws a hidden universe out of the shadows' (ibid.:66). That 'hidden universe' may perhaps be a 'still-missing people' (ibid.:176), or the hidden and neglected subjects (such as migrants) that art can ideally make visible and thinkable.

I insist, though, on supplementing Rancière with Deleuze (and Guattari) because of Deleuze's conceptual linkage of knowledge with movement and motion, and thus see these thinkers' theoretical views on an 'affect-sensation continuum'. As I outlined in detail above, it is important to bear in mind that what makes affect such a useful concept is that it connects knowledge and meaning with movement. More specifically, it relates to what we might call intensive movement. The generation and enhancement of affects not only produce joy; they also effectively shape one's capacity to have adequate ideas about oneself and the world ('what a body can do'). Heightened affects produce what are often called 'intensities' – 'intense feeling of transition' (Deleuze and Guattari 2013:30) that we pass through as relational, moveable bodies.[27] Although these intensities may not be observable by material extension, they produce a movement 'in an emotional, spiritual or libidinal sense' (Buchanan 2021:37). It is a different type of movement altogether that can at some point join up with extensive movement, but which has a different relation to power. Massumi explains this in terms of the change in capacity: '[A] power to affect and be affected governs a transition, where a body passes from one state of capacitation to diminished or augmented state of capacitation' (2015:48). As we know from Deleuze's and Massumi's reading of Spinoza, these states of capacitation determine our adequate understandings of ourselves and our subjectivity. But activating this transition requires a certain intensity, or a striking flow of intensified affects. Because art and literature are capable of producing affects and sensations, they thus induce a transition from one affective state – or 'state of capacitation' (Massumi 2015:48) – to another.

This change in affective states is an intensive movement. The activation of 'visceral forces' (affects) produces a change in our sensory and relational capacities, restructuring (or, to use Rancière's term: 're-distributing') the regime of what is visible and thinkable. Art and literature produce new sensible patterns and social understandings about the way our material world is arranged. Seeing knowledge, art, and intensive movement as inseparable from one another opens up a possibility for seeing kinopoetics itself as a making of movement. Such a theoretical connection between affect and literature assures that kinopoetics is not just about movement or focusing upon the migrant; it is also itself a moving poetics. If we accept the definition of poetics above – as both a linguistic and formal arrangement of a literary work, and a broader system of meaning – then poetics is directly connected with movement under this affect theoretical framework.[28] Writing and literature, as I will show in subsequent chapters, manipulate words, figures, space, and time to reconstitute modes of seeing and hearing; and it is the migrant figure who constitutes and invents this spatial, temporal, linguistic, and affective reconfiguration. By focusing on the migrant as a primary social and historical figure – and by affirming their active and creative capacity in constituting the material world they inhabit (rather than the other way around) – kinopoetics can then use migrant literature to intensively move the regime of visibility and thinkability. Kinopoetics thus induces an intensive movement across a threshold into a new space of meaning.

This emphasis on intensive and affective movement as constituting the distribution of the sensible overcomes certain representational limits. After all, treating knowledge and meaning as something that is not fixed, but is rather in a constant state of development and process, ensures that migrant motion is not necessarily something captured, but is rather felt or sensed. Through the affects and sensations produced, our intensities operate as a continuous becoming – a continuous process of changing from one state of capacitation and resonance to the next. A truly mobile epistemology, this affect-sensation continuum coincides with and registers migrancy with a knowledge assemblage that is also moving rather than fixed. Migration and mobility across geographic space is the extensive movement; the artistic generation of affects and a redistribution of the sensible is the intensive movement. Movement and migrancy are forces that circumvent liberal regimes of capture, recognition, and representation that operate on universalist terms (a point I will clarify in the next chapter).

Chapter Conclusion: How Kinopoetics Works

In the spirit of Spinoza (outlined above), *Poetics of the Migrant* confronts the following question: what can migrant literatures do? By thinking about how migrant literatures act upon or make actual changes in material and affective life, I will use this final section to outline the ways in which kinopoetics be utilised in the following chapters. I will list what a kinopoetic reading itself does, but also how its particular readings might generate alternative readings of the given literary texts. In particular, I will emphasise what kinds of questions and concerns kinopoetics addresses, and which terminological signs and indices will be deployed to this end.

Kinopoetics renders migrant movement visible through internal focalisation

The term 'internal focalization' recalls Gerard Gennette's narrative system. In particular, internal focalisation is more conventionally known as either first-person point of view or third-person limited point of view, whereby the internal thoughts of the character are known and made explicit to the narrator. In the case of kinopoetics, most of the texts I am reading and examining are those which internally focalise the migrant.[29] The result is that the migrant's intensive and affective life – their thoughts, feelings, and sensations – shape the perspective through which the story is realised.

Genette employs the term 'internal focalization' as part of a schematic where he answers the question: 'where is the focus of perception?' (1988:64). And in doing so, he offers one such type of focalisation, 'internal focalization', to suggest that it's a 'vision with' the character. These narratives operate with a 'selective omniscience, and a restriction of field' (ibid.:65). In kinopoetics, the texts' internal focalisations rely upon the perspective of the migrant who invents, creates, and produces the social system through which they pass. Furthermore, as Bal shows us, there are ethical stakes to be considered with respect to narrative perspective in terms of agency, power, responsibility, and authority, all of which coincide in shaping how the migrant figure produces the system of social relations (2021:28).

In the Magic Realist texts of Chapter 3, for example, we regard the nomadic subject as the agent whose perspective and thoughts invent and destroy reality in order to match the complexity of their social and historical intensity.[30] In the texts of urban city environments, in Chapter 4, it is the vagabond's wandering and mental geography that enunciates and rewrites the city's structures and regulatory systems. Finally, with the linguistic experimentation analysed in Chapter 5, the migrant, barbarian subject uses their own relationship to and position within language to evade the constraints of competency and mastery, on the one hand, but to also assert a new social relation and counterpower. In all cases it is perspective that organises social space and political relations in the text, making types of movement possible (see also Nail 2019:110). In turn, we might be guided by the migrant's subjective experience that may at times be unreliable or severely limited. Yet, we are affirming the migrant's active participation in the regime of social motion through which they are constructed and politicised, and therefore their sensory-motivity and intensive movement are what produce the distribution of the sensible world of migrancy they inhabit.

Kinopoetics (as a method) performatively declares the migrant as an affirmative and primary figure

As is made clear through kinopolitics, the migrant is analysed and affirmed as the primary constitutive figure of social history. In addition, this counter-history of the migrant treats their movement as the transformative, liberating, pedetic force against forces of power to which they are subjected. In kinopoetics, the internally focalised migrant character is also treated this way: their relational and active power confronts, shapes and challenges the social milieu, but their migrancy creates the bordering and circulating conditions through which the political assemblage functions. In the upcoming chapters, this will inform the discursive index on which I rely. As I will explain in the third section of Chapter 2, kinopoetics undertakes a reading of migrant literatures that is, perhaps, strange and unconventional, but nevertheless creates a poetics that performatively engages the affirmative movement of migrancy. The migrant figure's affirmative and deterritorialising potential is thus actualised through this critical method. By doing so, this ensures the methodological counter-poetics of kinopoetics, applying and shaping the critical procedures that incorporates a discourse of affirmation.

Kinopoetics (as an object of study) enacts intensive movement and a redistribution of the sensible

I outlined the relationship between kinopoetics, affect, and knowledge earlier in this chapter. In brief, the goal of kinopoetics is to create and produce intensive movements through affects; and by imparting intensive flows that shock, speed up, or slow down our relational affectivity (both personal and collective), literary texts are capable of (re-)distributing the sensible, changing the boundaries and hierarchies of inclusion and exclusion, as well as what is visible, thinkable, audible, and permissible. In the following chapters, various texts will do this in their own way. 'Destructive kinopoetics', by way of Magic Realism, changes the parameters of time and space in ways consonant with the migrant's singular and transformative movement. The migrant's nomadic renderings of the social milieu, which modify reality with magic, thus change the relational and epistemic conditions by which the social assemblage becomes knowable. In other words, reality becomes the migrant's reality, and in turn the enclosures of modernity, history, and identity are destroyed by the migrant's creative experimentation with time and space.

'Wandering kinopoetics' similarly brings the experience of urban settings and modernity out through the migrant's own intensive experience. The migrant within the city-scape exists as a vagabond, the criminalised outsider who is looked upon with suspicion. In focalising the migrant, letting them take their lead in their own vagrant subjectivity, their intensive life pushes and produces the distribution of space and, particularly, the borders that constitute life in the metropole. Rather than authorising or legitimising a perspective that controls and criminalises the vagabond's movement, the vagabond renders their own subjectivity. They bear witness to the suspicions and confrontations that characterise their out-of-placeness in the urban setting. Once again, this challenges the typical orderings of power within modernity whereby the juridical and legal system of policing and surveillance criminalises the vagabond, determining their circulation and movement on terms set by the State. Instead, the vagabond's kinpoetics creates and produces the experience of suspicion on their own terms – how they see, feel, hear, and know their own stigmatisation and suspicion in ways that may otherwise be imperceptible or unrepresentable. Thus, the typical arrangement of the population and the social milieu is redistributed, thereby also redistributing the sensible.

Finally, 'Stuttering Kinopoetics' changes the conditions of comprehension and communication. Undercutting basic standards of grammar, style, phonetics and syntax, migrant texts often deploy new language tricks that show the migrant's singular relationship to language (often, for example, code-switching between their native tongue and their new, received language). Crucially, though, a migrant figure will often invent and create new ways of rendering language, combining sounds, elongating vowels, or changing intonation. These ways of utilising language change the way that vibrations are made and the way in which language is heard – it is heard in atypical, foreign, and often incomprehensible ways. Nevertheless, the migrant's language thereby creates and asserts new ways of *making* meaning and understanding, often then rupturing the standards of grammar from within, but also activating sound waves and vibrations. Again, here, the migrant will unsettle or undo the relationship to meaning, thereby also (re-)asserting the migrant's creative, active, pressure on linguistic conventions.

* * *

In the chapters that comprise Part II, kinopoetics will function by satisfying all three of the above conditions – focalising the migrant, affirming their active pedetic motion, and enabling them to deterritorialise affective and epistemological enclosures. In each chapter, all three of these features of kinopoetics will be brought to the surface, acting again as a 'beam of light that draws a hidden universe out of the shadows' (Deleuze and Guattari 1994:66). In addition, all three of these aspects will be combined with or informed through an ontology of movement. In every instance of analysing the migrant figure and the migrant text, each analysis will centre or recentre the primacy of motion and movement; as such, migrancy and mobility are understood as the constitutive forces of political and social life. The upshot of kinopolitics is such that the counter-history of the migrant is given a political and ontological centrality. What kinopoetics adds to this is a critical methodology and object of study that makes the primacy of migrant movement thinkable and visible. Yet, what it also provides is a performative, pedetic transformation of the affective and epistemological life – those things that make the world legible and knowable. What kinopoetics assures, then, is the capacity to allow the migrant's extensive and intensive movement, carried in and through their literary texts, to then make migrancy, movement, and pedetic force visible and thinkable.[31]

Notes

1. Even in his 1981 *Introduction to Poetics*, Tzvetan Todorov retains this aspect of poetics, saying: 'In contradistinction to the interpretation of particular works, [poetics] does not seek to name meaning, but aims at a knowledge of the general laws that preside over the birth of each work' (6).
2. 'If one happens to not have seen the thing before, it will not give pleasure as an imitation, but because of its execution [e.g. rhythm and melody] or colour, or for some other reason' (Aristotle [c. 335BCE]1996:7).
3. 'Poetry [during the Medieval period] might, therefore, resemble a game in certain respects; but as long as poets play such word games in the service of public virtue, then, *contra* Plato, they perform a useful function in society' (Reed 2012:1060).
4. 'Everyone must allow that a judgement on the beautiful which is tinged with the slightest interest, is very partial and not a pure judgement of taste. One must not be in the least prepossessed in favour of the existence of the thing, but must preserve complete indifference in this respect, in order to play the part of judge in matters of taste' (Kant [1790]2007:37).
5. '[T]he feeling of the sublime is a pleasure that only arises indirectly, being brought about by the feeling of a momentary check to the vital forces followed at once by a discharge all the more powerful, and so it is an emotion that seems to be no play, but a serious matter in the exercise of the imagination' (Kant 2007:75–6).
6. 'The formalists', says Galin Tihanov, 'were the first to see literature as an autonomous domain of theoretical inquiry, steering away from aesthetics, sociology, psychology, and history and seeking support in linguistics' (Tihanov 2012:1239).
7. 'The goal of art', continues Shklovsky, 'is to create the sensation of seeing, and not merely recognizing, things; the device of art is the 'enstrangement' of things and the complication of the form, which increases the duration and complexity of perception, as the process of perception is, in art, an end in itself and must be prolonged' (2015:162).

8. This is largely due to Roman Jakobsen, who was a member of the Society for the Study of Poetic Language (*OPOYAZ*), where the Russian Formalists formed, and who later, upon meeting Claude Levi-Strauss, played a major role in the development of Structuralism after World War II.

9. According to Gérard Genette, 'structuralism as a method is based on the study of structures wherever they occur; but to begin with, structures are not directly encountered objects – far from it; they are systems of latent relations, conceived rather than perceived, which analysis constructs as it uncovers them, and which it runs the risk of inventing while believing that it is discovering them.' (Genette [1967]1997: 91).

10. In the multiplicity of writing', writes Roland Barthes, 'everything is *disentangled*, nothing *deciphered*; . . . writing ceaselessly posits meaning ceaselessly to evaporate it, carrying out a systematic exemption of meaning' ([1967]1997:123).

11. Of course, one glaring issue here is that this effort risks re-essentialising 'male' and 'female' categories as if they are fixed and coherent; and, as I will show in Chapter 2, it is these tendencies that migration literatures and poetics attempt to overcome.

12. In Chapter 2, Poetics of Migration: A Typology, I will discuss how négritude offers a place within the poetics of migration (what I designate as a 'poetics of migritude') to which kino-poetics responds.

13. As Edward W. Said writes, 'if you read and interpret modern European and American culture as having had something to do with imperialism, it comes incumbent upon you also to reinterpret the canon in the light of texts whose place there has been sufficiently linked to, insufficiently weighted toward, the expansion of Europe' (1993:60).

14. A more detailed outline of different strands of Postcolonial Studies, particularly those reflecting a turn toward Derridean deconstruction (in the works of Homi Bhabha and Gayatri Spivak), will be developed in the next chapter.

15. Because of the way this section is written, it is natural to think that the development of 'poetics' was a linear process.

Yet, it's important to note the extent to which these different fields interpenetrated and influenced one another, operating sometimes simultaneously or in parallel. For example, the emergence of Post-structuralism and Feminism, were not introduced in sequence, but rather existed within the same time period, inheriting the same (or similar) cultural ideas of the time. Similarly, Postcolonialism had strands that were much closer to that of the Structuralists than to the Post-structuralists; for example, many Postcolonial scholars were closely tied a more Marxist tradition or Psychoanalytic tradition than to the Derrideans/Foucaultians.

16. More about how this movement-oriented poetics works and how it departs from earlier traditions will be outlined in Chapter 2, section headed From a Poetics of Migration to a Movement-Oriented Poetics.

17. In *Theory of the Border*, Nail expands this notion of the junction to provide the foundation for the 'border' as such: 'The border is [. . .] a yoke or filter that allows some immigrants to pass through with only minor inconvenience, others to obtain work under illegal or exploitative conditions, and others still to be caught and held for years in detentions centres without charges. On the other side of the border, migrant labor flows are then harnessed through work junctions into a vehicle for production, profit, and social subordination. The flows that do not pass the border junction can end up in the detention junction[,] harnessed into a vehicle for profit for private prison contractors and private security forces responsible for deporting them' (2016:28).

18. 'Expansion by expulsion is the social logic by which some members of society are dispossessed of their status so that social power can be expanded elsewhere' (Nail 2015:37).

19. '[T]he name given to the Neolithic migrant is "the nomad" because it is the name of the figure whose emergence and movement are defined by its social expulsion from the territory' (Nail 2015:46).

20. 'The aim of these laws', says Nail, 'was to expand a specifically juridical control over the undesirable movement of peasants, beggars, paupers, heretics, minstrels, Jews, witches, and

rebellious travelers of all kinds grouped under the criminal name "the vagabond"' (Nail 2015:74).

21. 'All *potentia* is act, active and actual . . . [A]ll power is inseparable from a capacity for being affected, and this capacity for being affected is constantly and necessarily filled by affections that realise it' (Deleuze 1988:97).

22. 'This is why, even when one assumes the capacity for being affected to be constant, some of our power . . . increases or is enhanced by affections of joy' (Deleuze 1988:101).

23. More about this distinct ontology of primary difference will be discussed in Chapter 2 under the section headed Reassessing Postcolonial Theory through a Philosophy of Movement (second sub-section).

24. Ruddick, paraphrasing Deleuze, gives a more concrete example of how a transition from an inadequate idea to a 'common notion' is achieved (2010:30).

25. In *What is Philosophy?*, they write that a 'composite sensation, made up of percepts and affects, deterritorialises the system of opinion that brought together dominant perceptions and affections within a natural, historical, and social milieu' (Deleuze and Guattari 1994:197).

26. In *What is Philosophy?*, Deleuze and Guattari refer to the dominant social and historical opinions as *Urdoxa*. The idea here is that art and literature are meant to cut a 'slit in the umbrella' of *Urdoxa*; they 'tear open the firmament itself, to let in a bit of free and windy chaos,' and are 'needed to . . . carry out necessary and perhaps ever-greater destructions' (1994:204).

27. Ian Buchanan defines the Deleuzo-Guattarian idea of intensities in clearer terms: 'Intensities are the agitations of the mind and body (for the want of a better way of putting it) that move us in an emotional, spiritual or libidinal sense but we cannot name; they are the stirrings in our mental equilibrium that come before love and hate, anger and frustration; they are the sensations we long to sustain when we're on a "high" and cannot wait to escape or extinguish when we're stuck feeling "low"' (2021:37).

28. This turn toward movement, knowledge, and affect rests on a metaphysics that has been well-theorised and discussed in another field known as New Materialism. The suggestion here that texts and works of art induce and connect with our affective and relational knowledge, but also produce modulations across a social and political assemblage, is undergirded by a belief in a text's 'performativity'. One of the premises of performativity is that 'ontology and epistemology are inherently co-implicated and mutually constituting' (Gamble, Hanan and Nail 2019:122). In other words, the nature of what the world is and how we come to know its nature (that is, phenomenology) are not separate domains or forces. The consequence here, then, is that there is not necessarily a separation between an object that is moving and the phenomenology of its movement. These features are intertwined. The observation of migrancy within a text, then, brings together extensive movement and intensive movement, rather than keeping them as separate ontological domains. The migrant's movement across space and time is mutually constituted in and co-implicated with the distribution of the sensible wherein migrancy is made visible.

29. One exception to this will be Linton Kwesi Johnson's poem, 'New Cross Massakah', outlined in Chapter 5, section headed 'New Craas Massakah': Stuttering, Dancing and Rioting.

30. In this chapter, to illuminate this point, I make oblique reference to how this perspective is brought into one narrative field of vision, with Salman Rushdie's concept of 'stereoscopic vision'.

31. Parts of the chapter are adapted and modified from my 2019 article, 'Centrifugal Force and the Mouth of a Shark: Toward a Movement-Oriented Poetics.' *ARIEL*, 50(4):51–78.

CHAPTER 2

MOVEMENT INTERVENTIONS

To further set the background upon which kinopoetics is building, I will now examine some theoretical traditions to which a movement-oriented politics and philosophy offer a response. The foundational assumptions of sovereignty, citizenship, and statehood all develop within specific historical contexts, and require further elucidation. Furthermore, I also turn to previous analyses of migration and diaspora, showing what they have contributed to the field, but also how a philosophy of motion might intervene. From here, I will establish the discourses to which kinopoetics remains in constant dialogue. Throughout this chapter, readers should gain a sense for how kinopoetics fits into a broader tradition, how it responds to that tradition, and the myriad questions that it attempts to answer. I will start this first section with sedentarism, a concept which provides the ideological and discursive structure that underlies the legal and political system of migration-management, bordering, sovereignty, and nationalism. The upshot here is that kinopoetics and kinopolitics both aim to challenge this tradition, and it is from here that we can advance the theoretical discourse on movement and mobility.

In the second and fourth sections of this chapter, I will touch on two dimensions that dominate the theoretical study of migrancy and migrant literature. These fields have played an enormous role in my development as a scholar, and I hope to show how they still provide meaningful insights from which kinopoetics can draw. After both sections, they will be followed up by my attempt to intervene through a philosophy or politics of motion (third and fifth sections). From here, I hope to illustrate the debt that kinopoetics owes to previous traditions, but how it nevertheless offers an innovative approach to the study of migrant literature.

Sedentarism and Sovereignty: The Master Texts Behind the Nation

In a famous text, titled *Seeing Like a State,* anthropologist James C. Scott explains precisely how one comes to 'see' like a state. 'Originally', Scott writes, 'I set out to understand why the state has always been the enemy of "the people who move around", to put it crudely' (1998:1). Scott emphasises, throughout his book, the juridical and legal processes that state and administrative organs of power leverage to bring a society into a recognisable whole, a process he calls 'sedentarisation', or, a 'state's attempt to make a society legible, to arrange the population in ways that simplified the classic state functions of taxation, conscription, and prevention of rebellion' (ibid.:2). For Scott, the state, in order to function and exert its sovereign power, needs to create a ready-made index of citizens whom it can recognise and represent on its own, invented terms – quantifiable registries and categories that make citizens and the body politic representable as coherent entities. These processes ultimately create an easily controllable and manageable social structure. This process requires organising and systematising the social milieu and citizenry in terms that state power can recognise. The state institutes practices of registration, control, monitoring, indexing, and categorisation, to better keep control of, and secure, a sovereign territory. Moreover, sedentarisation is the foundation for visa schemes, restrictions on mobility, border control, and citizenship policies; and, in fact, the principle of settlement as a basis for immigration management emphasises the state's need for citizens to remain sedentary in order to be legitimised and recognised.

These practices have a long, complicated history in Western society, especially in the spatial (re-)structuring of nation-states. Ato Quayson traces, as many historians do, the formation of the nation-state to the 1648 Treaty of Westphalia.[1] Resulting from the development of nation-states as we know them was the concept of sovereignty, the governing principle around which nation-states are formed, and the principle that borders are meant to constitute and delimit. In classical political theory, borders mark the extent of sovereign political power; and sovereignty itself signifies a principle of non-interference from outside entities. Sovereignty is the central idea determining which societies count as states, giving them authority to determine which people are its citizens, and allow their national borders to remain recognised, protected, and uncompromised. How sovereignty is expressed and carried out by state power will be touched upon below; I will first outline the metaphysical relationship between sovereignty and the world-historical structure.

For a state entity to be legitimised as a state, it must maintain coherent features of *identity* that are recognised according to a broader historical conception of the nation.[2] This notion of recognition as providing an important feature of historical narrative can be traced back to Georg W. F. Hegel, whose dialectical structure of history is built upon a mutual recognition of, and struggle between, opposing forces.[3] Crucially, according to Hegel, the phenomenology (that is, appearance and recognisability) of history's eternal and guiding spirit (*Geist*) follows a linear process and teleological, rationalising structure; and the primacy of the nation (as identity) as defined in opposition to, but also in recognition by, its outside (difference) is built upon seeing the nation as a central, primary entity. A nation develops its 'character' based on a dialectical struggle of ideologies which then eventually resolve themselves, thereby producing the next temporal stage of history. As G. A. Cohen explains, the theory that Hegel promulgated would demonstrate a noticeable progress in 'values, culture, and politics' (2000:5) and, with it, a recognisable trend in improved material conditions. For Hegel, then, a nation is recognised as such based on its projection and achievement of progress; and its achievement of this process is through a dialectical struggle between the self and other (as with the famous master-slave dialectic).

Based on this dialectical structure of identity, we can underscore the connection to sovereignty, since sovereignty is a principle that mandates nation-states recognise one another as states. Again, according to Hegel, recognition by and through a struggle with the *other* is the basis through which identity is secured and legitimised. Similarly, the State bases its identity on its primacy and self-consciousness as an entity in opposition to that which is outside of its borders or sovereign boundaries. Such a notion of self-other dialectic leads Hegel to a metaphysics for recognising a people within world history.[4] In other words, for Hegel, a society and its people are deemed to have a history so long as they have a 'natural' membership within a specific state; that is to say that Hegel believed that membership within a political society 'should be based on birth, and at least seem given or natural, from the Latin root *nasci*, meaning birth' (Stevens 2019:110). The state is only identified and representable as a state according to its compliance with these recognisable features of sovereignty. Therefore, to be represented within world history, according to Hegel, a society has to have membership and identity within a recognised sovereign state.

Marx, too, notably adopted Hegel's dialectical structure to describe the historical development of political economy through proletarian struggle and revolution. According to Marx, instead of thinking of history as guided by solely a progressive change in social values and improved ideas (as Hegel does), 'growth in productive power is the force underlying social change' (Cohen 2000:345).[5] The point here, for Marx (especially in his earlier writings), is that the productive relations and circulation of capital and commodities ('base') condition the legal and political institutions ('superstructure' and ideology) of every historical epoch. Each historical stage, then, reflects the relative abundance or depletion of available resources and capital, coupled with the rationalisation (or management) of labour power, eventual technological acceleration, and the expansion of production. These processes within the political economy control and shape the distribution of material power, mobility, and freedom within society, thereby determining the composition of class and the nature of class struggle. Rather than, therefore, society consisting solely of one's membership to the state, Marx states in *The Grundrisse* that '[s]ociety does not consist of individuals, but expresses the sum of interrelations, the relations within which these individuals stand' (Marx [1857]1978:247). The governing principle for one's standing in society is not granted through the state, but is determined by the social relations of capital. For Marx, though, this conception of history as a dialectical struggle between capitalists and workers is characteristic of industrial societies of the Western world. He is describing how the development of productive forces govern the change and progress of history, thereby treating history as having a systematic, teleological, law-like pattern. Like Hegel, Marx understands his schema as a universal history, describing all historic stages as created by changing modes of production and material shift, negations, and contradictionss; and societies, again, are recognised as such, so long as their histories comply with this structure and trend toward expanded productive capacities and technological development.

Many have considered there to be a certain Eurocentrism following from this conception of recognition and teleological progress,[6] leading thus to the Hegel's oft-quoted racist assertion that Africa 'is no historical part of the world; it has no movement or development to exhibit' (Hegel qtd in Camara 2005:85). Dipesh Chakrabarty in his text, *Provincialising Europe*, takes Marx to task for his universal history as well:

> The coming of the bourgeois or capitalist society [for Marx] . . . gives rise for the first time to a history that can be apprehended through a philosophical and universal category, 'capital.' History becomes, for the first time, theoretically knowable. All past histories are now to be known (theoretically, that is) from the vantage point of this category, that is, in terms of their differences from it' (2000:30).

As Marx states in *The Grundrisse*, '[b]ourgeois society is the most developed and the most complex historic organisation of production' (1978:241). Chakrabarty responds to this, suggesting that we ought to, for 'bourgeois . . ., read "Europe" or "European"' (2000:30). The point, in Chakrabarty's reading of Marx, is that history's capacity to be recognised – that which makes history knowable and legible – is based on a society's achievement of a certain degree of capitalist development, resource abundance, proletarianisation, and industrial production. Crucially, though, this view of historic progress is similarly teleological, seeing all societies as developing toward the realisation of bourgeois production. Societies are considered 'developed' once they arrive at a mode of production that creates abundance and the ongoing generation of surplus-value. But (contra Chakrabarty) because capital and bourgeois power was, in Marx's time, firmly concentrated in Europe (Hobsbawm 1975:13–14), his understanding of historical progress derives from this context: one that obtained uniquely advanced productive capacities. As such, these were the only circumstances that properly lent themselves to Marx's model of capitalist expansion. Furthermore, we also know from Marx (as I examined in the third section of Chapter 1) that capitalist production depends upon the violent expropriation of land and dispossession of indigenous and colonised people through the process of primitive accumulation. This process, though, also creates an uneven global power and exchange relation, assuring the dominance of bourgeois capitalist societies over those whom they have expelled. Since the ruling class, or the bourgeoisie, sets and determines the exchange and property relations in a capitalist society, they also shape the governing ideology of that society. Ideology, here, produces the unconscious beliefs and understanding of society's structure; it is the 'the descriptive vocabulary of day-to-day existence, through which people make rough sense of the social reality that they live and create from day to day' (Fields 1990:110). Because of the pervasive dominance of the bourgeoisie as a ruling class, the world-historical narrative begins to bend according to the ruling class's ideas and to the principle of capital.

So, despite the limits that Chakrabarty finds in such a dialectical history, we can still adopt Marx's interpretive method in meaningful ways. Marxist theory can help underscore the fact that the pervasive image of historical development and sovereignty cannot be fully understood outside of the dialectical forces of capitalist, bourgeois society and ideology.[7] Although, as I stated earlier, the canonical origin of sovereignty is usually located at the Treaty of Westphalia, the material conditions for its historical enshrinement are in fact directly tied to the rise of colonialism (Loomba 1998:124). Of course, colonialism cannot be strictly understood or reduced to an economic imperative; we should rather realise that

> [c]apitalism . . . does not override and liquidate racial hier-
> archies but continues to depend upon, and intensify, them.
> Ideologies of race and the social structures created by them
> facilitate capitalist production. . . In colonial situations the
> state and its various institutions (such as educational estab-
> lishments) are especially crucial in maintaining these racial
> and class distinctions and ideologies necessary for creating
> capitalism. (Loomba 1998:124)

In other words, the expansion and establishment of European colonial rule throughout the world relied upon the administrative structures and organs of power that could legitimise racist ideology and settler control. As Cedric Robinson explains, in his diagnosis of racial capitalism, the ruling class of the sixteenth century took hold in the 'interstices of the state' (1983:20). In doing so, they consolidated power and wielded control by securing a class who eventually carried out the interests of the state itself.[8] European ruling power exported their ideology of racial superiority, while also extending their capitalist, bourgeois dominance over (what they saw as) peripheral nations. Colonialism, therefore, became intertwined with the stratifying logic of bourgeois capitalism, creating on a global scale a hierarchical system according to both race and class – axes of difference that assured the consolidated power of the bourgeoisie, and the dispossession and underdevelopment of the colonised.[9] A result of these differentiating, stratifying efforts was the emergence of racialist ideologies that justified and supported the ruling power of the European bourgeois class. These ideologies created the conditions through which specific (that is, bourgeois, European) forms of history, identity and politics could be recognised, authorised and proliferated on a global scale.

Out of these conditions of global hierarchy, capital rule and racial stratification developed the idealisation of sovereignty (Mongia 2007:396). Such a global power structure created a bordered regime, defining the sovereign boundaries and legible limits of nation-states around the world. In turn, the dominant, European hegemony determined which societies counted as nations and the rest of the world was handed over to their unelected control. This system placed a political and representative centrality on sovereignty as the constitutive principle for recognition. As a consequence, sovereignty granted states the capacity to determine the limits of sovereign territory – deciding who is left out of that territory and calling into question the capacity for mobile people to claim citizenship or recognition. Sovereignty is not only the principle upon which a nation or society can be considered a nation-state (and thus protected from foreign interference, 'discovery', or 'conquest'); sovereignty is also a regime of exclusion, determining that those who are not within the boundaries of sovereign territory are deemed threats or compromises to the nation's identity as a state (and not exempt from outside control or domination). Again, such a regime operates as an outcome of sedentarisation: those who are settled and stabilised within the state's territory fall under the scope of its protection, and can be readily recognised, monitored, represented and categorised – in short, they are made 'legible' (Scott 1998:2). Yet, sovereignty intersects not only with the legislative and juridical processes of the state; sovereignty is also reinforced through ideological and discursive forces of power. A society's capacity to be recognised as a sovereign, unified national identity is replicated within discursive and institutional practices of securitisation, racial violence, citizenship schemes, bordering, surveillance and identity-construction. Borders arise out of these practices to reproduce the hegemony's sovereign power, reducing the power of those who threaten sovereignty (Sharma 2019:77).[10]

The classic text for analysing the intersection between national identity, sovereignty, and discourse is Benedict Anderson's *Imagined Communities*, wherein he argues that the nation is 'an imagined political community – and imagined both as limited and as sovereign' ([1983]2006):6). For Anderson, although the members of this political community do not in fact know one another, they each nevertheless have an image of their shared communion – making this connection imagined, but no less real (ibid.). The formation of a nationalist ideology was synchronous with the emergence of sovereignty as a political value. Rather than a nation deriving its legitimacy from the monarchical order or divine rule, it instead fashioned a discursive and material regime of national identity through which its members could view themselves in relation to one another (Sharma 2019:78). Its identity as a nation – self-conscious and recognised, in the Hegelian sense – was forged by assuring that this identity contains a clear ethnic, linguistic, social, historic and ideological limit, enabling its citizens to position themselves against those who are outside. Similarly, sovereignty granted the national community its autonomy and legitimacy according to the bourgeois, European conception of statehood (as outlined above). These forces of identity-formation and political recognition set the foundation for nationalism, creating an ideology that attempts to maintain national purity and discursive practices of violent exclusion and hostility.

Nationalist policies, then, can rely upon the presumed political virtue of sovereignty, using it as the central governing principle in need of protection. We can extend this idea, in combination with the analysis of bourgeois sovereignty, to emphasise that it exists as both an effort of cultural homogenisation and differentiation, enabling the ruling power to determine what counts as a pure national identity, and devise a global hierarchy on these terms. The criteria for statehood and sovereignty emerged from the era of colonisation from which the ruling class determined how a society's history was meant to proceed and what form nation-states were meant to take. Thus, the conception of sovereignty emerged out of the material conditions of colonialism, allowing the consolidated European powers to divide the world's nations into differentiated, stratified categories of inclusion and exclusion; as a result, these nations export and externalise their ideology of racial superiority through which they justify imperial interference and domination. For Anderson, nationalism utilises the political apotheosis of sovereignty as a juridical and legislative incentive to leverage administrative, military, educational, and disciplinary power against those inside and outside who threaten national identity.[11]

Sovereignty, then, becomes an ongoing political project, creating axes of power, vulnerability, relationality, belonging and exclusion. Specifically, sovereignty helps inform the construction of immigration policies and citizenship schemes. Immigration policies create an image of a people who rightfully constitute the nation, determining degrees of belonging as well as the boundaries of national inclusion. Furthermore, though, across a variety of institutions of state power, a series of diffuse mechanisms continue to territorialise sovereignty and migrant subjectivity. In order to sufficiently manage and protect against this outside influence, national-state regimes have to replicate this image of their population and that of the migrant, justifying the interlocking techniques of territory, authority and security. These techniques coalesce in what Foucault called 'governmentality'. In *Security, Territory, Population*, Foucault defines governmentality as 'the way in which the conduct (*conduite*) of a set of individuals became involved, in an increasingly pronounced way, in the exercise of sovereign power' (2007:364). For Foucault, this exercise of sovereign power is an expression of 'biopower' through 'basic biological features [such as, mortality or health]' function as objects of 'a general strategy of power' (ibid:1). Governmentality, says Foucault, 'finds the principles of its rationality and the specific domain of its application in the state' (ibid.:365); and the 'new matrix of rationality' is deemed the 'Raison d'État' according to which the seat of state power exercises its 'sovereignty in governing men' (ibid.).[12] The point here, for Foucault, is that organs of political sovereignty necessarily call upon technologies of security so that a population can be properly defined and managed, disciplining or confining those who, in 'refusing to be the population, disrupt the system' (ibid.:44). Sovereignty, then, enacts governmentality over a 'multiplicity' by instituting codes of conduct and power relations by which the population must abide, and by upholding a territorial, economic, and moral authority.

Through this process the state power imposes and codifies restrictions on conduct and comportment, but it also facilitates the circulation of people and commodities through a 'physics of power' (Foucault 2007:49). As a result, any regime can be variable in its population, 'rich or poor, active or idle' (ibid.:96); but these aspects are 'only variables in relation to the territory that is the very foundation of the principality or of sovereignty' (ibid.). This foundational aspect of sovereignty produces the technological assemblages through which population management is achieved. One example, for Foucault, arises in the basis of statistics which was once the name given to the necessary 'knowledge of things that comprise the very reality of the state . . . the forces and resources that characterise a state at a given moment' (ibid.:274). A significant consequence for migration, then, is that citizenship and border controls come into contact with these securitising forces that manage the circulation of (human and non-human) movement (ibid.:325–6). So, the way that sovereignty exercises power over a territory is not only through the preservation of its national identity (population) and status as a recognised political entity; it also does so through the policing and management of circulation – where and how far people and things can move. These security forces coincide with disciplinary forces, producing complementary forces of (centripetal and centrifugal) movement that all function together in constituting a state territory and milieu. The coercive power of state and national territories relies on this management of circulation (Sassen 2008:41). Through this system, then, one finds that the state's combined efforts of citizenship management and securitisation all ensure a coherent population over which they can impose laws and codes of conduct. These intersecting forces then enable the administrative power and authority to institute practices of social control and discipline; and they also ensure and regulate economic activities, such as taxations and capital circulation. Additionally, these ideas tie in nicely with Anderson's suggestion that the nation's identity needs to retain a certain boundary of who counts as a member of the nation, and projects that image against the out-group. As a result, the concomitant treatment of migrants as failed citizens stems from these combined activities and techniques.

Migration controls and bordering exist as tools and techniques used by the sovereign state to make sure that a population abides by the codes of conduct and that they do not compromise the state's efforts of securitisation.[13] Immigrants confront this securitising and population management system in the form of assimilationism; that is, their conduct and composure is forced to comply with the nation's image, otherwise they are immediately subject to stigmatisation, criminalisation and hostility. The behaviour of immigrants is characterised as erratic, dangerous, uncivilised and disruptive – all aspects of conduct and behaviour that jeopardise sovereignty and security. Thus, because of the need to reproduce and sustain the authority of sovereignty and the state, these regimes also have to position their pronouncements and conduct in a way that makes the population coherent. Immigrants and outsiders do not conform to this coherent system. By 'refusing to be the population' (Foucault 2007:44), they are immediately deemed too disruptive and insecure for the state to manage. Sandro Mezzadra and Brett Neilson respond to this idea, noting that 'while for Foucault the people corresponds to the 'legal' logics of sovereignty and citizenship (and the language of rights), he posits population as the target of biopolitical government' (2013:173). The crucial point instead, according to Mezzadra and Neilson, is to recognise the difference between 'the concept of the population and the concept of the people' (ibid.).[14] This idea is comparable to Scott's assertion that these mechanisms for social discipline and management are the methods of sedentarisation that the state relies upon in order to properly function.[15] By ensuring that a certain population is realised and made legible, the state is able to limit the extent of that which it must enact sovereignty over; and because these state regimes operate in the service of the dominant group, they limit the subjects of sovereignty to those who are within that group and who conform to their ideology of national identity and community.

By limiting sovereignty, state power also confines its juridical and political responsibility, and controls what counts as life itself within that framework. This system creates what Giorgio Agamben (following Carl Schmitt) calls a 'state of exception'.[16] Taking cues from Foucault's conception of biopower, Agamben argues that the state of exception operates 'as the original structure in which law encompasses living beings by means of its own suspension' (Agamben 2005:3). According to Agamben, 'the first foundation of political life is a life that may be killed, which is politicised through its very capacity to be killed' (Agamben [1995]1998:89). This is the basis under which the sovereign power creates the conditions and boundaries of biopolitics – the capacity to multiply life (*bios*), making life itself the subject of political control (or lack thereof). Because political subjects grant authority to the state as the guarantor of political action, freedom and representation – and because these aspects bear directly on one's ability to live – the sovereign state is granted absolute control over life and death. This is especially the case in states of emergency, which expands the 'powers of the government' (Agamben 2005:5), creating a condition in which the 'distinctions among different powers (legislative, executive, etc.)' (ibid:6) are eliminated.

The dire consequences of this state of exception are dramatised in Achille Mbembe's concept of 'necropolitics':

> [T]he ultimate expression of sovereignty resides, to a large degree, in the power and the capacity to dictate who may live and who must die. Hence, to kill or to allow to live constitute the limits of sovereignty, its fundamental attributes. To exercise sovereignty is to exercise control over mortality and to define life as the deployment and manifestation of power (2003:11–12).

As I mentioned above, sovereignty operates for the nation-state as a regime of exclusion; and by operating on this principle, the state can determine that those whom it excludes are not worthy of life or may be killed. Examples of necropolitical cruelty abound, particularly in acts of war (Butler 2009:27) and incarceration (Gilmore 2007:247), and are especially pronounced across axes of race, class, gender and sexuality.[17] These forces of biopower and necropolitics converge in the realm of migration. Specifically, border and migration policies become 'dictatorial' systems in which 'migrants have no control over the definition of the laws and policies that concern their crossing of the borders of states of which they are not citizens' (Heller, Pezzani and Stierl 2019:67).[18]

Throughout this section, I have attempted to show the historic, ideological, and discursive continuities between sedentarism, sovereignty, colonialism, nationalism, biopower, and necropolitics, clarifying how these contribute to and shape the global conditions of migration that we have today. The consequences of sedentarism and sovereignty are revealed in the border policies and mobility restrictions that nation-states continue to utilise. Moreover, concepts of sovereignty and state protection provide support to nationalist policies and anti-immigrant sentiments: they provide the axioms through which the hegemonic group can justify its exclusionary violence. These ideas, though, did not arise in a vacuum; they emerged in the material conditions of colonialism, capitalism, and empire-building that helped replicate and export racist ideologies and power relations globally, thereby creating a differentiated world hierarchy. This discursive and ideological system places the nation as the primary centre around which all of global history is governed; and it is these systems that kinopoetics and kinopolitics are attempting to challenge. In order to do so, such a project requires that one 'strategically alter' the title of Scott's famous book (that I began this section with) from *Seeing Like a State* to 'seeing like a migrant' (Mezzadra and Neilson 2013:166). Such an enormous task demands that we embrace the counter-history of movement that Nail proposes through kinopolitics. But, additionally, kinopoetics presents an additional layer to this analysis: it offers the object of study and methodology that can make migrancy legible. In this way, kinopoetics can articulate what Antonio Gramsci calls a 'new culture' or, in other words, 'a new moral life', demanding that a migrant counter-hegemonic relation emerges alongside 'a new way of feeling and seeing reality' (1999:395). Migrant literature's narrative and linguistic hybridity, coupled with its ability to make us as readers intensively and affectively feel, see, and hear lives of migrant characters, is multi-faceted and methodologically unbounded enough to bring migrancy and a counter-history of movement to life. The next section gives an overview of already-existing traditions within the study of migrant literature and poetics.

Poetics of Migration: A Typology

Before venturing into kinopoetics, it is important to recognise that there is already a long-standing, well-established critical field for studying migrant literature; and within this field, several approaches can be said to operate within a 'poetics'. Depending on the specific literary object or the critical and discursive framework, what shape this poetics takes or what they emphasise can differ greatly. Nevertheless, within the study of migrancy and migration as a literary preoccupation, there are several types of approaches within this broader category – a category that I will call a 'poetics of migration'. But because there is not one general theory of migrant literature, the range of approaches have to specify their objects of study and their methodologies. Broadly speaking, within a poetics of migration, there are four types of poetics which I plan to identify: first, transnational poetics; second, poetics of relation; third, minor literature; and, fourth, poetics of migritude. This is by no means a comprehensive list; but I will summarise these poetics in an attempt to dramatise the diversity of approaches that operate within a poetics of migration. Within each sub-section, I will discuss a literary example to illustrate how each specific poetics produces a unique type of analytical framework.

Transnational poetics

As people move or migrate across different national boundaries and enter into different cultural spaces, they are exposed to a wide range of cultural codes. Within certain migrant literatures, authors tend to demonstrate this phenomenon, showing the encounter with languages, ideas and histories that come into contact across permeable borders. Furthermore, though, authors will often borrow from, or feel inspired or challenged by, different literary traditions. In his 2015 book

A Transnational Poetics, Jahan Ramazani detects a tendency among poets to borrow poetic devices, techniques, forms, and languages from other national contexts, producing a thoroughly transnational poetic form. Several poets, says Ramazani, 'conceive . . . the poetic imagination as transnational, a nation-crossing force that exceeds the limits of the territorial and juridical' (2015:2). For Ramazani, such an imagination has led authors to embracing a 'poetic transnationalism', which 'can help us both to understand a world in which cultural boundaries are permeable and to read ourselves as imaginative citizens of worlds that ceaselessly overlap, intersect, and converge' (ibid.:49). In other words, poets utilise different linguistic cues, stylistic patterns, and poetic devices to illustrate the constant exposure to and embrace of different cultural systems.

Derek Walcott's *Omeros*, for example, offers a quintessential example of poetic transnationalism. An epic poem written in 1990, *Omeros* illustrates the broad interconnectedness and encounters across nations at both the formal and stylistic level, as well as within the epic story itself. Through the intersecting lives of three main characters (and their friends and lovers) – Achilles, Philoctete, and Major Plunkett – plus the narrator (who shares biographical details with Walcott), *Omeros* presents a counter-epic of St Lucia. The story itself is set in a late twentieth-century context, a time long after St Lucia achieved independence, but when nevertheless tourism wields control over the island's industrial activities and daily life. *Omeros* foregrounds its transnational poetics, first, through various methods of character development: either by borrowing names from different literary and historic traditions (characters like Achille, Philoctete, and Helen), demonstrating various moments of transnational contact (Major Plunkett being a British colonial officer descending upon a recently-independent St Lucia; Achille and Philoctete both separately sharing African ancestry), or showcasing the author's own transnational experience (with an inserted narrator speaking in first person, describing his own distinctly transnational life in St Lucia, the United States and the United Kingdom). The names developed specifically from Homeric epics and Greek mythology (Achille, Hector, Helen, Philoctete) also speak to the inheritance of other national traditions converging and colliding within the text. As a counter-epic, *Omeros* invents an epic on behalf of St Lucia; but the shape of this epic must confront the various conflicts and wounds inflicted upon this island as a result of slavery, colonisation, and tourism. The setting itself, therefore, cannot exist without describing the formative role that other nations have always played in its development.

Crucially, though, *Omeros* instantiates a transnational poetics at its formal level.[19] Walcott borrows the infamous terza rima rhyme scheme from Dante's *The Divine Comedy* (that is: aba, bcb, cdc), but leaves the last line of the second stanza hanging with no preceding or subsequent rhyme:

> The bearded elders endured the decimation
> of their tribe without uttering a syllable
> of that language they had uttered as one nation,
>
> the speech taught their saplings: from the towering babble
> of the cedar to green vowels of *bois-campêche*
> The *bois-flot* held its tongue with the *laurier-cannelle*
> (Walcott 1990: 6).

Omeros presents here 'an almost free-form terza rima . . . combined with a polymorphous hexameter (Homer)' (Zillman and Scott 2012:1423), according to Lawrence Zillmann and Clive Scott. 'In this 'undone state'', Zillman and Scott continue, 'terza rima supports the thematics of wounded-ness and of the difficult curing of the present by the past' (ibid.). Using this Dantesque rhyme scheme, Walcott uti-lises tools derived from his exposure to other national, epic traditions, reinforcing the transnational poetics of *Omeros*. Other formal and intertextual aspects abound in the text, with gestures to Joyce, Homer and Hemingway, while also producing oral and lyrical elements akin to folk storytelling. These aspects confirm Rei Terada's insistence that *Omeros* constitutes a 'parable of poetic influence' (qtd. in Barnard 2014:44). With such an influence, the text confirms Rama-zani's insistence that 'cultural boundaries are permeable' (Ramazani 2015:49), and presents Walcott's own transna-tional imaginary. Such a 'nation-crossing force' (ibid.:2) is a characteristic feature of migration as such, considering the movement across national boundaries forces the migrant to be exposed to several languages, cultural codes, and ideas. As a poetic of migration, therefore, transnational poetics illustrates transnationalism as of many features that come with migration and migrancy, demanding that we confront the multiplicity of languages and literary forms will always come into contact. For authors making use of such a poetics, they can deliberately choose which formal and poetic devices they decide to utilise from different national contexts, but bend them to meet the particularities of their own setting – especially settings besieged by colonialism and violence.

Poetics of Relation

Like transnational poetics, a poetics of relation begins by rec-ognising the flexibility of language and identity that emerges within migration. Often this means we have to rework assump-tions and images of thought when it comes to identity. After all, if the migrant's political and social existence is not fixed to one particular place, language, or history, then she will often renegotiate her relationship to identity as such, not necessar-ily defining it on universally-valid terms. Such an idea reflects what Edouard Glissant calls a 'poetics of relation'. Deriving the image of thought from Deleuze and Guattari's notion of the 'rhizome', Glissant insists that 'identity is no longer completely within the root but also in Relation' (1997:18). Instead, says Glissant, 'every identity is extended through a relationship with the Other' (ibid.:11). Such an idea enables us to expand notions of identity-formation that, in the Western world, relied on universalising myths, filiation, continuity and coherence. According to Glissant, 'in the Western world the hidden cause (the consequence) of both Myth and Epic is filiation, its work setting out upon the fixed linearity of time, always toward a projection, a project' (ibid.:47).

The cultural legitimacy of the West, therefore, is asserted by 'describing in reverse the trajectory of the community, from its present to the act of creation' (Glissant 1997:47). As a consequence, the 'mythical community' only legitimates 'the individual' insofar as she is 'a link in the chain of filiation' (ibid.:47), and Western mythologies 'conceive of the individual only insofar as he is a participant in the community' (ibid.:48). Friedrich Nietzsche, for example, rather famously identified the how an individual arrives at what he deems a 'real historical sense': 'the sense of well-being of a tree for its roots, the happiness to know oneself in a manner not entirely arbitrary and accidental, but as someone who has grown out of a past, as an heir, flower, and fruit, and thus to have one's existence excused, indeed justified. This is what people nowadays lovingly describe as the real historical sense' (Nietzsche 1874:11). For Glissant, this linear, epic past maintains a strong currency in Western metaphysics, but has been used to catastrophic ends in justifying the worst tendencies of colonial power. In turn, Glissant imagines a poetics of relation that reflects a complex, non-universalisable notion of identity – one which emphasises the 'cultural multiplicity of our globalising world' (Kaiser 2012:131). In other words, Glissant resists the generalising gesture of Western metaphysics, filiation, and the 'originary myth of colonial power' (Bhabha 1994: 165), and pushes toward an extended, rhizomatic vision of identity.

Jamaican poet Louise Bennett offers a distinct example
to enliven a poetics of relation. On both the formal and linguistic level, as well as in her thematic engagement, Bennett
produces work that extends beyond the confines of colonial,
European discourse. Employing Jamaican Creole English
throughout much of her poetry, Bennett is keen to observe
that a localised linguistic context is not handed down from
imperial power, but rather expresses a relationality among her
local community. Placing profound importance on reflecting
the local dialect, Bennett stresses nevertheless its social position: '[F]or too long, it was considered not respectable to use
the dialect. Because there was a social stigma attached to the
kind of person who used dialect habitually. Many people still
do not accept the fact that for us there are many things which
are best said in a language of the "common man"' (qtd in
Morris 2005:xxi). Cultivating, therefore, her relationality as
someone whose linguistic circumstances derived from several
geographical and political encounters, Bennett's insistence
on creole as her chosen poetic language situates her within a
poetics of relation.

Bennett's poetics of relation, though, is best exemplified
in her poem, 'Back to Africa', in which she speaker addresses
herself to Miss Mattie, an 'Afrocentric *alazon*' (Ramazani
2001:121) – someone unaware of the irony of her Afro-
centrism – who is on a 'racial quest for origins' (ibid.).
Composed in 1947, 'Back to Africa' suggests 'that the "Back
to Africa" movement, strong at this time in Jamaica, may
also fall into simplistic racial polarities, merely inverting the
essentialism of colonialist racism' (ibid.:120–1). To put this
into Glissant's language, such a cultural movement betrays
a reliance on a myth of filiation, defining and legitimising
identity along a historic lineage and a coercively universalising metaphysics.[20]

In the opening lines of 'Back to Africa', the speaker begins
by suggesting that the 'back to Africa' movement is not only

wrongheaded; it is illogical given that saying 'back to' necessarily means a return:

> Back to Africa, Miss Mattie?
> Yuh no know what yuh dah seh?
> Yuh haffi come from somewhe fus
> Before yuh go back deh! (Bennett 1947:115)

So, at first glance, the speaker is simply making a point about
semantics. One cannot be said to be going back anywhere
if he or she was never there to begin with. But, as we will
see later on in the poem, the speaker problematises even the
conventional way of speaking about 'origins' and where one
comes from.

In the ensuing stanzas, the speaker continues to deride her
interlocutor, suggesting the cross-national and cross-cultural
relations that already culminate in and constitute Miss Mattie's
identity. The speaker concedes that although Miss Mattie's has
a 'great great great Granma' who was African, it is also the
case that her 'great great great Granpa' (Bennett 1947:115)
was an Englishman. Moreover, as Miss Mattie's family history proceeds and develops closer to the present, Miss Mattie's
family history splinters in even more directions through family marriages, thereby suggesting that the 'great grandmodder
fader' on her father's side 'was Jew', and her 'granpa' by her
mother's side 'was French parlez-vous' (ibid.). By tracing Miss
Mattie's familial line that extends outside of African origins
and which take on different ethnic codes, Bennett is not just
questioning Miss Mattie's ties to Africa; she's rather suggesting more broadly the sheer incoherence of a simple, uniform
familial lineage, given the myriad national, cultural and
ethnic identities that intermingle within a family's history.
Bennett is largely embracing a poetics of relation that challenges the dominant view about family history necessarily
having a single national and mythic origin.

Switching then to a more affirmative tone, the speaker in Bennett's poem uses the next five stanzas to stress 'the importance of knowing where "home" is' (Schenstead-Harris 2017:139). Noting that we cannot base our home upon people who share our 'countenance' (Bennett 1947:115), nor simply based on where our 'great granpa' originates, even if he is 'Englishman' (ibid.:116), Miss Mattie is instead encouraged to realise that she has a home all along:

> Ef a hard time yuh dah run from
>   Teck yuh chance! But Mattie, do,
>   Sure a whey uh come from so yuh got
>   Somewhe fi come back to! (ibid.: 116)

This insistence conveys a crucial feature of the poetics of relation Bennett demonstrates in 'Back to Africa'. Here she challenges not only the desire to return to one's mythic past; she takes a step further in suggesting that Miss Mattie's relational surroundings – her community, 'de balance a' her family, and her 'whole generation' (ibid.:115) – converge in her immediate surroundings. In other words, her relational proximity to the present community provides a meaningful framework for her identity, enabling her to reassess entirely how she conceives of identity as such. She need no longer conceive of her identity on Eurocentric, linear terms, based on the myth of filiation; instead she can accept that identity can have a rhizomatic structure, conceived along a horizontal plane that connects with and attaches to her relational community and milieu. Conceived broadly as another poetics of migration, poetics of relation supplies an important dimension here, as it interrogates the structure of how identity is legitimised and formalised within systems of power – particularly assimilationist power structures within the nation-state, and the purity of identity embedded in colonial discourse. In this sense, a complex, fluid, multi-directional identity that might exist for a migrant subject is achieved and articulated through a poetics of relation.

Minor literature

Much like transnational poetics and poetics of relation, minor literature also re-evaluates the critical approach to literature and rejects the idealisation of standard language and unifying national identities. Often misunderstood to refer to a literature written by 'minorities', the concept of minor literature actually suits a poetics of migration quite well. The concept is given its most detailed treatment in Gilles Deleuze's and Félix Guattari's text, *Kafka*, in which Franz Kafka's writing stands as an exemplary case of minor literatures – a term they derive from 'a diary entry of Kafka's devoted to "small literatures" ("kleine Litteraturen"; in French translation, "littératures mineures"), such as Czech and Yiddish literature' (Bogue 2012:294). From an examination of Kafka's writings, though, Deleuze and Guattari extrapolate a larger theoretical concept of minor literatures.

In the middle chapter of *Kafka*, titled 'What is a Minor Literature?', Deleuze and Guattari argue that minor literature has three characteristics: first, minor literature works from within the standardised and codified structure of a national literature and language, and attempts to challenge its dominance through non-standard language: 'A minor literature doesn't come from a minor language; it is rather that which a minority constructs within a major language. . . [T]he first characteristic of minor literature . . . is that in it language is affected with a high co-efficient of deterritorialisation' (Deleuze and Guattari 1986:16). The author of minor literature undoes the territorialising structure of a national literature – including its standardised grammatical rules, its assertions to mimesis, and its canonisation – and invents an entirely new literary and linguistic space. In doing so, authors induce certain instabilities in language – grammatical and syntactic anomalies for 'strange and minor uses' (ibid.:17). Minor literature detaches language from its native soil and destabilises conventions of language.

Second, minor literature is meant to reflect an inherently political quality, whereby the political conditions and structures are foregrounded. In other words, the world created in minor writing 'forces each individual intrigue to connect immediately to politics' (Deleuze and Guattari 1986:17). Authors of a major literature, according to Deleuze and Guattari, address 'individual concerns within a quotidien social milieu' (Bogue 2012:294) – illustrated in novels such as, say, George Eliot's *Middlemarch*, in which the everyday, 'provincial' interpersonal conflicts take centre stage, while the larger political structure is relegated to the background. In minor literatures, by contrast, the political concerns are a central, constitutive focus (think of, say, Kafka's *The Castle*, where the power structure weaves through K's life).

The third, and final, characteristic is that 'everything' in minor literature 'takes on a collective value' (Deleuze and Guattari 1986:17). This is meant to suggest that no expression or enunciation 'belong[s] to this or that "master"' (ibid.), but rather they enable a collective voice to assert itself. As Deleuze puts this in a later text, minor literature envisions the capacity to invent a 'people who are missing' (Deleuze 1997:4.). While Deleuze and Guattari may not use these words, this third characteristic functions in order to assure that dominated collectivities are empowered and made legible through literary expression.

Several critics have noted the efficacy of the concept of minor literature when speaking in relation to migration, transnational, and diasporic literatures (see Seyhan 2001; Ramazani 2001; Moslund 2010). To connect minor literature within this typology, I turn to A. K. Ramanujan – an Indian poet who, during his time living in the United States, illustrated what Salman Rushdie famously calls a migrant author's 'stereoscopic vision'; that is, migrants 'are capable of writing from a kind of double perspective: because they, we, are at one and the same time insiders and outsiders in this society' (1992:19). To put this in Deleuze's and Guattari's terms, the migrant (or, minor) author invents a space within a major language and literature, but destabilises and deterritorialises its unitary self-image from within. Turning to Ramanujan, I will reflect upon his poem 'Waterfalls in a Bank', for its mixed metaphors and useful commentary for a minor literature.

Starting on the word 'and', as if to demonstrate someone mid-conversation, the speaker in the poem enters Hyde Park Bank in Chicago:

> 'And then one sometimes sees waterfalls
>   as the ancient Tamils saw them,
> wavering snakeskins,
>
>   cascades of muslin . . .' (Ramanujan 1995:189)

Right from the beginning, the speaker perceives the decorative, artificial waterfall in the lobby of the bank as having a metaphorical connection to 'wavering snakeskins' and 'cascading muslins', just as 'the ancient Tamils saw them' (ibid.). This linkage between a man-made waterfall and wavering snakeskins indicates the split, stereoscopic vision of Ramanujan's own life. The added space between the first two lines gives both the visual impression of a rippling waterfall, and at the same time makes a gap with the reference to 'ancient Tamils' – a gap where meaning must be transferred. Generally speaking, 'wavering snakeskins' is a metaphor that would not immediately register with someone who has not read the ancient Tamil texts; yet, it demonstrates a translation of cultural codes between two distinct national spaces (Chicago and India) and peoples (Modern-day US bank customers and ancient Tamils). Ramanujan, as a translator of Tamil texts, was attentive to the etymological connection between metaphor and translation, both terms conveying the idea of 'carrying-across'. In his case, the wavering snakeskins is carried over into a different context, in much the same manner that a waterfall is transplanted from its natural environment into a commercial business environment, however artificially. From this point, it is not enough to merely point out how waterfalls would be seen differently from their natural habitat; Ramanujan wants to also show the stereoscopic vision of this waterfall that arises from the point of view of someone who has navigated different national and historic contexts.

What is also occurring is the minorisation of this particular scene, as Jahan Ramazani explains: 'Ramanujan decommodifies and indianises the confined waterfall in an American bank, putting metaphor to work in a kind of reverse colonisation' (2001:78). By bringing in a metaphor derived not only from an Indian context, but an Ancient historical frame, the poem presents something beyond mere juxtaposition. By doing so, Ramanujan activates Tamil memory: 'The bank's waterfall not only occasions memories of the East but soon becomes itself a metaphor for postcolonial recollection' (ibid.). What occurs here, then, is an effort to assert a power that 'takes on a collective value' (Deleuze and Guattari 1986:17), speaking on the behalf of a people whose texts and cultural memory has been abandoned to colonialism, but who regained power through being translated and metaphorised. The social and spatial structure is then inflected, reshaped, and recast under a new, minor light, de-authorising the immediate commercialised and Americanised context, and injecting a metaphor that does not 'belong to this or that master' (ibid.), thus enunciating a collective social value for those who speak from the minoritarian persepctive.

At first glance, 'Waterfalls in a Bank' seems to foreground the everyday, quotidien reality inside of a bank – something which Deleuze and Guattari associate with 'major litera- ture'. Yet, Ramanujan translates the commercialisation and commodification of life that banks generate into a broader, historical and political context, leaving them inseparable and operating within the same field of stereoscopic vision:

> As I transact with the past as with another,
>   country with its own customs, currency,
> stock exchange, always
>
> at a loss when I count my change: water-
>   falls of dying children, Assam
> politics
>
> and downtown Nairobi fall through me. (Ramanujan 1995: 189)

The use of the verb 'transact' here enacts a continuous, gen- erative negotiation between past and present, alongside the circulation of currencies immediately taking place within a bank – an environment always politicised, especially when one considers the economically displacing struggle for the immigrant who has to deal with exchanging currencies, bur- dening fees, and economic and financial imbalance. Both the past and the present are measured against one another as a means of exchange, quantification and evaluation; and his 'transaction' is also a 'trans-action' – an action that operates in two places at once. 'At a loss when' he counts his change, the speaker is watching the actual balance of his bank account lose money, as a result of the exchange rates and devalua- tions between different countries. Yet, as an immigrant, he is also 'at a loss' with the proper words, language, customs, and metaphors to satisfactorily express or represent himself – to advocate for himself in a new setting. He has, perhaps, run out of monetary value as he has also run out of linguistic and political value. Finally, 'at a loss' has another idiomatic meaning: feeling oneself stunned or shocked into stillness, unable to properly react or respond. This lack of symbolic as well as financial currency leaves the speaker exposed, perpetually negotiating between past and present, home and arrival country. In both cases, the exchange results in a loss – giving up aspects of a past, never full assimilated, adjustments and adaptations to satisfy the commanding social system and commercialised regime. 'Assam politics' and 'downtown Nairobi fall through' him, suggesting that these aspects come rushing forward (as with a waterfall), clouding and affecting the context he is in. Of course, the references to Assam and downtown Nairobi recall ongoing and contemporary political conflicts that involved separatist struggles, indicating that his mind veers toward violent insurgent movements occuring in recent memory. The present is an always politicised, collective struggle as 'every individual intrigue is connect[ed] immediately to politics' (Deleuze and Guattari 1986:17); that is, as an immigrant subject, he carries an abiding postcolonial memory as well as a displacing financial power struggle that is inescapable from his line of vision.

Integrating unusual and unconventional metaphorical translations, combined with an activation of collective voices, and foregrounding social value, Ramanujan's 'Waterfalls in a Bank' illustrates a minor literature, suitable as another type of poetics of migration. Much like a transnational poetics and a poetics of relation, minor literature, too, provides a theory and method for viewing not only formal techniques of language and metaphor, but also reflects a complex power relation that migration produces for the migrant subject. Confronting the dominant structure of literary canonisation ('major literature'), while also complicating and deterritorialising linguistic convention, minor literature reflects the migrant's capacity to assert her power and resist the overcoded, dominating presence of the nation's 'custom, currency, stock exchange' (Ramanujan 1995:189), in which she will always be at a loss.

Poetics of migritude

The last, and final, type of poetics of migration I will examine reflects a revolutionary, anti-assimilationist desire and attitude that often arises from migrant subjectivity – what poet and author Shailja Patel calls 'migritude.'[21] Although Patel does not use this concept to reflect a theory of migrant literature, I would like to suggest that it can give us a language to speak about form and meaning within and throughout migrant texts, as well as a methodology of approaching these texts, constituting a *poetics* of migritude.

Many readers who see the term 'migritude' will no doubt recognise a connection to the concept of 'négritude', associated with Martinican theorists Aimé Césaire and Frantz Fanon, and Senegalese poet Léopold Sédar Senghor. This conceptual paradigm arose in the 1930s as an effort to reclaim Pan-African identity as something which need not be measured according to the hegemony of assimilationist standards, but rather retains its own power and force. Patel embraces anti-colonial paradigm, which resonates within a French-Caribbean diasporic context, and affirms her own background – being a Kenyan-born immigrant to the United States – as one vitally in contact with, reinforced through, and challenged by the lasting legacy of anti-imperial struggles. Because of her own transnational location and deep anti-colonial sensibilities, she is equipped to enter the conceptual space that has been opened up within this already-existing, Pan-African context – reinforcing the mobility and widespread circulation of the négritude paradigm. 'Négritude', according to Césaire, is 'a resistance to the politics of assimilation' (1972:72); and, above all, it is 'a concrete rather than abstract coming to consciousness' (ibid.:76). What this sentiment reveals in itself is a desire – a desire not to assimilate, and a refusal to embrace the 'civilising' and hegemonic violence of colonisation.

In her poetry collection from which this concept emerges, aptly titled *Migritude*, Patel 'not only grafts an ideological connection between [négritude and migritude], but opens up temporal and spatial dimensions of interconnectedness between a period of anti-colonial independence movements and the neo-colonial/imperial structures in which we continue to be embedded' (Qadir 2018:222). Her intellectual encounter with an already-existing paradigm (négritude) bespeaks a rich global connection and solidarity demanded of those who wish to overcome the violence of assimilationism. By inventing the concept of migritude, Patel not only brings the voices in her poems into relation with migrants who exist throughout the world (and throughout history), but she also inherits, expands, and modifies the traditions that attach her to anti-colonial and anti-imperial struggles – shedding light on 'the generations of migrants who speak unapologetically, fiercely, lyrically, for themselves' (Monegato 2010:143). Migritude offers a performative alliance with anti-capitalist and anti-colonial struggles, rather than deference to the Anglo-European hegemony. As a poetics, therefore, a poetics of migritude constitutes an anti-assimilationist mode of critical analysis, and also similarly suggests a particularity to the literary object that goes against a hegemonic structure.

In an interview, Patel stresses the overt connection with négritude. She notes that, on the one hand, the idea of migritude contains within it a play on the idea of 'migrant attitude, or migrants with attitude' (Patel 2014). Patel continues, though, showing how the conceptual framework of négritude supplied her with the necessary intellectual tools for migritude: 'I was asserting the same thing for migrants and for migrant movements, saying there is a voice, a worldview, a space that migrants inhabit that is unique and powerful and defined by itself . . . not by how close they've come to assimilation, not even by where they came from, but by the state of being a migrant' (ibid.) The aspirational ideal that undergirds migritude presents us with a political value-system that prioritises and emphasises the self-claimed migrant consciousness. In the foreword to *Migritude,* Vijay Preshad clarifies the connection of Patel's work to the tradition of négritude:

> *Migritude* draws from this heritage [of négritude] to suggest that there is a 'compass of suffering' shared by migrants of color into the heartlands of power. It shows how this compass binds them in unexpected ways. The term migritude suggests the horizontal assimilation engineered by migrants as they smile at each other, knowing quite well what is carried on each other's backs (2010:iv).

In other words, as Preshad clarifies, Patel's book 'is not a cultural anthropology of migrant lives, but rather a philosophical meditation on what it means to live within the concept of Migrant' (ibid.). *Migritude,* as a text, expresses and performs this internal, subjective desire to remain within the space of migrancy, to embrace its history and power for itself.

Migritude is a collection of poetic fragments originally showcased on stage as performance art in 2006. The text itself brings together small vignettes, reflecting upon the speaker's refugee movement – her family's displacement from Kenya, and her eventual relocation to the UK and the United States. Throughout the collection, Patel not only illustrates the movement of people, but also the crucial cultural importance of what the migrants bring with them – the jewellery and the saris that are packed – all of which embody what Ato Quayson and Girish Daswani call 'the affective economy of diaspora' (2013:2). Throughout the entire text, Patel showcases and projects various dimensions of migritude, reinforcing the singularity of migrant existence that attempts to resist and delegitimise the authority of assimilationism. This act of resistance reflects a poetics of migritude, affirming the subjective experience of migration that is not measured according to the demands of assimilationism – demands that are built into the cultural and legal discourse of immigrant life.

Perhaps no better demonstration of a poetics of migritude exists than Patel's poem 'The Making (Migrant Song)'. Throughout the poem's beginning, the speaker displays a defiant tone, embracing her cultural heritage and non-assimilation to the US (where she has now moved). First, we get a detailed account of how migrants perform their migrancy, according to the narrator: 'We overdress, we migrants. We care too much how we look to you . . . We absorb information without asking questions . . . We try to please . . . We don't contradict so we don't show you up. You mistake this for a lack of intellectual confidence' (2010:34). Here the speaker introduces the crux of her migritude: the refusal to assimilate. Inhabiting the space and subjectivity of migrancy, the speaker is hyper aware of her separation from, but also disgust toward, the politics of assimilation. Marking her separation from the citizens in the arrival country (United States), she then moves toward expressing the outrage and anger that this forced veneer of diffidence engenders:

> So I make this work from rage/for every smug, idiotic face I've ever wanted to smash into the carnage of war/every encounter that's left my throat choked/with what I dared not say/ I excavate the words that hid in my churning stomach through visa controls/ words I swallowed down until over the border/they are still there/ they knew I would come back for them. (ibid.:35)

She continues, noting that 'This is for the hands/hacked off the Arawaks by Columbus and his men . . . I make this work/ because I still have hands' (ibid.). Stating that 'this is for' the Arawaks suggests not only a solidarity with and a deep historical-political connection to the plight of the enslaved and colonised; this also suggests a sense of responsibility to them. Patel makes her work because of the intellectual and historical conversation her work engages across time and across space, offering a space for their silenced history to re-emerge and be recognised.

Shifting from first defining the characteristics of 'we migrants', toward then expressing her motivations and desire to create this work of poetry and performances, showcases her own concrete 'coming to consciousness' as Césaire would put it. After a prolonged period of self-restraint, the narrator has reached a boiling point of resentment and humiliation at the oppressors' 'smug, idiotic face[s]' (Patel 2010:35). Such encounters, then, fuel her internal ruminations on her migrant existence and the connections felt among migrants more generally. What is then conveyed through this poem's ending, with the switching voice and tone, is the conviction to maintain her migrant identity, and to proffer the desires and motivations that permeate her inner subjective, conscious experience, regardless of any external pressures from the receiving country. Declaring her migritude, the speaker discloses the moral and political impulses that pervade her existence, establishing her relation to anti-colonial and migrant struggles throughout history. Migritude, much like all historical struggles, is an ongoing, perennial struggle that one maintains across time and space.

It is also worth noting the unique formal character of 'The Making' that further performs a poetics of migritude. The first part of the poem ('We overdress, we migrants') is written as a prose poem, utilising full stops and repetitions on the word 'we' to demonstrate line breaks, despite conforming visually to a linear prose form. Such a formal device enables the poem itself to instantiate its own migritude, leaving readers unable to discern a clean generic categorisation. 'The

Making' is, therefore, an in-between poem/vignette – both prose and poetry – existing not within the specific bounds of one specific genre. Much like the migrant, who resists being measured according to how well they adjust and assimilate to the arriving nation, this piece as such cannot be measured according to any specified written form. The form therefore embraces its undefinable characteristic and refuses categorisation within any particular form. This is a manner by which 'The Making' is a meta-poem (or meta-prose-poem) – presenting, formally, its own attitude and arguing for its own existence and resistance. Similarly, when the form of the poem changes later ('So I make this work from rage/for every smug idiotic face. . .') we have it also demonstrating an in-between form in a different manner. The use of back-slashes (which we generally use to mark line breaks when a poem is quoted within a piece of prose) demonstrates artificial line breaks. This suggests another metapoetic device. In this sense, the ability to label this part a 'poem' stems from an imitation of a poem – yet remaining uncommitted to that form. The migrant subject attempts to adopt the social decorum of the arrival country, but they do as a performance merely to avoid suspicion or ridicule.

Fitting within this typology, a poetics of migritude is not limited to Patel's poetry, but can be expanded and adapted as a critical procedure for analysing and evaluating migrant and diasporic literature more generally. In this case, a poetics of migritude encourages a staunch anti-assimilationist 'attitude' (much like the combination of 'migrant' and 'attitude' built into the concept itself) that is both markedly shown in the poetry and language itself, but also in how we as critics approach the texts. A poetics of migritude is uniquely suited to empower migrant subjects to 'speak unapologetically, fiercely, lyrically, for themselves' (Monegato 2010:143), supplying an additional approach and system of meaning for studying migration.

From a Poetics of Migration to a
Movement-Oriented Poetics

The previous section was meant to outline a few already-existing critical and theoretical traditions that operate within the study of migrant literature, and specifically ones which function as a poetics. This typology dramatises and confirms the sheer diversity of approaches, conceptual tools, and literary objects that exist within a poetics of migration, and show even the coinciding analytical constellations in the era of Postcolonial criticism. In their own ways, each of these poetics induce a particular critical approach usefully applied to the displaced social and political position of the migrant; and they illuminate the cultural and linguistic complexity that comes with cross-national movement.

Kinopoetics, as I will outline below, builds atop many of these traditions, but takes them a step further. The idea of a kinopoetics is meant not only to highlight and stress the particularities and complexities of migrant life. Nor does it simply produce a political framework for describing forces of dispossession in which migrancy is a part. Rather, kinopoetics is an approach toward migrant literature that activates and makes movement. It builds upon a counter-history of the migrant and a movement-oriented politics (that is, a kinopolitics), and suggests that the regime of thinkability and visibility is made possible through forms of extensive and intensive movement. The methodology of kinopoetics will specifically rely upon its own set of discursive and critical practices. As Linda Hutcheon teaches us in *A Poetics of Postmodernism*, the critical procedures of postmodern theory and criticism rely on their own discursive indices: '[Postmodernism] is usually accompanied by a grand flourish of negativised rhetoric: we hear of discontinuity, disruption, dislocation, decentring, indeterminacy, and antitotalisation. What all of these words literally do (precisely by their disavowing prefixes—*dis, de, in, anti*) is incorporate that which they aim to contest' (1988:10).

Kinopoetics will also arrive with an attending set of terminological signals, but they should, instead, reframe the critical analysis with affirmative rhetoric. I will less frequently deploy terms that are used in a discussion of migration, such as 'marginalised', 'excluded', 'negating', 'outsider', 'relegate', 'subaltern', 'alterity', or 'subordinated'. Although these terms are in no way invalid to my analysis, these more reflect the reactive forces of kinopower and expansion by expulsion. Instead, I will more frequently tend toward more affirmative rhetoric to performatively undergird the migrant's active movement: 'push', 'pedetic force', 'pressure', 'activate', 'create', 'experiment', 'deterritorialise', 'invent', 'potential', or 'becoming'. Attaching these terms to the migrant's movement, the critical and methodological *poetics of kinopoetics* assures an affirmative orientation toward the object of study. The internally-focalised migrants in these texts are given a relational and active power to confront, shape and challenge the social milieu. By virtue of their migrancy, they will *create* and place pressure upon the conditions through which the political assemblage functions. Kinopoetics, therefore, will move beyond a poetics of migration and reorient these critical approaches toward a movement-oriented poetics, further affirming migrancy as a socially-constitutive and active process.

Postcolonial Theory: Identity, Representation and the 'Holy Trinity'

Earlier in this chapter I mentioned Edouard Glissant's concept of 'relation-identity.' In his text, *Poetics of Relation*, Glissant positions relation-identity against the Western metaphysics of identity – a universalising image of the subject developed in connection with a unifying history. This

gesture that Glissant is making coincides with the broad history of Postcolonial Theory wherein questions of identity,
history, and subjectivity are interrogated. Broadly speaking,
several theorists and thinkers in this domain challenge the
basis for subjectivity and identity that is taken for granted
in philosophy and theory. The conception of identity that
runs through several strands of continental philosophy and
political theory tends to be essentialising. That is, it assumes
a universal, unchanging essence to all identities; and this
resulting essentialism creates a limited view into what can be
readily considered a legitimate form of identity. For example,
by defining subjects in terms of their capacity for 'reasoning' or based upon standards of culture, art and language
which have historic roots in European colonial history tends
to neglect people who do not comply with or conform to
these regimes of identity-formation.

The sedentary metaphysics assessed in the beginning of
this chapter is a direct consequence of the essentialist and
Eurocentric notions of identity. We will recall that one of
the underlying theoretical assumptions of a sedentary metaphysics is a static notion of being and history, and that these
ideological and discursive forces create differentiated power
structures globally, but also subject immigrants to exclusionary violence and dispossession. In the field of Postcolonial
Theory, there have been sustained critiques of the legacy of
colonialism upon Western conceptions of identity. One of
the earliest of such analyses is Frantz Fanon's *Black Skins,
White Masks*, in which he challenges the ontology of being
– that is the understanding of what being *is* and of what it is
composed – that excludes racial Others ([1952]1986:81–2).
For Fanon, this colonial conception of identity is what leaves
the colonised Other unrecognised by regimes of power. The
identity of the colonised subject cannot be readily understood
based on the colonial ontology of existence and subjectivity,
thereby placing their existence under subjugation or erasure.

For the global imperial regime, such an exclusionary ontology is a useful ideological tool to replicate their power and superiority, while also justifying the violence and dispossession of the colonised. So long as those over whom they wield power are not considered to have recognisable or legitimate qualities that fit within an ontology of being and identity, the Western imperial powers can restrict their concerns and political responsibility to a limited population. Moreover, this restricted ontology dovetails effectively with a notion of threat, contagion, invasion, and terror that comes to define the non-white colonial subject. Because this ideological system of exclusion, sovereignty, and colonial dominance relies upon a notion of identity that can be recognised and legitimised, this system in turn also has to ensure that there are notable boundaries to this identity and subjectivity. Thus, by discursively associating the 'differing' subject with crime, threat, contagion, or inferiority, hegemonic power kept itself in a constant, dialectical struggle with this differing subject. Indeed, so long as the nation-state is founded upon the same ideological and discursive regime of exclusion and settlement (as shown in the previous section), both the migrant and the colonised will be subject to regimes of racialisation and nationalisation, thereby permanently aligning their historical and political identities.

This type of analysis from Fanon regarding identity, recognition, and difference continues to run through Postcolonial theories; and several notable scholars each had their own means of addressing this issue. Through the remainder of this section, I will take a brief look at ways in which the conception of difference, identity and essentialism were discussed in the realm of Postcolonial Studies; and to do so, I will consider the ideas of three major thinkers – the so-called 'Holy Trinity' (Huddart 2011:60; Chrisman 2021:30) of Postcolonial Theory: Edward Said, Gayatri Spivak, and Homi Bhabha. Crucially, this analysis will have two major considerations.

First, I will consider how these theorists examine the relationship between colonial discourse and its coercive exercise over identity and difference (some of which was touched upon in the previous section). I will examine and attempt to summarise what some of them considered the problems to be with regard to identity and difference through a postcolonial lens. Second, though, I will also touch upon how some (particularly Bhabha) suggested or proposed alternatives to these modes of differentiation and identification. I will consider the terms and concepts that theorists employ to circumvent the essentialising problematics of colonial, hegemonic discourse. To put this another way, I will examine how Postcolonial Theory attempts to resist or overcome the discursive practices of colonial identity-construction. After these two considerations are accounted for, I will then move on (in the fifth section) to suggest the way that kinopolitics and kinopoetics extend and modify these concepts. As we will see, several of these concepts turn out to be quite useful to kinopolitics, contributing to the theoretical questions and ideas that it is in conversation with. Yet, I will also combine these theoretical concepts with the philosophy of movement and ontologies of motion theorised by Nail, Deleuze, and others. Such will allow me to delineate the concerns for migrant subjectivity that will be laid out through the rest of this book.

Edward Said

Said carries on the concerns for identity construction that extends through several strands of Post-structuralist theory. Yet, as Patrick Williams points out, '[u]nlike ... Post-structuralist theorists who would see the process of identity construction as ... involving the Self's dominatory will to power over the Other', Said is more concerned with how identity construction 'translates to dominance in the real world' (2004:278). In *Culture and Imperialism*, Said explores how regimes of power weaponise representations of foreign cultures in order to wield dominance over them:

> All cultures tend to make representations of foreign cultures the better to master or in some way control them. Yet not all cultures make representations of foreign cultures and in fact master or control them. This is the distinction, I believe, of modern Western cultures. It requires the study of Western knowledge or representations of the non-European world to be a study of both those representations and the political power they express. (1998:100)

For Said, such representational constructs have been used to devastating effect with respect to colonised subjects and, particularly, those of his home in Palestine. 'One of the things that most concerns Said,' Williams continues, 'is the way in which assertions of identity can come to reify identities involved. . . [R]ecourse to a reductive or essentialised identity risks bringing into play "atavastic passions" which scarcely belong to the secular rational world Said hopes for' (2004:278). For Said, the real-life consequences of identity formation arise in the material forces of domination, war and colonisation.

Although Said's approach toward different 'nationalisms' and territory-formations vacillates throughout his oeuvre (Hallward 2001:55–56), '[p]erhaps nothing is so consistent' in his writings 'as the critique of what he calls "murderous essentialisms"' (ibid.:53). Such essentialisms are, according to Said, attempts to 'freeze the Other in a kind of basic objecthood' (Said qtd in Hallward 2001:53). His perhaps most famous analysis of this endeavour arrives in his sustained critique of the essentialising colonial project in his book *Orientalism*. Said argues that 'Orientalism staked its existence, not on its openness, its receptivity to the Orient, but rather on its internal repetitious consistency about its constitutive will-to-power over the Orient. In such a way, Orientalism was able to survive revolutions, world wars, and the literal dismemberment of empires' (1978:222). In this way, the coercively manipulated and forged image of the Orient was a replicated and coherent identity over which the Western imperial powers could assume complete knowledge and power. This image helped produce 'stereotyped knowledge about the Orient' (Williams 2004:273), and arrived with a set of ideas about their intellectual capacities and 'civilisational stagnation' (ibid.:273). Because this image was then consistent, repeated, and usable to the imperial system, this essentialising project of Orientalism was made all the more efficient and possible. 'In a quite constant way', says Said, 'Orientalism depends for its strategy on this flexible positional superiority, which puts the Westerner in a whole series of possible relations with the Orient without ever losing him the upper hand' (1978:4). Consequently, a coherent, usable, and repeatable image of the Orient contributes to a much broader colonial project of essentialism, determining identity and existence based on a coherent image and language. In a theoretical through-line connecting Fanon to Said, we can see that this concern with essentialism was of vital significance to the postcolonial project, as thinkers in this tradition question the basis under which forms of existence and identity were defined on generalisable terms. Forms of state and imperial power rely on conceptions of identity in order to forge regimes of representation and hegemonic power. How subjectivity is constructed by these systems of power determines the relative degree of autonomy and recognition across a globally-differentiated world-system. As a result, the struggle against imperialism is always a struggle for recognition within these highly stratified global power structures.

Gayatri Spivak

Writing ten years after Said's *Orientalism*, one of the most famous challenges to the critical discussion of colonial subjectivity came from Gayatri Spivak's essay, 'Can the Subaltern

Speak?'. Originating in the collection titled *Marxism and the Interpretation of Culture*, Spivak directs her essay as a response to the postcolonial project of the Subaltern Studies collective. The Subaltern Studies collective arose in the early 1980s as an endeavour to research 'the histories of subaltern insurgency in colonial and postcolonial South Asia' (Morton 2011:215). In an interview, Spivak suggests that the use of the term 'subaltern' provides a meaningful category for her analysis, and she is compelled toward this subject based on her combined readings of Antonio Gramsci and the Subaltern Studies collective:

> I like the word 'subaltern' for one reason. It is truly situational. 'Subaltern' began as a description of a certain rank in the military. The word was later used under censorship by Gramsci: he called Marxism 'monism', and was obliged to call the proletarian 'subaltern'. That word, used under duress, has been transformed into the description of everything that doesn't fall under a strict class analysis. I like that because it has no theoretical rigour. (Spivak qtd in Morton 2011:216)

For Spivak, picking a category that 'doesn't fall under a strict class analysis' is crucial, as she is eager to overcome limited connotation built into the term proletarian, 'which conventionally denotes the masculine working-class subject of nineteenth-century Europe' (Morton 2011:216). Instead, 'subaltern', for Spivak is a metonymic category to include all those who are 'removed from all lines of social mobility' (Spivak 2012:430). Indeed, much of what informs Spivak's objections to Marxist historiography – which includes, as we shall see, the Subaltern Studies collective – is her insistence that one not too readily assume that there is a ready-made subaltern subject that can be represented and analysed.[22] One cannot assume, according to Spivak, a rigidly defined subject that can be spoken of and for simply by virtue of producing a history 'from below'. Spivak, then, distances herself from the efforts to do so particularly in the Left, post-Marxist intellectual tradition.

She begins her famous essay, therefore, by challenging the assumptions of Foucault and Deleuze who, in a co-interview titled 'Intellectuals and power', imply that 'intellectuals must attempt to disclose and know the discourse of society's Other' (Spivak [1988]1994:66). Because of the ongoing critical work of Foucault and Deleuze that, in different ways, attempts to undo the homogenising discourses of power, they run into a 'constitutive contradiction' (ibid.:69): 'In the name of desire, they reintroduce the undivided subject into the discourse of power' (ibid.). In their case, Deleuze and Foucault assume 'two monolithic and anonymous subjects-in-revolution: "A Maoist" and "the workers struggle"' (ibid.:66). As a result, they replicate a hegemonic gesture that assumes an easily recognised and representable subject, thereby collapsing the 'pluralised "subject-effects"', even in the name of 'undermining subjective sovereignty' (ibid.). Put another way: Spivak suggests that the 'much-publicised critique of the sovereign subject thus actually inaugurates a Subject' (ibid.). By trying to give a thorough-going analysis and rigorous uncovering of the discursive forces that constitute a sovereign subject, Deleuze and Foucault actually end up repeating and reasserting the existence of an already coherent subject that can be represented, critiqued, spoken for, and identified with.

The upshot of Spivak's polemic builds on her complex analysis of representation as such. In her mind, a discussion of power relations and discursive structures of subjectivity ought to occur separately from a discussion of representation: 'If such a critique and such a project are not to be given up, the shifting distinctions between representation within the state and political economy, on the one hand, and within the theory of the Subject, on the other, must not be obliterated' (Spivak 1994:70). In other words, for Spivak, an important mistake that critics often make is confusing the efforts to speak for a subject as opposed to speaking as a subject. As a result, theorists and philosophers blur the lines between two modes of representation which ought to remain separate, or whose distinctions should be held much sharper. To set out on this point, Spivak responds to the famous quote from Marx's 'Eighteenth Brumiaire', wherein he states regarding the proletariat that 'Sie können sich nicht vertreten; sie müssen vertreten werden', or 'They cannot represent themselves; they must be represented' (Marx [1852]1978:608). What interests Spivak here is the term used in German, 'vertreten' as opposed to 'darstellen', noting that the former tends to convey speaking 'as', while the latter connotes 'speaking for'. Such a distinction is elided in Marx's use of the term, and continues to be collapsed in Marxist as well as liberal political discourse. However, Spivak does not stop at merely asking us to keep these types of analyses separate; she is, rather, suspicious of whether one can ever truly represent (either in the sense of speaking for or speaking as) in a world beset by uneven power relations. By entering into the discussion of representing the subaltern, Spivak suggests that we enter into an age-old complication regarding the nature of representation.

Considering we can use representation to mean political, economic, and juridical representation, it remains up to this globally-differentiated system to determine whether representation can accommodate a wide range of subject positions. Elected officials, for instance, rely on a generalised category, demographic models and statistics to get an intelligible sense of the constituents whom they 'represent' (in other words, speak for). However, the problem remains that in disproportionate systems of capitalist and imperial power, political representation – in our everyday ideology – tends to stand for both speaking as *and* speaking for, thereby reducing the subject's ability to 'speak' to mean simply their capacity to participate in liberal democracy and capitalism. The problem then is that this faith in the voicing capacity of liberal democracy leads to what she calls an 'essentialist, utopian politics':

> In the guise of a post-Marxist description of the scene of power, we thus encounter a much older debate: between representation or rhetoric as tropology and as persuasion. Darstellen belongs to the first constellation, vertreten – with stronger suggestions of substitution – to the second. Again, they are related, but running them together, especially in order to say that beyond both is where oppressed subjects speak, act and know for themselves, leads to an essentialist, utopian politics. (Spivak 1994:71)

As a result, even in our academic theorising we commit the same epistemic mistake, as we conjure up categories and concepts that attempt to fully represent subjectivities who are distant from us in terms of desire and power. We commit the same problem we set out to solve when we, as Spivak says, 'inaugurate the Subject' in our critique of the subject (1994:66). By relying on concepts like the 'proletariat' or the 'working class', we assume that these terms are generalisable; and Spivak suggests that 'subaltern' uniquely expands to meanings and subjects that are not reducible, but rather exist across historical and spatial contexts and conditions, neither of which can be specified, located, or fully comprehended.

These tendencies in both political discourse as well as 'post-Marxist' analyses create, for Spivak, forms of 'epistemic violence'. On Spivak's terms, epistemic violence is the 'persistent constitution of Other as the Self's shadow' in which the 'intellectual is complicit' (Spivak 1994:75). According the Spivak, '[t]he clearest available example of such epistemic violence is the remotely orchestrated, far-flung, and heterogeneous project to constitute the colonial subject as Other. This project is also the asymmetrical obliteration of the trace of that Other in its precarious Subject-ivity' (ibid.:76). Once again, in terms reminiscent of Said, she suggests that there is a collaborative effort across different colonising institutions (educational, juridical and cultural) that replicate and export an image of the Other, over which the regimes of power can justify their domination. For Spivak, though, attempting to locate this subject as simply one side of a dialectical strug- gle repeats the imperial gesture she is working tirelessly to avoid. This issue becomes especially a problem for a concept like 'subalternity' because, by definition, it cannot be called upon or invoked in any way that does not commit the same epistemic violence. So, even in the well-meaning campaign to tell the history of the subaltern, as the Subaltern Stud- ies collective aims to do, they cannot avoid the fundamental contradiction at the heart of representation: the problem of speaking for a subject slipping into speaking *as* that subject.

Following a tradition inaugurated by Derrida and Emman- uel Levinas, Spivak consigns the subaltern subject to the space of an incomprehensible Other. In terms of axes of difference, the analytical force of any single, locatable identity-signifier loses its power when deployed globally, especially in third- world contexts:

> Can the subaltern speak? What must the elite do to watch out for the continuing construction of the subaltern? The question of 'woman' seems most problematic in this context. Clearly, if you are poor, black and female you get it in three ways. If, however, this formulation is moved from the first- world context into the postcolonial (which is not identical with the third-world) context, the description 'black' or 'of color' loses persuasive significance (Spivak 1994:90).

This complex situation, cross-cut with layers of stratifica- tion and differentiation, results in abandoning the subaltern subject, keeping them perpetually distant from power. To answer the question she asks in the essay's title, Spivak ends by suggesting that any regime of power that attempts to give representation to the subaltern will always fall short. Spivak's essay was (and still is) an invaluable contribution to Postcolonial Theory discourse; the complexity of this essay reflects the difficulty of her subject matter, as she seeks to actively avoid the same epistemic trappings she is critiquing. At the same time, Spivak is recognising the impossibility of sufficiently accounting for the subaltern subject in a way that does not commit epistemic violence. According to Spivak, so long as intellectual activities (even those which are ostensibly based upon anti-colonial, anti-imperial criticism) try to produce a ready-made subject for analysis, they will always replicate the same subject they want to empower. So, for Spivak (and those who follow her line of thinking), the subaltern remains unable to speak so long as we are still at an impasse in our critical and conceptual language. One cannot, therefore, expect to produce a universal speaking subject with which subaltern subjects can identify without returning to an 'essentialist, utopian politics' (Spivak 1994:71). Without having a representational regime suitable to subaltern particularity, the best we can hope for is an ethics of incomprehensibility whereby the Other remains a silenced figure beyond our ability to hear.

Homi Bhabha

Based on reading Spivak, it would seem that what Postcolonial Studies could use is a concept that can accommodate the subjectivity of the colonised, the subaltern, or the Other, without reducing them to a coherent category that is simply opposed to or contrasted with Self and identity. Homi Bhabha's 1994 text, *The Location of Culture*, gives a sustained treatment of 'hybridity' in one early attempt to produce such a conceptual framework. Although Bhabha is not the first to employ this term toward the postcolonial subject, hybridity for him 'becomes an interpretive mode for dealing with what

[he] calls the juxtaposition of space, and the combination of "time lag" out of which a sense of being is constructed that constantly oscillates between the axioms of foreign and familiar' (Papastergiadis 1999:192). In his case, hybridity was 'initially used to expose the conflicts in colonial discourse, then extended to address both the heterogeneous array of signs in modern life and the various ways of living with difference' (ibid). For Bhabha, hybridity is not a pre-given state, and it does not just refer to the existence of diverse, coherent cultural identities coexisting in one particular place (Huddart 2011:66). Rather, hybridisation is an ongoing process of identity co-construction and contestation, creating contradictory and sometimes tensional temporal and spatial configurations that emerge in processes of colonisation and globalisation. Crucially, though, for Bhabha, hybridity has the capacity to confront and intervene in the colonial exercise of authority and processes of differentiation, thereby reducing the colonial power (Bhabha 1994:163). He then goes on to insist that hybridity retains a certain power derived from its capacity to 'terrorise authority with the ruse of recognition, its mimicry, its mockery' (ibid.:165). He notes, in other words, that it is the power of hybridity to 'so disturb the systematic (and systemic) construction of discriminatory knowledges that the cultural, once recognised as the medium of authority, becomes virtually unrecognizable' (ibid.:164).

Much of Bhabha's response hinges on his analysis of cultural stereotypes which not only brings him into critical relation with Said, but also produces a palatable set of concerns about cultural representations that pervade consumer media and journalism. For Bhabha, stereotypes produce 'modes of differentiation, realised as multiple, cross-cutting determinations, polymorphous and perverse, always demanding a specific and strategic calculation of their effects' (1994:96). What Bhabha is concerned with, in particular, is the manner in which the coloniser's 'civilising' mission and the creation of stereotypical knowledges merge and coincide. After all, the 'objective of colonial discourse is to construe the colonised as a population of degenerate types on the basis of racial origin, in order to justify conquest and to establish systems of administration and instruction' (ibid.:101); and, therefore, stereotype 'plays a public part in the racial drama that is enacted every day in colonial societies' (ibid.:112). Yet, on the other hand, according to Bhabha, the stereotype is an object of fixation for the coloniser that can then facilitate coercive assimilation and discrimination. It helps to set up a 'discursive form of racial and cultural opposition in terms of which colonial power is exercised' (ibid.). However, in their efforts to replicate and solidify these racial and cultural oppositions, the coloniser produces a 'colonial fantasy' (ibid.:117) which hybridisation immediately disrupts. Hybridisation creates, therefore, an ambivalent disruption for both the coloniser and the colonised, engendering a condition of constantly reinventing subjectivities. The breakthrough that hybridisation ensures is a way to treat identity that is necessarily disruptive, plural and non-universal but problematises any clearly demarcated binaries and oppositions. Hybridity and hybridisation are achieved through singular instances of coinciding power-relations and subjectivities, but are necessarily too complex, and therefore preclude being able to conceive of a representable dialectical relation.

In some ways, we can see here that Bhabha is responding to tendencies that both Said and Spivak are diagnosing, attempting an early model for demonstrating the complexities of colonial identity. Hybridity seems, according to Bill Ashcroft, Gareth Griffins and Helen Tiffin, to provide a 'model for resistance, locating this in the subversive counter-discursive practices implicit in the colonial ambivalence itself and so undermining the very basis on which imperialist and colonialist discourse raises its claims of superiority' (2007:110). Such a concept provides here a useful departure for Postcolonial Theory, assuring that the colonial relation is explained with enough complexity to avoid a one-sided, unidirectional perspectives on power and identity, and operates beyond essentialist and universalisable categories. As a concept, then, hybridity offered a useful departure for Postcolonial Studies, providing a 'model for resistance' that attempted to overcome the very problems that the field set itself against initially.

Although Postcolonial Theory covers a wide range of perspectives, analyses and concepts, Said, Spivak and Bhabha offer the most well-known frameworks and concerns that carried the field for decades. All of the questions they addressed themselves remain within the field today in Postcolonial Theory, and across the range of academic disciplines that critique colonial discourse and power. Furthermore, as I stated in the introduction, the 'migrant turn' in the late 1980s – that is, the renewed concern for migrancy and migration in literary and cultural studies – joined up with the explosion of Postcolonial Studies, confronting the same discursive and conceptual problems that Postcolonial theorists responded to: questions of identity, nation, borders, displacement, otherness, representation, and language, to name a few. Kinopoetics and kinopolitics ought not be ignorant of the preoccupations of Postcolonial Studies and theory, as they raise important, unavoidable problems that bear directly on the questions of migrancy, poetics and visibility. As we saw through all three of these thinkers, there has been a long-standing need to address the basic questions and assumptions that underlie any ostensibly political analysis. On the other hand, one might imagine ways in which kinopolitics and kinopoetics might extend these conceptual contours or modify them in certain ways. In particular, kinopolitics and kinopoetics are also concerned with overcoming essentialism, questioning the ability for representation, and highlighting complex and hybrid subjectivities. Yet, what is of interest within the counter-history and counter-poetics that I am envisioning here is an emphasis on motion and movement, modes of orienting ourselves to the world that overcomes the metaphysics of fixity and settlement. In the following section, I will detail the ways in which this emphasis on motion and movement – not just in the political sense, but also ontological sense – extends and modifies the theoretical contours of Postcolonial Studies in ways that are dialogical and mutually reinforcing.

Reassessing Postcolonial Theory through a Philosophy of Movement

Having evaluated and summarised some of the basic tenets of Postcolonial Theory, I would like to argue that, while I derive considerable intellectual and political inspiration from Said, Spivak and Bhabha, their theories can be recuperated through a philosophy of movement. By supplementing their theories in this way, I find there are meaningful avenues and terrain for analysing the subjectivity of the migrant, while also overcoming essentialisms and generalisations. Below I will re-evaluate Said, Spivak and Bhabha (and the concepts with which they are associated), drawing out a theoretical tradition with which I will remain in dialogue throughout this project.

From anti-essentialism to an ontology of motion

Said's sustained pre-occupation with anti-essentialism and the real, material consequences that it involves are a huge part of Postcolonial Studies more broadly, and it remains an important concern within the field today. On the one hand, theorists and writers want to overcome the dangers associated with essentialism. Yet, on the other hand, there is also often a question of how to envision a subject who can be affirmed and accounted for, yet whose identity does not subject them to the capture of power or domination. Another way to ask this question (from a philosophical perspective): is there an ontology of existence that is non-essentialising and non-universal, yet is capable of affirmation? Or, are we simply caught choosing to negate and critique essentalism without offering an alternative theory of the nature of being?

In his later text, *Being and Motion*, Nail addresses himself precisely to this question. Following several changing tides in philosophy and research which attempt to consider, analyse, and foreground mobility and movement, Nail finds there remains a deeper, foundational set of problems: 'At no point in history have beings ever been anywhere near as mobile as they are today, so what does this say about the nature of our reality? If being is defined by the historical primacy of motion today, yet existing ontologies are not, then we need a new ontology' (Nail 2019:16). Crucially, for Nail, academic research in the humanities and social sciences had consistently relegated motion as a secondary concern; this research has 'systematically marginalized, and explained motion by some other foundational category' (ibid.:53) and consequently 'failed to define the very mobility of being and its own immanent ontological practice' (ibid.). One political or ideological reason for this can be traced, again, back to the first section of this chapter, in which, as we saw, the metaphysics of fixity and sedentarism became the central organising system for history, identity, and politics. This established interest in stasis directly connects with the ideological underpinnings that permitted colonisation throughout the globe. Indeed, though, for Said and Postcolonial theorists, colonialism also expressed itself in the essentialising tendencies that attempted to define, interpellate, and subjugate the colonised nations, creating an image of their existence that could be easily controlled and dominated. The upshot of Said's critique is to overcome the problems of essentialism.

Indeed, in Said's text *Culture and Imperialism*, he does note that migration and mobility have introduced the capacity to confront and resist the effects of essentialism and Orientalism. This capacity was an attending outcome of the agitating efforts for decolonisation carried out by 'unassimilated subjects' who are 'rejected by the established order (Said 1993:332). The way Said characterises migratory figures is as if they negate the established order based on their difference from, and subordinate position to, it. When framed in this manner, nation and identity still retain a historical and political centrality. In Said's work, such a centrality creates tensions (but not necessarily contradictions) for his critique. Hallward explains that this is particularly the case in Said's treatment of Palestine: 'The admirable consistency of his commitment [to the Palestinian liberation cause] cannot mask, however, an apparent inconsistency or ambivalence regarding the decisive questions of *territorial* sovereignty and an independent Palestinian state' (2001:54). On the one hand, Said observes a 'national Palestinian mobilisation against occupied territories, if only as an essential means to the eventual secular, supra-national goal' (ibid.:55); yet, the challenge remains being able to square this advocacy with the fact that much of Said's work involves a 'vigorous refutation of nationalist arguments for sovereignty' (ibid.:56). I would argue that this tension exists largely due to the sustained imprint of sedentarism upon the work of Postcolonial critique, whereby sovereignty and nation are still given political primacy, if only to critique, negate or oppose it.

Yet, in the context of kinopolitics, this relationship is reversed to constitute the migrant figure as an affirmative figure. This takes a radical departure from Said in that it encourages us to think of the regimes of state and national formation as secondary, reactive processes, and the migrant's movement as the constitutive transhistorical force for social formation. Instead of repeating a gesture that assumes that stasis, settlement, nation and identity are historically primary – and treating the migrant merely as a negating, marginal figure – kinopolitics and kinopoetics take the critique to a radical reversal, helping assure the pedetic force and transformational potential of the migrant. Kinopolitics and kinopoetics do not merely stop at critiquing or refuting essentialisms and identity-construction; they re-envision the entire social, political, and ontological state of the world as one characterised by movement and motion. Yet, despite what might appear to be a totalising theory, I would hasten to add that the way kinopower and pedetic force are represented does not impose epistemic violence, in the way that Spivak would suggest. So, in the following section, I will highlight how moving beyond representation can render the subaltern subject knowable, without constituting them within a regime of power (that is, without committing epistemic violence).

Beyond representations and making the subaltern knowable

Spivak's critique of the Subaltern Studies project, alongside her general resistance to academics who wish to define the subaltern subject on universal terms, hinges on her analysis of representation. She problematises representation in any political sense to produce any meaningful space for 'speaking' and subaltern agency, especially amid a system where representability relies on terms and conditions set by the regime of colonial and capitalist power. The point is that such a regime can never claim to capture the subject; and to imagine that it can will only bolster the self-legitimacy of liberal political institutions. Spivak is right, I would argue, in suggesting that representation does not have the capacity to sufficiently account for or recognise the subaltern subject, so long as uneven power relations continue to exist, and so long as representation demands that universal subject to be replicable. Yet, what kinopoetics might be able to offer in assuring that meaning and knowledge are conceived as operating in motion (as I suggested in section four of Chapter 1) is recognising that representation's inadequacy may not necessarily be a problem.

The stakes of representation are connected to what is made thinkable, visible, audible and knowable in society – in other words, it is a system of meaning. What Spivak sees as representation's epistemic violence stems from its inability to accommodate the subaltern subject without reproducing and perpetuating its conditions of subalternity. Yet, it should not follow that we are necessarily left abandoning the subject entirely. Rather, we have to reconfigure and reimagine the metaphysics under which the system of visibility, audibility and knowability is achieved. Above I tried to map this out in the already existing field of affect studies. Through this domain, meaning and knowledge are not restricted under the bounds of a representational regime; they are not fixed within pre-established categories and coherent linguistic boundaries. Rather, affect is a manner through which imperceptible parts of the world are made knowable, and whereby knowledge of something is achieved as a process in and through movement.

In *Being and Motion*, Nail describes this in the context of various 'flows of sensation'. He notes how we come to recognise the qualities of sensation that something creates:

> When a flow folds back and intersects with itself, it produces a sensation of something: the sensed. Events produce a flash or streak of sensation that disappears immediately without being connected to some particular thing. It is a flash of light or color without a clear source, a feeling of urgency without a plan or programme of action, an ambient sound without discernible instrument, and so on. Affects sustain these sensations, but if they are not yet conjoined to any others, they are still not necessarily things. (Nail 2019: 110).

The crucial idea, which also connects with the anti-essentialism noted above, is that 'outside of . . . affective kinetic sensibility there is no transcendent essence of the thing. Things are made of affects, not the other way around' (ibid.:111). How we come, then, to understanding something or someone, particularly a being of marginal ontological and political status (such as the migrant or subaltern subject), is not through the 'transcendent essence' of it, made coherent and legible in representations. Rather, we encounter 'affects' that sustain the sensation of something which gains their 'kinetic identity in the persistence or flow of their affects' (ibid.).[23] We can come to understand the nature or quality of a being without the authority of a transcendent regime of representation to which it must comply or cohere. Instead, we arrive at our sensation and perception of something or someone by its affects – its relational power, its external and sensible qualities, and the potential immanent to its movement.

So, what we are able to overcome in this instance is the problem that Spivak sees with regard to the epistemic limits of representation. Kinopoetics and kinopolitics share the treatment of representation as an inadequate mode of meaning, visibility and comprehensibility. Yet, this does not follow that there is no system under which a 'still-missing people' (Deleuze and Guattari 1994:176) can be made legible. Making something legible requires instead the movement of affects and the deterritorialisations of perception and sensation. Deleuze articulates this in *Difference and Representation*, stating that '[m]ovement, for its part, implies a plurality of centres . . . a coexistence of moments which essentially distort representation: paintings or sculptures are already 'distorters', forcing us to create movement – that is, . . . to ascend or descend within the space as we move through it' (1997:56). The capacity to 'distort representation' means that art and aesthetics are capable of disrupting and deterritorialising the transcendent authority of representation by issuing forth affects and percepts that flow outward – affects that, in turn, speed or slow our intensive movements and relational power. One wants to distort representation because representation is a transcendent system of meaning through which power governs, captures, and controls identity and 'denies that which "differs"' (ibid.:53). Instead, affects unleash differing forms of existence and movement in the world, assuring a 're-distribution of the sensible' (Rancière 2004:85) – deterritorialising, rather than conforming to, the pre-established representational system of identity. Because affects and flows of sensation are multidirectional, relational, and irreducible, they activate beings which share these qualities. So, insofar as affects and the distribution of the sensible are systems of meaning under which forms of subjectivity are made legible, visible, and audible, the subaltern can speak, in their production of affects and sensations that are not restricted to representation, but are nevertheless epistemologically and affectively available.

Hybridisation and regimes of mobility

Finally, in Bhabha's analysis of hybridity and hybridisation, there is a rather useful image of thought that kinopolitics and kinopoetics ought to retain. In particular, I still want to assume that the migrant overcomes and disrupts the 'colonial fantasy' (Bhabha 1994:117) that develops in modes of discrimination and discursive practices. Hybridity and hybridisation offer another 'anti-essentialist perspective' (Papastergiadis 1999:190), addressing 'the historical positions, cultural conditions and political conjunctures through which all identity is constructed' (ibid.). We should not deny that the mutual co-construction and negotiated forms of identity constitute migrancy, especially in the convergence of cultural subjectivities in and through migration and movement. Hybridity, then, exists as both this discursive process of co-construction and, at the same time, an outcome of regimes of mobility.

For Bhabha, hybridisation is an ongoing process of reinventing subjectivities. The concern with process over stasis coincides easily with the kinopolitical framework and is not exclusive to Bhabha's model of hybridity (see also Hall 2015:394 and 402). On the other hand, we might also wonder whether this distinction between process over stasis is made too easily and too readily. In other words, we might consider whether this a process metaphysics is not merely a description of migrant and diasporic subjectivity. Rather, we might ask: is existence itself better understood as a process? Recall once again that sedentarism and static conceptions of social ontology and identity are an outgrowth of state, imperial forces that impose themselves upon immanent movement from without.[24]

To go a step further, I suggest that one cannot so easily locate or isolate a static 'being' at all, much less locate it strictly in the citizen, non-diasporic subject. Here I once again turn to Deleuze. The reason for this reliance on Deleuze is that, as Nail explains, 'Deleuze was the philosopher of process and becoming par excellence' (2019:45). For Deleuze, instead of treating becoming-as-difference as something 'running alongside continuity' (Hall 2015:396) and essence, he shows 'the ontological *primacy of becoming* over being' (Nail 2019:45; emphasis added). In other words, existence itself is becoming and process. Existence as we know it is a constant transformation and ever-changing assemblage, rather than containing a locatable essence, origin, or purity: 'Everything becomes because everything is a force of becoming' (Nail 2019:45). Because of process's primacy, '[m]ovements, becomings, . . . pure relations of speeds and slownesses, pure affects, are below and above the threshold of perception' (Deleuze and Guattari 2014:327). And since we are, as bodies, 'a set of speeds and slownesses between unformed particles, a set of nonsubjectified affects' (Deleuze and Guattari 2014:306), the becoming that characterises our existence is imperceptible. This primacy of process helps to realise that subjective existence is not susceptible to representation but is apprehended through affects.

Yet, it is important to clarify that there is a distinction to be made between process and motion; or, more precisely, they may differ in emphasis. For Nail, Deleuze's process philosophy has three limitations which cover motion, matter and history. Philosophers in this process philosophy tradition (including Whitehead) 'provide robust theories of becoming, but neither provides an ontology of motion' (2019:49); and Deleuze's 'theory of motion is extremely uneven and fractured . . . it is explicitly subordinated to stasis, time, immobile speed, vital force, and other such attributes' (ibid.:47). In terms of bringing hybridity into a kinopolitics and kinopoetics, thinking of it as a process is a helpful and useful starting-point. Yet, combining it into patterns of motion and movement might be a separate difficulty.

Incidentally, many within what is known as the New Mobilities Paradigm have addressed this very problem. Scholars within the New Mobilities Paradigm inaugurated the emergence of an explicit methodological framework that foregrounds human and non-human movement within the humanities and social sciences. They offer an interdisciplinary approach toward mobility, 'argu[ing] for the ubiquity of mobility as a structuring principle in every aspect of human and non-human life' (Merriman and Pearce 2017:503). Broadly speaking, this field involves 'interlinking migration, transport and tourism studies' in order to address 'emerging challenges and discourses concerning environmental, development, justice and security issues at local and global levels' (D'Andrea, Ciolfi and Gray 2011:150). So, while migration is one concern within the mobilities paradigm, they are more interested in widening the scope of research to technological and communicative forms of mobility. Because of the ever-growing nature of mobility research in recent years, including many 'theoretical influences, approaches, methods and disciplinary perspectives', the New Mobilities Paradigm has really begun to 'challenge any easy alignment of mobilities research with a neatly demarcated realm called the social sciences' (Merriman and Pearce 2017:495). And, furthermore, the New Mobilities Paradigm addresses the manner by which subjectivity is cultivated through mobile, globally-transmitted media images and (im)mobilising transportation infrastructures –features of motion and transport that are integral to our globalising world.[25]

A concept that is related to hybridity, what Nina Glick Schiller and Noel B. Salazar call 'regimes of mobility', was given sustained treatment in a 2013 issue of the *Journal of Ethnic and Migration Studies* as a contribution to the New Mobilities Paradigm. In doing so, scholars 'move beyond categorical opposites such as fixity and motion, self and other, and communalism and cosmopolitanism' (188), in a way that neither 'normalises fixed relationships between people and territory nor naturalises movement' (Glick Schiller and Salazar 2013:188). Rather, the 'regimes-of-mobility' approach illustrates the 'ever-changing relationships between mobility and immobility' (ibid.:189). Here we note a similarity with hybridity, in that it is about a mutually-constructing relationship between different forms of subjectivity; but, crucially, their methodological and thematic concern is the 'dynamic between sedentariness and movement', whereby they can 'explicitly critique the dichotomy between mobility and immobility' (ibid.:189–90). We can adopt, then, a kind of hybridising theoretical model that is equally concerned with ongoing transformations and changes within cultural identity. Yet, for a paradigm explicitly concerned with movement, it changes the focus from the dialectical relationship of coloniser/colonised to that which is explicitly about different speeds and flows of mobility. If, then, a kinopolitics and a kinopoetics were to continue to rely on hybridity as an explanatory model – one that is anti-essentialist, non-universal, and heterogeneous – it

might well think of it less as a process of renegotiating relationships between the inside and outside, but rather between
the changing material flows of mobility and immobility (that
is, a regime of mobility).

Chapter Conclusion: Kinopoetics and the Migrant Tradition

In attempting to construct this theory of kinopoetics, I am
also attempting to engage but also write myself out of previous traditions. A movement-oriented philosophy, ontology and
poetics helps resolve some internal tensions within these fields,
ultimately offering the emancipatory possibilities toward
which previous theories strive. Although I do not rely heavily
upon the poetics of migration outlined in the second section
of this chapter, nor necessarily the Postcolonial theorists summarised in the fourth, I hope it is nevertheless clear to readers
how much these theories have inspired my scholarship and
development of kinopoetics. Throughout Part II, readers will
notice ways in which kinopoetics still engages similar theoretical concerns that these other traditions have raised, but
attempts to revise them through new concepts, terms, and
perspectives. For example, in Chapter 3 and Chapter 5 I find
it still quite meaningful to rescue the dimensions of poetics of
migration that provide useful terms and ideas that are consistent with kinopoetics; and throughout the analysis chapters,
I will remind readers of these concepts.

In *Poetics of the Migrant*, I am not entirely prepared to
castigate the entirety of Postcolonial Theory, but recognise
still many of its limitations.[26] Broadly speaking, in order
for kinopoetics to properly take its position as a theory and
method for studying migrant literature, I insist that it remains
in dialogue with the other dominant traditions within the
field. Kinopoetics not only remains indebted to these previous thinkers and writers; it is also actively carrying on their
ideas, albeit through the discourse and method of movement.

Notes

1. '[T]he nation-state as we know it today is a fairly recent product of human history. The Treaty of Westphalia of 1648 that set up the earliest model of nation-state sovereignty was based on the two central principles of territorial integrity and the absence of a role for external agents in domestic affairs. However, the treaty also signally ignored the widespread and intensified movements of population that were taking place in the same period, from the mass outward European migrations to the New World, to the Atlantic slave trade, both of which were in full flow at the time' (Quayson 2013:141).

2. 'Central to sovereignty', says Radhika V. Mongia, 'is the notion of recognition: an entity can only be sovereign if it is recognised as such by other sovereign entities' (2007:394).

3. 'We have now to see how the process of this pure Notion of recognition, of the duplicating of self-consciousness in its oneness, appears to self-consiousness. At first, it will exhibit the side of the inequality of the two, or the splitting-up of the middle term into the extremes which, as extremes, are opposed to one another, one being only recognized, the other only recognizing' (Hegel [1807] 2010:540).

4. See Introduction.

5. As Marx states in the 1859 Preface to *Critique of Political Economy* 'In the social production of their life, men enter into . . . relations of production which correspond to a definite stage of development of their material productive forces. The sum total of these relations of production constitutes the economic structure . . . on which rises a legal and political superstructure' (Marx 1859).

6. I disagree with Chakrabarty and others' assertion that Marx's analysis of bourgeois development is Eurocentric. It rather suggests that a system of resource abundance that is, at the same time, immiserating and exploitative was only available in Europe at the time he was writing; and Marx contended that this advanced stage of development was a prerequisite for achieving communist revolution. This situation was one (as Marx was well aware) obtained thanks to surplus gained

from the cruel forces of colonisation, slavery and expropriation. Marx by no means celebrated this fact (see Marx [1847] 1955; see also Anderson 2020) and regarded this contradiction as central to the advanced nature of nineteenth century capitalist development.

7. Moreover, Vivek Chibber has convincingly challenged Chakrabarty's dismissal of Marx, indicating that the material relation to capital accumulation is severely understated and, perhaps, misunderstood. (2013:176–206)

8. 'The bourgeoisie of the sixteenth century accumulated in the interstices of the state. And as the state acquired the machinery of rule . . . those who could soon constitute a class settled into the settled into the proliferating roles of political, economic, and juridical agents for the state' (Robinson 1983:20).

9. 'The tendency of European civilisation through capitalism', says Robinson, 'was thus not to homogenise but to differentiate – to exaggerate regional, subcultural, and dialectical differences into "racial" ones' (Robinson 1983:26).

10. In turn, nationalist and right-wing political parties (such as UKIP, outlined in the Introduction, section headed Poetics and Politics) have been able to effectively deploy bordering ideologies of sovereignty in their own efforts to instill racist paranoia (Yuval-Davis 2018:137).

11. Even today, countries who brandish their military action and intensify immigration policies do so on the basis of sovereignty (see Introduction).

12. Foucault elaborates and historicises these aspects at length: 'In the seventeenth century, at the end of the wars of religion – precisely at the time of the Thirty Years War, ever since the great treaties, the great pursuit of the European balance – a new historical perspective opens up of indefinite governmentality and the permanence of states that will have neither final aim nor term, a discontinuous set of states appears doomed to a history without hope since it has no term, states that are not organised by reference to a reason whose law is that of a dynastic or religious legitimacy, but rather by reference to the reason of a necessity that it must face up to with *coups*

that, although they must always be concerned, are always risky. State, *raison d'État*, necessity, and risky *coups d'État* [i.e. the sovereign's way of demonstrating its prevalence over legitimacy (265)] will form the new tragic horizon of history' (Foucault 2007:266).

13. 'Migration', says Sharma, 'is the specter that haunts the nationalist fantasy of perfection' (2019:79); while '[t]he nation, it is fantasized, would be perfect were it not for the supposedly smelly, noisy, lazy, and overly fecund migrants' (ibid.).

14. Mezzadra and Neilson continue: 'To be governed, the population has to be known, and since it is an elusive statistically unstable entity, it has to be continually traced in its movements and dissected into discrete groups. The more unstable and mobile the population to be governed becomes, the more finely tuned and sophisticated the knowledge devices deployed must become. In the case of migrants, a vast assortment of technologies have been deployed toward this end' (173).

15. Such methods coincide with technologies of recording, managing and monitoring the population, including 'passports, visas, health certificates, invitation papers, transit passes, identity cards, watchtowers, disembarkation areas, holding zones, laws, regulations, customs and excise officials, medical and immigration authorities' (Walters qtd in Mezzadra and Neilson 2013:173).

16. '[T]he state of exception . . . allows for the physical elimination not only of political adversaries but of entire categories of citizens who for some reason cannot be integrated into the political system' (Agamben 2005:2).

17. A comprehensive overview of some of these forces of necropolitics as they relate to marginal identities can be found in *Queer Necropolitics* 2014, edited by Haritaworn, Kuntsman and Posocco.

18. As a result of these political forces, areas like the Mediterranean Sea, the US-Mexico border, and several refugee camps and detention centres all constitute spaces outside of the the scope of sovereign responsibility, resulting in death and violence to vulnerable migrants. In the Mediterranean, 'states have exercised unprecedented levels of violence across

the entire trajectories of illegalised migrants', resulting in a 'record number of 5,096 deaths in the Mediterranean' (Heller, Pezzani and Stierl 2019:51) in 2016 alone. These policies and increased pressure on borders do not exist because of an unruly and unmanageable refugee crisis; the answer is the reverse. It is only because of a restricted regime of sovereignty whereby movement is dictated by 'the richest states on earth over the movement of the populations of the poorest, instilling a de facto regime of global apartheid across the globe's multiple centres and peripheries' (ibid.:67), that there is a bottleneck of refugee movement forced through the violent, dangerous *terra nullius* of the Mediterranean sea.

19. Ramazani's *A Transnational Poetics* uses 'poetics' in more of a conventional sense – that is, with respect to devices of poetry and the formal and linguistic qualities.

20. Moreover, this relationality helps calibrate some of the re-essentialising overcorrections that emerged in previous eras of feminist poetics (see Chapter 1, section headed Poetics: A Diachronic Study).

21. Parts of this sub-section have been lifted from a previously-published chapter: Potter, 2021, '"Don't Get Too Comfortable": Regimes of Motility in Shailja Patel's *Migritude*'. Pp. 176–188 in *Cultural Mobilities Between Africa and the Caribbean*, eds Birgit Englert, Sigrid Thomsen and Barbara Gföllner.

22. See Chibber 2013 for a thorough-going and rigorous critique of this.

23. See Nail 2019, p. 139.

24. See first section of this chapter, Sedentarism and Sovereignty: The Master Texts Behind the Nation.

25. For my own intervention into this paradigm, see Potter, 2021.

26. Furthermore, Postcolonial Theory has already been a target of several vociferous critics (most vocal being Vivek Chibber and Aijaz Ahmad).

PART II

CHAPTER 3

DESTRUCTIVE KINOPOETICS

*The figures who inhabit the
world's borderscapes are not
marginal subjects that subsist on
the edges of society but central
protagonists in the drama of
composing the space, time, and
materiality of the social itself.*
—Sandro Mezzadra and Brett Neilson,
Border as Method. P. 159

Magic Realism and the Migrant

A genre developing predominantly (though not exclusively) out of Latin America, Magic Realism contains formal and thematic aspects that fit within a kinopoetics. Novels within this tradition are wide and varied, yet emerge broadly out of a critique of, and aesthetic response to, the limited confines of bourgeois mimesis and Eurocentrism. Gabriel García Márquez, one of the best-known practitioners of Magic Realism, considered the suitability of the genre to the Latin American and Caribbean context: 'Latin American and Caribbean writers have to admit, hands on hearts, that reality is a better writer than we are. Our destiny, maybe our glory, is to try to imitate it with humility, and as best we can' (2019:235). Márquez delivers this statement at the end of an essay in which he notes that the reality experienced in the Latin American context exceeds the imagination of anyone who might dwell elsewhere, especially in the Global North. He continues: 'In the Caribbean, the original elements of the primal beliefs and magical conceptions previous to the discovery [in other words, European expansion and colonisation] are joined by the profuse variety of cultures that came together in the years following it in a magic syncretism the artistic interest and actual artistic fecundity of which are inexhaustible' (ibid.:233). Márquez here is conveying the fact that writers working in this specific geo-political and historical context find themselves needing to reflect the extraordinary nature of their surroundings – the 'magical syncretism' that emerges once a region finds its identity reshaped by global political forces and regimes of mobility. The complexity, non-linearity, and sheer strangeness of life within this part of the world, according to Márquez, are the identifying features that inhabitants grow to live with, such that literature had to reflect them while simultaneously treating them as a banality.

Understanding that Magic Realism is meant to convey both complexity and mundaneity at the same time helps us better understand the major concerns its authors address. Distinct from Science Fiction and Fantasy, Magic Realism's distinguishing feature remains its dialogic relationship to Realism. Yet, there remains a difference between how Realism and Magic Realism work, particularly in terms of their gesture toward hegemonic power:

> An essential difference . . . between realism and magical realism involves the intentionality implicit in the conventions of the two modes . . . [R]ealism intends its version of the world as a singular version, as an objective (hence universal) representation of natural and social realities – in short, . . . *realism functions ideologically and hegemonically*. Magical

realism also functions ideologically but . . . less hegemoni-
cally, for its programme is not centralising but eccentric: it
creates space for interactions of diversity. In magical realist
texts, *ontological disruption serves the purpose of political
and cultural disruption*: magic is often given as a cultural
corrective, requiring readers to scrutinise accepted realistic
conventions of causality, materiality, motivation. (Zamora
and Faris 1995:3; emphasis added).

These differing 'modes' of hegemonic and counter-hegemonic
writing have two different implications: one specific to literature, and one toward the broader ideological and historical
system. Within literature, the formation and legitimation of
Realism as its own, self-contained genre intersects with
collaborative effort between publishing and education, especially in the nineteenth century. These combined institutional
forces created a standardising, mimetic narrative system that
conformed to the bourgeois conceptions of reality, language,
and structure. In turn, writers, readers, and publishers alike
were able to discern a recognisable narrative that confirms
the qualities of Realism and reality as such. Yet, to return
to Magic Realism, the mode of rendering a narrative that
'serves the purpose of political and cultural disruption' (ibid.)
undercuts the metaphysical basis of history and nation-states
analysed in Chapter 2. Recall that we found through Hegel,
Marx, and others that the standard conception of history
and identity was based both on teleological progression and
on a population's settlement within a nation's boundaries.
Such a conception coincides with political centrality of bourgeois capital and the development of industrial modes of
production. Yet, because teleological, linear historic narrative combined with the primacy of nations is the governing
system by which identity, personhood and human rights are
defined – in other words, bourgeois liberalism – the result is
also a globally-differentiated and hierarchised system of history and identity.

Maintaining this hierarchised system, too, coincided with the Enlightenment project from which philosophers derive the concept of Realism in this first place. A tradition of thinkers such as John Locke, David Hume, Jean-Jacques Rousseau and Immanuel Kant began to place a premium on scientific method and empirical knowledge, insisting on standard laws of objectivity and universality to which all moral, physical, and political knowledge could adhere. Although critiques of the Enlightenment project have been thoroughly taken up elsewhere (see Adorno and Horkheimer 1972), it is important to note that this academic and philosophical context is the one wherein the virtues of Realism emerged – the intellectual interest in reflecting and promoting an objective, empirical, and rational understanding of the material world based on universalisable standards. Such a project, again, cannot be understood outside of the historic context of imperialism, world-building, and liberal development; there had to be an ideological condition through which Enlightenment ideals crystallised. As a result, one must come to realise that we cannot dispense with the Enlightenment project entirely, so much as recognise it as incomplete. The interest in establishing Realism as a genre similarly was, after all, an interest in creating a vision of 'reality' upon which publishers, writers, and readers could all agree. Ian Watt's classic history of Realism and the development of the novel form helps draw this out. The Realist narrative mode in the nineteenth century became 'the sum of literary techniques whereby the novel's imitation of human life follows the procedures adopted by philosophical realism in its attempt to ascertain and report the truth' (1957:30). These authors, thus, meant to assume but also perpetuate the notion that reality as such was so self-evident as to be taken for granted by all who come across the text.

So, because this conception of Realism was invented through the ideological spread of imperial power and development, there remains a need for those whose lives are permanently dominated, stratified and disempowered by imperialism to disrupt this conception of reality (Faris 1995:180). Magic Realism, then, positions itself not necessarily as hostile to Realism as such, but rather an expansion and modification of Realism through magical means.[1] This generic endeavour aims to reflect, with as much mimetic fidelity as possible, the 'magical syncretism' that Márquez describes. Authors in this tradition do not merely challenge the metaphysics of history, identity, and representation; they also undermine the foundational physical parameters of reality – time, space, causality and mortality. The outcome is a suspension not just of reality, but specifically the taken-for-granted aspects of reality, thereby enabling the writer and reader to critique the ontological assumptions of modernity (see Chakrabarty 2000:43). Creating a magical modification of realism ensures that writers treat magic with the same indifference and crudeness that Realist authors treat the mundaneity of bourgeois life. By doing so, these authors destabilise 'inherited notions of imperial history' and instead produce one in which 'the silenced, marginalized, or dispossessed voices within the colonial encounter form the record of "true" history' (Slemon 1995:414). This 'true' history models the conditions of social and political life presented on terms set by the perpetually dispossessed and disempowered.

Throughout the twentieth century, several authors made use of the Magic Realist genre, whereby two modes of knowledge and ideological exist side-by-side. Salman Rushdie's *Midnight's Children*, Márquez's *One Hundred Years of Solitude*, Jorge Luis Borges' *Labyrinth*, Toni Morrison's *Beloved*, Arundhati Roy's *The God of Small Things* all remain classic texts in this tradition. Although these fictional texts differ in their style, themes, language, and spatial-historic context, they share an interest in challenging the stability of Westernised, imperial history, while also attempting to provide a 'cultural corrective' (Zamora and Faris 1995:3). These can, for example, revive a lost history of a people – a history stifled and silenced by the workings of imperial power – by rendering time itself non-linear and unstable. Or, these texts give magical power to powerless communities and individuals, such that they can (re-)claim autonomy and justice. In either case, texts within magic realism tend to make it easy to imagine magic and reality existing side-by-side in paradoxical, yet complementary ways. The result is what Rushdie called 'stereoscopic vision': two seemingly unstable or conflicting images of the world that converge within a person's (or speaker's) field of vision.[2] This stereoscopic vision becomes necessary for the text, as the people represented are forced to renegotiate a reality that has abandoned or displaced them. As Gloria Anzaldúa teaches us, a 'tolerance for ambiguity' and 'contradictions' enables us to achieve a new consciousness: only by 'remaining flexible' can we 'stretch the psyche vertically and horizontally'. This new way of thinking involves moving from 'convergent thinking, analytical reasoning that tends to use rationality to move toward a single goal (Western mode), to divergent thinking, characterised by movement away from set patterns and goals toward a more whole perspective, one that includes rather than excludes' (2012[1987]:101). So, by conjuring a familiar world adjusted through magical forces, Magic Realist texts are able to claim power in a way that liberal or modern reality as such cannot offer.

This empowering quality that Magic Realism has makes it well-suited to kinopoetics and a counter-history of migration. In a global society beset by regimes of immigration management, deportation, border controls and sovereignty, being able to claim an affirmative politics for the migrant requires seising history and identity from imperial power and ideology. Several migrant authors – notably Rushdie, Junot Diaz, and Maxine Hong Kingston – have used Magic Realism to remarkable effect, allowing the complexities and disruptions in the migrant's life to shape and redesign the social milieu through which they move. This capacity stems largely from what Rushdie has already shown us – that '[m]igrants must, of necessity, make a new imaginative relationship with the world, because of the loss of familiar habitats' (1992:125). In his own novel, *Midnight's Children*, we can plainly see this new imaginative relationship in his character Saleem Sinai, the protagonist born *temporally* between two nations; that is, he is born at the midnight turning-point between India pre-Independence and India post-independence. Born at this pivotal point, Saleem joins an imaginative relationship with the other children of midnight: '[A]ll over the new India, the dream we all shared, children were being born who were only partially the offspring of their parents – the children of midnight were also children *of the time*: fathered, you understand, by history. It can happen. Especially in a country which is itself a sort of dream' (Rushdie 1981:159). This in-between place and time is one that motivates these children to invent their own relationship to history and the nation's place in it. The conditions of their role in history are such that they cannot be said to be merely inheriting the positions of their parents, families, or society. They are instead children of a historic moment that could only exist for them in their unique place between the nation(s). As a result, Saleem Sinai sees himself as not one person from one unifying, linear identity, but as an entity containing fragments and multitudes. Speaking, then, of himself in third-person, he writes:

> Because a human being, inside himself, is anything but a whole, anything but homogeneous; all kinds of every-whichthing are jumbled up inside him, and he is one person one minute and another the next. The body, on the other hand, is homogeneous as anything . . . Thus we enter into a state of affairs which is nothing short of revolutionary; and its effect on history is bound to be pretty damn startling. Uncork the body, and God knows what you permit to come tumbling out (ibid.:328).

Saleem's in-between configuration ties his body and self to the nation, creating effects on the external world which 'will be no less profound' (ibid.). It is because of his in-between relation to the nation – in other words, his place beyond its spatial and temporal borders, that rests between to national histories and identities – that he claims 'a place at the centre of things' (ibid.:330). The place and time in which he enters the world is such that he navigates a national space that is not only unfamiliar to him, but also not yet actualised in itself. As a result, his centrality to its history reverses the relationship to the nation: Saleem creates and affects the unfolding political changes, rather than vice versa. His centrality in its history is precisely because he (and the other midnight's children) have been born along with the nation itself. So, Saleem's 'new imaginative relationship with the world' (Rushdie 1992:125) is such that it quite overtly changes the world into which he enters – its identity and defining features fragment, divide, and become eternally changing and inventing, just as he too has to construct the self anew. Rushdie renders a world in *Midnight's Children* in which two realities converge into one – the real history of India pre- and post-independence, but which is instead shaped by Saleem Sinai's magical gifts. This narrative form complies with the subjectivity of those who navigate changing national and political identities, and who find themselves negotiating between its (spatial and temporal) borders. Moreover, Saleem's internally conflicting and fragmented identity requires that he shape the world to fit his own experience of it; his 'place at the centre of things' (Rushdie 1981:330) is his version of history, created and invented to comply with his own internal splits and divisions. A person who takes their place in a nation that is not settled and whose history is not uninterrupted or linear has to also invent their self-identity alongside the nation. Much like the migrants whom I will be analysing this chapter, Saleem's invention of India's history and identity is a necessary part of having to live at and through its borders.

Rushdie's insistence, then, that the migrant make a 'new imaginative relationship with the world' is helpful in understanding the prevalance of magic realism among migrant authors. Placing two (or more) models of reality side-by-side helps make visible and thinkable the familiar strangeness – what Freud called 'unheimlichkeit', or the uncanniness ([1919]2010:825)– that often characterises migrancy. Entering into a new national space means relearning the material reality that we might often assume to be taken for granted. Arriving from a different country, one already has a set of customs, languages, cultural references, rules and expectations that might have to be reconsidered upon migration. Dispelling or disabusing oneself of these previous assumptions and behaviours is an active, not passive, process, requiring sometimes a certain force or confrontation with the reality previously known and understood. Authors are highly aware of this and will often use magical elements to elucidate the idea that having lived in two different nations which have their own, sometimes conflicting or contradictory features, often feels like living with two realities at one time. As a result, being a migrant helps clarify the sense in which there are multiple ways of conceiving of the world which are not restricted to one understanding of history, language, identity or power.

The type of kinopoetics, therefore, that this engenders is what I shall call a 'destructive kinopoetics'. As a poetics, it destroys, disrupts, and deterritorialises knowledge, power, and affects through the narrative genre of magic realism, operating as a critical challenge to, or modification of, an Enlightenment project. I conceive of the migrant here as one whose active movement and force against regimes of kinopower produces a counter-history at which they are the centre. Throughout the remainder of this chapter, I will examine two magic realist novels which focalise the migrant amid changing political and material circumstances, and which utilise magic elements as a means of disrupting reality.

In doing so, I will orient myself toward the migrant figure by affirming their destructive, creative power to undermine the assumptions of liberal history and ideology. Such an undertaking will allow me to both examine and enact a destructive kinopoetics.

The first novel will be Mohsin Hamid's 2017 novel, *Exit West*. Set at a time reminiscent of the (so-called) 'refugee crisis' that reached its apex in 2015, Hamid imagines this moment through two characters, Nadia and Saeed. The desperation, fear and anguish that they undergo as refugees is typical of those experienced by refugees who endured such turmoil in 2015. Yet, portals and doors that suddenly appear throughout the world, instantly leading to other countries, change the entire dynamic for migration and refuge. These 'magical' portals render migration free, safe, instant and increasingly more available (although at first a source of profiteering) in a manner that destroys and undermines the typical bureaucratic and regulatory systems of migration in the present day. Problems and conflict abound no less, but crucially (as I will show) compel readers to take a critical look at today's migration patterns and regulations. The narrative juxtaposes the reality of immigrants in the novel – one augmented or modified through magic doors – in a way that reconfigures the metaphysics of sovereignty and bordering. The second novel I will examine, Chitra Banerjee Divakruni's *The Mistress of Spices* (1997), a novel that follows the life trajectory of Tilo, a young woman whose movement from India to Oakland, California is a journey imbued with mystical power and energy, but also destruction. In her case, her passage from one nation to another requires her to take a vow as a 'mistress of spices', granting her exceptional powers of spice-making and mind-reading, but also bringing her immediately into old age. The novel, as I will detail below, provides a template for Tilo to enact a pedetic force of magic and mysticism that empowers her and draws her into the textures of her community. The dynamics of the narrative, rendered through her lens and controlled by her magic powers, ensure that we see her as a positive, affirmative force of creation in her society.

In both novels, I will show how the migrant characters invent, create and push through the conditions and constraints of expansion by expulsion, enacting their pedetic, relational force and power. They are the ones who Mezzadra and Neilson describe (in the epigraph shown at the beginning of this chapter) when they envision figures 'who inhabit the world's borderscapes' as if they are 'central protagonists in the drama of composing the space, time, and materiality of the social itself' (2013:159). Yet, too, each text generates a new vision of space, time, personhood, power and movement, reorienting and destroying the metaphysical boundaries of modernity, nationalism and sedentarism. Before proceeding with the literary close readings, I will more thoroughly develop the theoretical underpinnings of destructive kinopoetics, and especially emphasise how it operates as an affirmative and transformative kinopoetics. To do so, I will have to connect the operations of this kinopoetics alongside a long-theorised and highly-contested migrant figure: the nomad.

Nomad(ic) Destructions

The nomad is one of the figures that emerges in a counter-history of the migrant. This figure, again, is known for being expelled from social power, but who enacts pedetic force through raids. The force corresponding to the valourisation of the nomad is the centripetal force. To repeat, centripetal force re-channels the flow of agriculture and land into a consolidated center, bringing them in from the periphery, in a centripetal motion; and the feature whose movement makes this redirection and circulation possible is the nomad.[3]

In terms of their relation to the building and directing of resources, materials and spaces, one can find an early account of the nomad's relationship to forces of labour and development in Marx's *Capital*:

> [The nomadic population is] a class of people whose origin is agricultural, but whose occupation is in great part industrial. They are the light infantry of capital, thrown by it, according to its needs, now to this point, now to that. When they are not on the march, they 'camp.' Nomad labour is used for various operations of building and draining, brick-making, lime-burning, railway-making, etc. A flying column of pestilence, it carries into the places in whose neighbourhood it pitches its camp, small-pox, typhus, cholera, scarlet fever, etc. ([1867]1990:818)

In this passage, Marx reveals the economic position of the nomad as one 'thrown by' capital, but who are also excluded for being a 'flying column of pestilence' that brings in 'small-pox, typhus, cholera, scarlet fever, etc.' Similar to the 'industrial reserve army' that he also theorises in *Capital* (ibid.:781), the nomad here exists as a valourised 'light infantry' called upon to fulfill capital's development aims. Even for Marx, the nomad is a creative force; their energy and power is harnessed to build and develop the social and political junction, and are therefore the coordinated unit pulling along centripetal force. Seen here as builders who march and stop only to 'camp', the nomad is identified by their capacity for supplying labour for building, constructing, and developing the various vessels for transport and storage. These features of the nomad are included, indeed, in both the historic as well as conceptual image of the nomad, as we will see. First, however, distinguishing the historic figure of the nomad and the conceptual figure of the nomadic subject is important for this analysis. While they are related, one must be careful not to collapse this distinction.

Nail locates the historical emergence of the nomad in the Neolithic period. This period, as Lewis Mumford notes, 'is preeminently one of containers: it is the age of stone pottery utensils, vases, jars, vats, cisterns, bins, barns, granaries, houses, not least great collective containers like irrigation ditches and villages' (Mumford qtd in Nail 2015:41). Crucially, though, the Neolithic period of centripetal force was a time of agricultural expansion; and '[s]ince centripetal social force is primarily concerned with accumulation, territorial expulsion remains an *indirect* phenomenon' (Nail 2015:45). As a result of this accumulation and agricultural expansion, the expelled figure – the nomad – was created as a byproduct, or as a leftover. There remained a scarcity of resources and territorial flows that needed to be managed, but to which the nomad hunter-gatherers could not gain access. Under these political conditions of expansion by expulsion (outlined in Chapter 1), the nomad emerges and develops. However, according to Nail, 'nomadism is also a product of the migrant's positive desire to leave and to live in a different way: transhumance. The nomads invented a new form of social motion based on continuous movement within a system of relays between seasonal pastures and desert oases' (ibid.). So, while their political expulsion was an indirect result of territorial expansion and agricultural accumulation, the determining feature of the nomad's movement is its inventive and creative desire to abandon the conditions they are in and to instead live differently. Yet, by living differently, the nomad's ingenuity and, perhaps, desire for self-direction produces a new existence beyond the territorial and centripetal forces of kinopower.

'The method of territorial expansion by expulsion', Nail concludes, 'is thus to accumulate through the destruction of the periphery. Once enough of the periphery has been destroyed or displaced, humans must move on: itinerantly expanding and expelling' (Nail 2015:47). The outcome of this is that the nomad's capacity to build, invent, drain and

construct is not, as Marx suggests, supplying the labour needs
of capital accumulation, but precisely their expulsion resulting from territorial accumulation. They did, however, by
virtue of having actively left territorial society, cultivate 'the
newly discovered art of animal raising' and, in turn, invented
'an entirely different form of social motion' (ibid.:130). With
this form of social motion came the pressure, pedetic force,
and counterpower that comes to define nomadism. After all,
'[t]here is no stable ground to rely on', says Nail, 'so the
nomad must become its own ground in a continual oscillation of rigorous self-transformation and self-cultivation of
pressure and counterpressure' (ibid.:134). This creates a crucial point about the nomad's position as a historical figure of
transformation. Nomadism meant being able to apply forms
of (counter-)pressure, create waves of collective power, oscil-
late circuitously between desert oases and seasonal pastures,
and infiltrate territorial power through raids. As a result, this
ensured the first capacity for the nomad to emerge as one
(but indeed not the only) transformative figure in social history. Enacting a force against territorial, centripetal power,
the nomad produced, through pedetic force, conditions for
resisting kinopower.

The existence of this historic figure is not directly appli-
cable to the theoretical discussion of (kino)poetics, affect, and
Magic Realism. What instead helps is theorising the nomad in
a way that does not simply confine them to a unique moment
or mode of production, and instead widening the scope to
suggest a 'nomadic' conceptual and political figuration that
can go beyond a specified historical period.[4] This does not
necessarily mean abandoning history entirely; but this, again,
can run alongside the counter-history of the nomad in order
to make its singular nomadism legible and thinkable. One
of the most famous discussions of the conceptual figure of
the nomad comes out of Deleuze's and Guattari's 'Treatise
on Nomadology' in *A Thousand Plateaus*. In this chapter,

Deleuze and Guattari set out to effectively describe the figure who is 'Deterritorialised par excellence' (Deleuze and Guattari [1987]2014:444). They write:

> The nomad has a territory; he follows customary paths; he goes from one point to another; he is not ignorant of points (water points, dwelling points, assembly points, etc.). But the question is what in nomad life is a principle and what is only a consequence. To begin with, although the points determine paths, they are strictly subordinated to the paths they determine, the reverse of what happens with the sedentary. . . [T]he nomad goes from point to point only as a consequence and as a factual necessity; in principle, points for him are always relays along a trajectory (ibid.:443).

Here, Deleuze and Guattari posit the nomad's tendencies toward movement as distinct from those desires which condition the dominating structures of *polis* and sedentarism. The latter are ideological and metaphysical tendencies I outlined thoroughly in Chapter 2, in the first section. In brief, though, Deleuze and Guattari characterise sedentarism as the attempts to measure, territorialise and direct flows of motion; it 'determines paths' insofar as sedentarism enables 'reterritorialisation *afterward*' (ibid.:444) – that is, creating a well-defined, locatable space wherein subjects can be made legible to the organs of state power and placed within an identifiable, categorisable frame. Sedentarism is a technique employed by *polis*, the regime of control that attempts to fashion and develop a territorial flow that is stable, recognisable, controllable, and profitable. 'Nomadism', they write, 'is a movement, a becoming that affects sedentaries, just as sedentarisation is a stoppage that settles the nomads' (ibid.:500). This sedentarist regime operates by way of a 'striated space' that is 'both limited and limiting': 'it is limited in its parts, which are assigned constant directions, are oriented in relation to one another, divisible by boundaries, and can interlink; what is limiting . . . is this aggregate in relation to smooth spaces it 'contains', whose growth it slows or prevents, and which it restricts or places outside' (ibid.:445). In other words, the State creates forces of reactivity that attempt to restrict and confine the nomadic mobility so that their identities can be represented according to a regime of social control or mode of production.

The nomad, instead, enacts 'deterritorialisation' – that is, they continuously produce their own affective and epistemological 'smooth space' (that is, open-ended, clear space of frictionless intensive movement) and 'line of flight', using affects as 'weapons' (Deleuze and Guattari 2014:466) to destroy or tear open any reactive boundaries ('absolute reterritorialisations') imposed afterward. In doing so, the nomad invents a movement that cannot be readily captured, directed, defined, or appropriated by regimes of power. Instead, the nomad operates in the same way as a metallurgist whose 'operations are always astride the threshold' (ibid.:478), and who are therefore capable of overcoming the limitations of form through 'continuous development' (ibid.:479). This is a significant feature of the nomadic figure for purposes of kinopoetics. The nomad's capacity to build, make or create is at the same time – and perhaps paradoxically – an ability to destroy. The nomad's ability to build requires creative and inventive power; by creating new ways of living and new forms of motion, the nomad in turn does so in a manner that is automatically and autonomously disrupting representational fixities and norms. Rather than working on something derived from pre-established plans or blueprints, the nomadic artist, or metallurgist, works to immanently build from within, by way of productive, relational connections. Their act of creative development is a constant process of producing affects which, because they are in constant motion or process, cannot abide by axioms of power. So, they are actively and constantly 'deterritorialising' in their creative pursuits because the tools they fashion, the art they create, and their way of life all exist outside of, beyond, or beneath the boundaries of norms and forms. If any reterritorialisations do occur, they occur on the basis of relative, momentary stabilities and actualities, but are conceived on the nomad's terms. Where they go and what they build does not have a pre-established design or limit in mind; instead, their project or motion is completed on autonomous terms, rather than according to a mapped out plan or principle.

Nomadism and sedentarism are not binaries, however. They are manifestations of power produced and valourised within particular shifting, changing, and overlapping assemblages, and not restricted to one specified figure, identity or organisation. The 'smooth space' and the 'striated space' are two types of territorial assemblages whose political content is conditioned through arrangements of desire. It is important to note, in this respect, that nomadism is a double-edged sword. After all, State power is capable of being nomadic, continuously expanding its yoke of influence and power (through, for example, expanding security apparatus and military garrisons). In other words, invading forces of state power share nomadic qualities: they can clear spaces (both physical and conceptual) to accelerate frictionless movement.[5] Capital, too, differentiates in a way that often 'tends toward a smooth space defined by uncoded flows, flexibility, continual modulation, and tendential equalisation' (Hardt and Negri 2000:327). The nomad, furthermore, finds occasion for stasis and relative reterritorialisations. It is just that they do so 'only as a consequence and a factual necessity' (Deleuze and Guattari 2014:443). As I will show through this chapter, the characters (Saeed, Nadia and Tilo) uphold counter-power as nomadic subjects, inventing and creating liberatory opportunities. Their liberatory character derives from an assemblage of desire and affect that pushes them to overcome the limitations of state and national power. So, as we evaluate the nomadic qualities made visible in and through these texts, I will pay close attention to the desire, or dominant social drives, inherent within this movement. The centripetal force of kinopower, by contrast, is not of a liberatory nature, but rather based on an ambition to expand (or, deterritorialise) by expulsion. Yet, the nomad subjects who apply pressure through counter-power assert their affirmative capacity and pedetic force through solidarity, connectivity and relationality.

This affirmative capacity to build while also destroying is what makes Magic Realism a suitable genre to the nomad figure. Magic Realism challenges the normative boundaries of Realism, including the foundational parameters of time and space; as a result, so arises a capacity to reshape the arrangement and distribution of the sensible world, including its hierarchies and spaces of belonging. By doing so, authors in this tradition imagine and invent a narrative where lived experiences and intensities coincide in new, unexpected ways. They break through the conventions and ideological assumptions of Realism, thereby overcoming the pre-ordained system of norms, identity, language, and representation set by a regime of Western, bourgeois ideals. Magic Realism, then, 'create[s] a new Earth' (Deleuze and Parnet 1977:36) and is, in turn, 'imbued' with a 'process of demolition' (ibid.:39); it affirms and makes legible an existence that, in its manner of modifying and altering reality, destabilises the foundational structure of modernity. For this reason, I have designated Magic Realism as enacting a 'destructive kinopoetics', making it the first kinopoetic type that I will be building. It complies with the overall methodological system and object of study for kinopoetics (as outlined in the previous two chapters), reinforcing the counter-history of kinopolitics, and the affirmative, transformative, relational power of migrancy, affect, and intensive movement. Furthermore, the characters envisioned in the two novels I examine also enact an active and creative force. They decide or invent the reality as they see it, on their own terms. So, in terms of both the narrative form of Magic Realism, as well as the configuration and internal focalisation of migrancy, these texts – in their destructive kinopoetics – enact the transformative, pedetic power of the nomad. The nomadism that these texts perform, both in terms of their narrative structure and in the migrant character's focalised movement, exists in a way that is deterritorialising – sometimes affirmative and positive, sometimes violent and cruel. Throughout the rest of this chapter, I will insist that destructive kinopoetics is one way to render migrancy visible – both in its nomadic workings and in the migrant's nomadic movement.

Exit West: *The Desire to be Anywhere, but Not Here*

Hamid's *Exit West* opens amid a city 'swollen with refugees but still mostly at peace, or at least not openly at war' (2017:1) where we are introduced to Saeed and Nadia, whose burgeoning relationship, travels, and personal development frame the proceeding narrative. They encounter each other in the familiar setting of an 'evening class on corporate identity and product branding' (ibid.). Within the first page of the novel, the speaker gestures toward the wider social climate and expectation of events to come. The characters we meet, and their immediate surroundings, anticipate an existential change to the circumstances in which they live, and the reality they expect to emerge out of it:

> It might seem odd that in cities teetering at the edge of the abyss young people still go to class . . . but that is the way of things, with cities as with life, for one moment we are pottering about our errands as usual and the next we are dying, and our eternally impending ending does not put a stop to our transient beginnings and middles until the instant when it does (ibid.:1–2).

The poetics of the last sentence in this passage is worth pondering. Emphasising 'eternally impending endings' repeats on the rhyme 'ending', challenging the presumed finality of endings as such. Rather, they occur 'eternally', as if returning time and again, without a fixed point at which 'we' settle. Secondly, the repeated '-ing' sound that connects 'impending', 'ending', and 'beginning' assures that present, future, and past are interconnected and co-creative rather than existing on a linear timeline. 'Impending', 'ending', and 'beginning' create a syllabic sound of expansion, contraction and expansion again – a deterritorialisation, reterritorialisation, and deterritorialisation – that shows the experience of flows followed by (temporary) junctions, or outward pulsating movements followed by merely a momentary fixity. Endings, neither in time or space, can be said to be fixed or absolutely final; rather, endings are – like middles and beginnings – equally transient, producing instead breaks, irruptions, or shifts in direction without stopping, settling, or remaining. One arrives at a point, not necessarily as a permanently settled state, but rather as a relay to more points, even other beginnings and middles – 'until the instant that it does' which, in this case, means death. This poetics foreshadows the nomadic existence and alternative reality that Saeed and Nadia navigate throughout the novel. In both their own romance, as well as their passage to other cities and nations, endings are never as they seem, as they do 'not put a stop to transient beginnings and middles'. Rather, as we will see, one questions whether in life, love or even migration there need necessarily be a beginning, middle or end.

As the narrative proceeds, Saeed's and Nadia's relationship begins to solidify, and throughout the novel the trajectory and evolution of their relationship unfolds. From the time they are introduced and through their worldly travels, the complexities and conflicts of romance start to emerge in a way that reflects a Realist framework, unperturbed by sentimentality. Similarly, though, the narrator describes the violence surrounding them with similar coldness and matter-of-factness. Saeed works up the nerve to speak to Nadia 'for the first time. Their city had yet to experience major fighting, just some shootings and the odd car bombing, felt in one's chest cavity as a subsonic vibration like those emitted by large loudspeakers at music concerts, and Saeed and Nadia had packed up their books and were leaving class' (Hamid 2017:2). 'Just some' and 'odd' are words typically deployed to describe commonplace events, or randomness and spontaneity that can be forgotten the moment that it happens. That they are used to describe 'shootings' and 'car bombings' shows that the inhabitants in this city are desensitised in how they relate to violence. Michael Perfect notes that, '[m]uch like the refugees in the novel's opening line, that violence is framed as subordinate to the development of Saeed and Nadia's relationship, sandwiched as it is here in the middle of a two-sentence paragraph that begins and ends with interactions between the two protagonists' (2019:191). The conflict, uncertainty, and violence relegated to the background, almost as an afterthought, at first seems like something they can ignore as they move on with the mundaneity of their lives.

Even from the start of their relationship, their desires are directed outward, beyond the confines of their home country and city. Saeed and Nadia have their first date at a Chinese restaurant, and Saeed is amused by Nadia's choice of restaurant:

'I like it,' he said, indicating their surroundings. 'Sort of mysterious. Like we could be anywhere. Well, not any-where, but not here.'
'Have you travelled abroad?'
He shook his head. 'I want to.'
'Me too.'
'Where would you go?'
She considered him for a while. 'Cuba.'
'Cuba! Why?'
'I don't know. It makes me think of music and beautiful old buildings and the sea.'
(Hamid 2017:20)

This brief dialogue provides some meaningful foreshadowing for the ensuing narrative; but it also makes a broad statement about the two characters' relationship to their circumstances. Saeed's first reaction to the Chinese restaurant, suggesting 'we could be anywhere. Well, not anywhere, but not here', is a banality not lost on readers who have ever travelled abroad. Like most multinational corporations, Chinese restaurants are a staple of nearly every country, and their presence globally provides a sense of stability and consistency that tourists recognise.

Yet, there is another layer of significance to this phrase, 'like we could be anywhere'. One aspect that immediately stands out upon reading *Exit West* is the deliberate choice to hide the name of Saeed's and Nadia's hometown: it is given no name at all, other than 'their city' (Hamid 2017:2) or 'Saeed and Nadia's city' (ibid.:48). Through some aspects of deduction, readers could easily conclude that the city is likely in Pakistan (Hamid's country of origin) based on the developing conflict at the time as well as its time zone connection to other cities mentioned in the novel. However, Hamid's decision to give names to every other city to which Saeed and Nadia travel except for their city and country of origin invites us to question entirely the basis of home, identity, settlement and citizenship in the first place. Critics such as Claire Chambers have noted that leaving the city nameless 'enables readers to involve themselves in the co-production Hamid espouses in his art' (Chambers 2019:244). Amanda Lagji, in a similar vein, has noted that this 'generalising gesture encourages readers to see similarities between places that could serve as the novel's setting' (Lagji 2018:223). A (destructive) kinopoetic reading allows us to interpret this aspect somewhere between Lagji's and Chambers's readings. Lagji's reference to a 'generalising gesture' finds confirmation in the dialogue noted above: just as the setting for their first date in a Chinese restaurant also produces a generalised quality that could easily be anywhere, so too does the city's namelessness. Furthermore, readers' active participation in comprehending and making visible previously unseen places and people ensures that we can produce and invent this nameless place along with the story's narrator, just as Chambers suggests. In the destructive kinopoetics, though, this namelessness leaves open the possibility and potential for nomadic invention and creativity. Not only are we the readers capable of filling in this gap with our own imagined city, mapping it onto our own version of which city would likely fit its characteristics. Saeed and Nadia, too, are rather nomadic migrants who get to invent, produce, create and build their version of home on their own terms. That the city is framed as their city, one over which they have possession, and which belongs to them (rather than the other way around), reflects their affective relation to the city – a relation that is more active and affirmative, rather than passive and coerced. As the novel proceeds, we find the characters inventing and reinventing their version of home that is not in a fixed geographic location, but rather expanded and renegotiated as they both grow together.[6]

Furthermore, their affective relation to home is not one confined within the spatio-political boundaries of their city and country of origin (wherever that may be); rather, their desires are directed outward, in a place that could be anywhere, '[w]ell not anywhere, but not here' (Hamid 2017:20). Their city is 'swollen with refugees' (ibid.:1), wherein '[r]efugees had occupied many of the open places in the city' (ibid.:23). We know they live amid 'times of violence' (ibid.:28) such that eventually 'militants' began 'taking over a holding territory throughout the city' (ibid.:48), creating what the narrator calls 'this death trap of a country' (ibid.:69). Once these hostile and unstable circumstances are known to the reader, the narrative gives us a sense for the characters' desires. Nadia begins to rethink her sense of safety and stability within her home country: 'Nadia was herself coming to acknowledge that this was no longer a city where the risks facing a young woman living independently could be thought of as manageable, and equally important she worried for Saeed each time he drove over to see her and back again' (ibid.:72). Nadia's rumination here reflects the typical way that news media and world leaders come to understand and recognise the internal life and motivation of refugees. Out of desperation and a need to find safety, refugees (according to this broad generalisation) have no other choice but to leave. Yet, the narrative of *Exit West* is careful not to reduce Saeed's and Nadia's appetite for leaving as merely a response to uncertainty and instability. While it is true that the circumstances in their city are unlivable and unmanageable, thereby creating the necessity to seek refuge elsewhere, this reaction is not the only basis for wanting to leave home. In fact, throughout the beginning of the novel, we can locate their affective relation toward escape in their desires to exist in different places.

As already mentioned above, this desire to travel or be in another part of the world expresses itself in their conversation about travelling while they sit in a Chinese restaurant – a setting that already gives them the feeling that they are anywhere but their home, or that, more precisely, home as such could really be anywhere. In that moment, we can locate their relational desire toward the outside or to a different place. Furthermore, we are also told in an early chapter about Saeed's and Nadia's attachments to their phones. Taking place during, presumably, the famous refugee crisis of 2015, the novel's contemporary setting allows the characters to have the same technology that we, as modern readers, would come to expect, complete with internet-enabled smartphones that provide social media as well as surveillance capabilities. Nevertheless, both Saeed and Nadia in their own ways use their mobile phones to access the world beyond their city: 'In their phones were antennas, and these antennas sniffed out an invisible world, as if by magic, a world that was all around them, and also nowhere, transporting them to places distant and near, and to places that had never been and would never be' (Hamid 2017:35). Saeed, for his part, tries to resist the 'pull of his phone' (ibid.), and only in the evenings does he use it to 'disappear . . . down the byways of the internet' (ibid.:36). Nadia, by contrast, used her phone without restricting her access to global events:

> It kept her company on long evenings, as it did countless young people in the city who were likewise stranded in their homes, she rode it far out into the world on otherwise solitary, stationary nights. She watched bombs falling, women exercising, men copulating, clouds gathering, waves tugging at the sand like the rasping licks of so many mortal, temporary, vanishing tongues, tongues of a planet that would one day too be no more. (ibid.:37)

Saeed and Nadia here see their phones as windows or portals to the outside world. They view images or videos of places they have yet to actually live in, and imagine that those parts of the world have either 'never been and would never be' or as 'tongues of a planet that would one day too be no more'. In either case, they gain instant, unbridled, unlimited (or in Saeed's case, semi-unlimited) entry into cities and situations they never had an opportunity to experience. Even if they are not (yet) physically in those other places, they are already in an affective and imaginative relation with parts of the world beyond their home city. Liliana Naydan writes here that the digital screens in *Exit West* creates a paradoxical condition in which all migrants live: 'they live as simultaneously connected to and yet disconnected from one another, their homes, and the nations to which they migrate' (2019:434). This description of their phones and digital screens occurs in the novel before we learn of the doors that begin to appear and through which people can pass through to escape their city and transport to another city entirely. This narrative ordering has two effects: on the one hand, it reminds us that their aspirations or desires for being elsewhere are simulated through their phones and communication access; and, on the other hand, the digital screens anticipate and foreshadow the passage of the doors that crop up later.

What is interesting to note, when we finally learn of these doors, is how similarly they are described to the transporting and seemingly 'magic' (Hamid 2017:35) power of phones. For this reason, the description of the doors in the first time they are mentioned, and the characters' reactions to them, is worth quoting in full:

> The effect doors had on people altered as well. Rumours had begun to circulate of doors that could take you elsewhere, often to places far away, well removed from this death trap of a country. Some people claimed to know people who knew people who had been through such doors . . . Most people thought these rumours to be nonsense, the superstitions of the feeble-minded . . . Nadia and Saeed, too, discussed these rumours and dismissed them. But every morning, when she woke, Nadia looked over at her front door, and at the doors to her bathroom, her closet, her terrace. Every morning, in his room, Saeed did much the same. All their doors remained simple doors, on/off switches in the flow between two adjacent places, binarily either open or closed, but each of their doors, regarded thus with a twinge of irrational possibility, became partially animate as well, an object with a subtle power to mock, to mock the desires of those who desired to go far away, whispering silently from its door frame that such dreams were the dreams of fools (ibid.:69–70)

These doors, as we come to learn, allow migrants free, safe, and instant passage from one country to another. The way they are described when the city inhabitants learn of them (though not the first time we, as readers, learn of them) is reminiscent of how new types of technology are described when they emerge on the market. After all, digital technology and smartphones, as they were introduced, 'altered' the way people began to think; and their power and capacity to make information, connectivity – but also more nefarious surveillance capacities – available seemed to be 'nonsense' and 'superstition'. Yet, when these characters are experiencing the new doors, digital screens and cell phones were an everyday banality. At the same time, note the intensive and affective similarities between the doors and digital technology crystallise in this above passage. The 'new' doors changed the way the characters looked at 'simple doors', which were merely like 'on/off switches', 'binarily either open or closed', just as the emergence of smartphones creates new ways of looking at basic phones whose main functions are far simpler. Referring to doors in our houses, closets, or buildings as having on/off switches and operating on a binary system treats them more as electronic computing machines with algorithmic properties instead of mere physical barriers with knobs and hinges. Similar to smartphones, though, the new doors created a longing in users and people for different possibilities that were previously unavailable, modifying and changing one's perspective on the present material circumstances.

For Saeed and Nadia – the main, focalised figures and migrants in the story – the doors stand for something different. We already know that, through their smartphones, their appetite for travel, and the pleasure they take in being 'anywhere, but not here' (Hamid 2017:25), they desire and long for leaving their city. Knowing this about the two main characters complicates the typical, standard perspective through which we view refugees: that their only rationale for departure is a calculated decision for self-preservation. The assumption of such a perspective is that migration is merely a matter of 'decisions that will serve his or her own interests and for which he or she can be held responsible' (Collins 2017:2). For quite some time, however, the migration studies field has tried to distance itself from viewing the migrant as a 'utility-maximising individual' (ibid.), or a 'decision maker who chooses to migrate in a relatively autonomous or individualistic way' (ibid.). The attribution of individualist or autonomous motivation obscures the complexity of affective and relational attachments that immigrants might or might not have toward their homes, to varying degrees (we see these differing attachments especially with Saeed and Nadia). Instead, we can widen the scope of understanding the internal, affective life of migrants by examining their *desires*. Specifically, as Francis Collins does in a 2017 special issue of the *Journal of Ethnic and Migration Studies* devoted to 'aspiration, desire and the drivers of migration', I shall also think of desire 'as a social force' (2). Also following after theories of Deleuze and Guattari, Collins 'conceives of desire as the energies that draw entities – human, non-human, symbolic – into relation with each other and in the process generates social forms and affects' (ibid.:2–3). I, too, share in Collins's (and, by extension, Deleuze and Guattari's) insistence that desire should not necessarily be 'characterised by 'lack' and the striving for an impossible ideal' (ibid.:4), but rather as 'the very force that animates the world – it is not an effect of power, but rather a force involved in the production and arrangement of social forms' (ibid.:4). In other words, desire here acts as an outward, active flow that produces, invents, builds, shapes, and creates the social world of affective, relational speeds and slownesses. It is neither merely a rational process of self-preservation, nor is it merely a need to escape hardship. Instead, desire is a process of inventing and connecting through relation and affective power, in addition to responding to needs for safety and refuge. 'From this perspective,' writes Collins, 'existence is not determined through transcendence or by underlying collective interests, but rather by unconscious drives that emanate from particular 'assemblages', arrangements of bodies, things, and ideas. Desire, then, acts to bring different bodies together in new and transformative formations' (ibid.:4). As I outlined in Chapter 1, this conception of politics and power is built upon an understanding of affect and movement as a constitutive force of social and political subjectivity. In brief, this affective, relational framework helps refine the analysis of political and social life, including the basis for freedom, joy, knowledge and collective power. Desire and affect, then, are the main forces – 'the relations of speed and slowness' (Deleuze 1988:125) – that constitute political subjectivity; they also act upon the material assemblage, deterritorialising its liminal, structuring, and axiomatic power. As a destructive force, desire is a reinventing and rebuilding capacity to construct a new world; and, as a kinopoetics, *Exit West* uses magic to generate a new material and affective arrangement. Locating where and how strongly desire is 'plugged into [an] existing social field' (Deleuze and Guattari [1983] 2013:44) and how to activate desire into a collective assemblage remains part of the political challenge.

In *Exit West*, though, the existence of doors or portals which suddenly appear to carry migrants through a safe passage, from one country to the next, can be read as an outcome, effect, or actualisation of Saeed and Nadia's desires. We already know that both of them, before they knew about the existence of the doors, were eager to exist elsewhere and move beyond their home city. Reading them as nomadic subjects, Saeed's and Nadia's desires to be 'anywhere, but not here' (Hamid 2017:25) are really their forces which 'animate' the world – forces 'involved in the production and arrangement of social forms' (Collins 2017:4). As nomadic figures, they create and invent the world, actively shaping the material and relational assemblage. Their affective movements act as weapons upon the striating and territorialising forces of sedentarism. So, instead of thinking of these doors as objects that enable or ensure the conditions for Saeed and Nadia (and other migrants) to move freely, a destructive kinopoetics reverses this relationship. Nadia and Saeed's desires for, and affects toward, existing elsewhere are the constitutive forces that created the doors to other countries – not the other way around. The migrant, in this case, is not merely a subject to material conditions or transcendent, ideological systems that govern how they can move. Rather, the migrant, and particularly the nomadic subject, invents movement through pedetic force, affecting, creating, pushing, and deterritorialising the social assemblage. Their desires, as a result, act upon the assemblage, or the 'arrangement of bodies, things, and ideas' (Collins 2017:4) and bring it into new formations. In their case, Saeed and Nadia's attachment to other places, seen in the way that they use their phones to access other worlds, people, events, and ideas, rearranges the assemblage through which they live, thereby activating the emergence of the doors. Such openings in the fabric of space and time are made possible because desires and affects act upon the social assemblage; and the existence of the doors emerges from the nomad's pedetic power for creating and inventing lines of flight and, therefore, transforming the social assemblage.

We can note, too, how the passage through the doors is described in the text. At first, as she walks up to the door, Nadia 'was struck by its darkness, its opacity, the way that it did not reveal what was on the other side, and also did not reflect what was on this side, and so felt equally like a beginning and an end' (Hamid 2017:98). She is told that 'the passage was both like dying and like being born', and as she passes through she 'experienced a kind of extinguishing as she entered the blackness and a gasping struggle as she fought to exit it, and she felt cold and bruised and damp as she lay on the floor of the room at the other side' (ibid.). The doors themselves do not resemble moving checkpoints, and one is not aware of the passage of space the way they would if they are travelling on a train or aeroplane. Instead it is 'equally like a beginning and end', felt as though one is 'both like dying and being born'. These sensations produce an experience that is not subject to linear time, and are not confined to the regulations of passage that govern international movement and travel. The movement through the door is 'a beginning and an end', which is a direct parallel to the novel's opening sentence analysed above. Again, this gestures us toward questioning and challenging the Realist conceptions of linear time and the management of time in migration and travel. Previous to the doors, Nadia and Saeed were drawn to their phones' instantaneity and digital access that do not require physically leaving home (which can cost money and time, but can also subject them to dangers). Through their phones, they developed and realised their internal desires. The doors, then, became the ultimate actualisation of these 'unconscious drives that emanate from particular 'assemblages" (Collins 2017:4); in this case, it is the assemblage built around digital screens, social media, and their users' interactions with them, making possible the activation and generation of their desires. Nadia and Saeed wanted always to be 'anywhere, but not here' (Hamid 2017:25); their digital screens assured and activated the becoming-nomad that, then, forced open time- and space-circumventing doors. The nomadic figures create the doors from one country to the next, inventing the possibilities for their movement, and affirming their relational power to move; and, in turn, they use their pedetic social force destroy the metaphysics of time and space.

A destructive kinopoetics treats the migrant figures of *Exit West* as nomadic figures, and affirms their centrality and primacy in producing the forces of deterritorialisation and reterritorialisation that constitute the social and political assemblage. Saeed and Nadia's desires act upon the world and the city they inhabit, pushing its material and physical limits to then enable their capacity to move. From a counter-historical kinopolitics, they are the primary constitutive figures that produce the emerging regime of social motion – in this case, a borderless regime of free movement. A destructive kinopoetics sees that these figures' desires are the forces that created the doors, animating a new regime of motion that is open, free, multidirectional, and multi-linear. Taking a step back, this also functions, formally for Magic Realism, as the product of the internal focalisation, wherein the 'vision with' (Genette 1988:65) Saeed and Nadia makes possible and grants access to these affective movements. As a feature within these novels, and the generic tendency of Magic Realism, this contributes to the stereoscopic vision that *Exit West* makes available. Their nomadic power conjures the means for smooth passage between borders and between nations; and such power extends indefinitely in order to transform the world they inhabit. As a Magic Realist device, the doors or portals are the magical objects that update and modify the existing reality – they, in other words, destroy the commonplace assumptions of time, space, movement, nation and travel. The destructive power is the nomad's pedetic force through which she affirms her movement and manifests the conditions for transformation. Saeed's and Nadia's primacy in this story, then, are not just as a confluence of forces, but as active agents pressing and pushing against the assemblage with their own nomadic power. Having now underscored the source of free movement located in Saeed's and Nadia's nomadism, I shall now analyse more thoroughly the wider political consequences of their activated desires. As we will see, the destructive power of their nomadism, actualised in the doors, will reshape the globe and force a new vision of society, changing our sensible and affective relation toward nations, borders and migrants.

Exit West: *Making the Open Bordered World Thinkable*

As the doors appear in the story, the world the characters inhabit begins to dramatically change. Although similar conflicts arise in conditions of immigration – intercultural hostilities, alienation, and struggles for belonging – the wider legal, juridical and political systems of migration management disappear entirely. The necessity for this disappearance emerges when the desperation sets in among the city's inhabitants:

> Conversations focused mainly on conspiracy theories, the status of the fighting, and how to get out of the country – a since visas, which had long been near-impossible, were now truly impossible for non-wealthy people to secure, and the journeys on passenger planes and ships were therefore out of the question, the relative merits, or rather risks, of the various overland routes were guessed at, and picked apart, again and again. (Hamid 2017:50)

Saeed observes these conversations at his workplace, and both he and Nadia start to notice that the urgency of escape is starting to affect their daily lives. At the same time, they also begin to learn about the challenges different nations face amid crises of this nature. After all, 'an unprecedented flow of migrants was hitting the rich countries, who were building walls and fences and strengthening their borders, but *seemingly to unsatisfactory effect*' (ibid.:71; emphasis added). Eventually, because of the existence of doors/portals that connect nations and bring migrants seamlessly through them, no effort on the part of any securitising, migration-management regime was going to be enough to stop the flight of migrants and refugees around the world. Once people come to know and accept the availability of free, safe and instant migration and movement, the outcome is that states have no capacity for restricting migration.

Once these magical doors impose themselves on the world they inhabit, a new regime starts to take shape. The world Hamid builds in the narrative is otherwise a familiar one to readers: an ongoing refugee crisis in response to political conflict, civil war, and climate change, and a widespread panic among receiving nations (adding fuel to reactionary, right-wing, anti-immigrant political impulses). Furthermore, the characters are otherwise unextraordinary people, progressing through a romantic partnership filled with commonplace emotional complications. Even their upbringing, education, career paths and courtship follow standard, formulaic patterns of twenty-first century modernity. As I noted above, people in the novel were aware that procuring visas was 'near-impossible' and 'truly impossible for non-wealthy people to secure' (Hamid 2017:50), while the 'relative merits, or rather risks, of the various overland routes were . . . picked apart' (ibid.). Their capacity to imagine the world differently from how it actually is remained, therefore, unreachable. Similarly, for readers, the narrative presents a world exactly as it was throughout the years that the story takes place, complete with reactionary backlash against migration in countries like the United States, the United Kingdom and Austria, intercultural conflicts, and the increasing desperation to regulate and manage movement. Yet, with the introduction of the doors, the free movement of people changes the structural arrangement of people, borders and nations as such, forcing upon (both readers and the characters) then a new way of imagining global migration and mobility.

The intervention *Exit West* makes into the discourse on migration, borders, human rights, and nation-states is one which asks us to consider a world of open borders and free movement. In the realm of immigrant rights activism and theorising, advocacy for opening borders – that is, making the unrestricted passage between nations available to all, eliminating the securitising, criminalising, and militarising aspects of borders – has had a long, contentious history. 'The idea of movement as a human right is not new', writes Reece Jones. Rather, '[a]s soon as humans began to divide up the land of the world into separate political spaces, others questioned the legitimacy of these divisions' (2019:13). The 'open borders' position 'envisions no, or hardly any, restrictions on cross-border migration while at the same time not necessarily striving toward a borderless world' (Heller, Pezzani and Stierl 2019:56). The challenges leveled against such a position are often taken to imagine both its feasibility and pragmatism, as well as market considerations from left- and right-leaning commentators (Jones 2019:5–12). The concerns range from wondering how the absolute wages of the working class would suffer from the influx of migrant labour, to how to mitigate cross-cultural conflict and strife as people come into more intense contact. These closed-border positions all suffer from the same epistemological problem and symptom: namely, an inability to think beyond a coherent idea of the nation as a bounded entity of uniform identity. As Alex Sager points out in his 2020 book *Against Borders*, 'Our imaginations fall frequently under the thrall of state-centered ideology,' and serious thinkers seldom engage 'social scientific work that has challenged the nation-state-centered worldview' (2020:3). As a result, those who wish to envision a world of free movement and mobility between countries have to contend with a deeply-ingrained structure of statehood, sovereignty, and borders. Furthermore, we have developed a cultural and social imaginary around the clear division between nations and people, treating borders as if they are natural parts of the modern world; and thus the juridical, political, and material boundaries created through this state-based paradigm govern how we view the world at large. However, as Nail writes, this way of conceiving borders as simply 'the outer territorial borders of states' or identifying them 'with abstract lines and demarcated boundaries'

(2016:14) ignores its material history and functional development. Nail continues:

> The border as a social process of division is not reducible to state power . . . Rather, the border is *what divides*. It is a process that states try to harness, but that often eludes them. Not only does the border precede the state historically since humans have been making borders for thousands of years before states existed, but it also precedes the state logically as the technical delimitation required in the first place for the social division called 'the state' to exist at all. (ibid.)

What Nail is conveying here is a need to disarticulate borders from states, noting that they need not necessarily be intertwined, despite the fact that we tend to think of borders, states, and sovereignty as continuous (see previous chapter). Yet, crucially, for Nail and other scholars in critical borders studies, there exists a need to clarify the political and social function of borders: to divide. Specifically, nation borders reinforce divisions of (il)legality, political citizenship, and social belonging. In order, then, to advocate for an open bordered world, one has to acknowledge not only the legal stakes of bordered states, but also the social and cultural aspects which govern how we imagine a globalising world – one in which there are clear divisions between those who are citizens, and those who we deem migrants, foreigners, or outsiders. Free and autonomous mobility and movement, alongside the continuous intermingling of people, are capacities unachievable within the framework of a closed bordered, hypermilitarised, and liberal democratic paradigm (even those which allow relatively free movement, such as within different EU and US member states).

In *Exit West*, the characters, too, are rendered as people living within a world divided by borders, and within which visas, travel restrictions, nationalist resentments, and detention centres are part of the fabric. At first, after leaving their home city, they pass through a door ending up immediately in Mykonos, Greece. Upon arrival, they approach a refugee camp and join the throng of new arrivals:

> [T]hey saw what looked like a refugee camp, with hundreds of tents and lean-tos and people of many colours and hues – many colours and hues but mostly falling within a band of brown that ranged from dark chocolate to milky tea – and these people were gathered around fires that burned inside upright oil drums and speaking in a cacaophony that was the languages of the world, what one might hear if one were a communications satellite, or a spymaster tapping into a fibre-optic cable under the sea.
>
> In this group, everyone was foreign, and so, in a sense, no one was (Hamid 2017:100).

As they settle into their surroundings, Saeed and Nadia slowly begin to adjust to the circumstances, 'set[ting] up their temporary home there' (ibid.:102) and occasionally exploring 'the island as if they were tourists' (ibid.:108). As they grow accustomed to their living circumstances, Saeed and Nadia form an insight about how the world might be changing in front of their eyes: 'Sometimes they saw rough-looking groups of men and Saeed and Nadia were careful to keep their distance, and by evening they were always sure to sleep at the periphery of one of the big migrant camps, of which there were many, and to which anyone might belong, joining or leaving as they saw fit' (ibid.:108–9). This short passage foreshadows how their life proceeds while the passageways and doors continue to open and proliferate around the globe. Eventually, absent any real, material restrictions on movement and mobility, everyone would become a migrant, and every place would be one 'to which anyone might belong, joining or leaving as they saw fit' (ibid:109). This insight about an open-border world clarifies one reason why, in the text, the narrator deliberately avoids naming the home city of Nadia and Saeed (as I mentioned in the previous section). After all, with their capacity to continuously move, their identities and sense of place are actively invented and produced, thereby deterritorialising a settled notion of home, nation, and selfhood. Because of this, the vision of 'home' as such comes with them as they enter into new spaces, territories, and surroundings; they install a 'temporary home' (ibid:102) and make their surroundings a place of comfort, rather than it being a default uncontested place from which they originate.

Saeed and Nadia only spend a short time in Mykonos before arriving in London. Passing through another portal/door, they end up in a bedroom within a larger communal living space. Here, too, a sense of home begins to crystallise, perhaps more intensely for Saeed:

> To have a room to themselves – four walls, a window, a door with a lock – seemed incredible good fortune, and Nadia was tempted to unpack, but she knew thety needed to be ready to leave at any moment, and so she took out of their backpack only items that were absolutely required. For his part Saeed removed the photo of his parents that he kept hidden in his clothing and placed it on a bookshelf, where it stood, creased, gazing upon them and transforming this narrow bedroom, at least partially, temporarily, into a home. (Hamid 2017: 120).

A stark contrast from the refugee camp in Mykonos, Saeed and Nadia slowly come to forge their own home environment that provides the comfort, security, and stability they come to look for. Leaving out pictures of his parents, Saeed even begins to consider their place with a bit more permanence; he decorates the room with pictures of his life and family, bringing his identity onto the physical space in which they are dwelling. After a few nights, other familiar elements begin to turn their new residence into a home. One morning 'they heard in the distance someone making a call to prayer, at dawn, perhaps over a commandeered karaoke machine, and Nadia was alarmed, waking from a dream and thinking for a second that she was back home in their own city, with the militants' (ibid:125). The memories of home penetrate their soundscape, creating a combination of familiarity, on the one, and fear, on the other. The sounds of home awaken Nadia, as if she is alarmed by the lingering traumas of a home captured by militants; yet, instead, the everyday quality of a call to prayer acts as a juxtaposition of two realities side-by-side. Home is thus both a place whose familiarity is sought after, reinvented and redefined; yet it is also a phantasmal presence that follows them, reminding them of violence.

The non-identity of their home city in *Exit West* is further connected with the idea that home could be anywhere. In this sense, their actual home (nameless) could be any place, and similarly home as such is not a fixed temporal or spatial location. At one point, Saeed wonders aloud to Nadia about moving to a different house on Vicarage Gate, 'known to be a house of people from his country' (ibid.: 148). He thinks he 'was really accepted by this house' (ibid.:149), and is immediately offered a space for himself and Nadia to sleep on the floor there. We learn here that, for Saeed, his affective attachment to his home city is much more pronounced than that of Nadia's. As he discusses his idea to move to the new house with her, we witness a dialogue in which, by its end, Saeed reconsiders his relation to home:

> 'Why would we want to move?' she said
> 'To be among our own kind,' Saeed answered.
> 'What makes them our kind?'
> 'They're from our country.'
> 'From the country we used to be from.'
> 'Yes.' Saeed tried not to sound annoyed.
> 'We've left that place.'
> That doesn't mean we have no connection.

They're not like me

. . .

'Here we have our own room,' she said,. . . 'Just the two of us. It's a big luxury. Why would we give that up to sleep apart?'. . .

Saeed had no answer for this. Considering it later, he thought it was indeed odd that he would want to give up their bedroom for a pair of separated spaces, with a barrier between them, as when they lived in his parents' home, . . . (ibid.:149–50)

This back-and-forth between Nadia and Saeed eventually leads Saeed, as well as readers, to the understanding that 'home' does not necessarily relate to where one is in fact from – as if by sheer virtue of having been born somewhere permanently fixes one's 'connection' as Saeed calls it. Instead, as Nadia impresses upon him, what makes a home is the ability to produce comforts that can keep them safe and together, regardless of whether they are surrounded by people who are from the country they 'used to be from' (ibid.:149). This moment makes plain a rift between Saeed and Nadia, particular with respect to their subjective conceptions of home. As some critics have pointed out (Sadaf 2020:643; Lagji 2018:226), the characters' differing degrees of connections and affects can be traced along axes of gender. From the perspective of kinopoetics, their unique subjectivities can be seen as different manifestations of desire: one future-oriented and self-liberating (Nadia); one toward relative, and perhaps nostalgic, stability of his past (Saeed).[7] Nevertheless, throughout the story, Nadia and Saeed's nomadic desires and affects produce, construct, and design their own, subjective conceptions of home, not as a pre-given place, but as a necessity for their lives to continue. Home becomes then an ever-changing assemblage (rather than an essence), invested with affects and desires, and coinciding with the actual, material conditions through which they pass. Both the world at large as well as their conception of home is, therefore, deterritorialised and one in which its discursive and material borders are open to change, passage, and reinterpretation.

Returning again to the larger geo-political context rendered in the narrative, Saeed and Nadia start to observe how the world is slow to adapt to an open-border paradigm. Nevertheless, the free movement of people appears to proceed unabated, despite any attempts from government officials to put a stop to it. Other characters, too, continue to face conflict as they are reticent to embrace this new world. As they start to adjust to their new dwellings in London, Saeed and Nadia quickly begin to observe the cultural and linguistic dynamics of their group home. At first, a 'sort of camaraderie evolved, as it might not have had they been on the street, in the open, for then they would likely have scattered, and the devil take the hindmost, but here they were penned in together, and being penned in made them into a grouping, a group' (Hamid 2017:124). Such a dynamic parallels the formation of diasporic enclaves that, as this narrative sees it, would likely still emerge even in a regime of open borders. Later, Nadia observes the experience of the communal living space:

> Nadia experienced the environment of the house as a bit like that of a university dormitory at the start of classes, with complete strangers living in close proximity, many of them on their best behaviour, trying to add warmth to conversations and strike poses of friendship, hoping these gestures would become more natural over time. Outside the house much was random and chaotic, but inside, perhaps, a degree of order could be built. (ibid.: 129)

London society at large acts as a counterweight to this sense of collective order, and the political world as a whole is less adaptive to the arrival of migrants. The very same nationalist resentments that in fact exist in English society, especially

in the lead-up to the 2016 Brexit referendum, are depicted
in the narrative. At first, the fears of nativist reactionaries
seem to come true, as 'London houses and parks and disused
lots were being peopled in this way, some said, by a million
migrants' and, at the same time, 'legal residents were in a
minority' (ibid.:126). As a result, local newspapers refer to
these high concentrations of migrants as 'black holes in the
fabric of the nation' (ibid.). Such a label reinforces an image
of a solidified national identity and essence being cracked by
the arrival of immigrants, a notion which many fear will further metastasise once borders are open to movement. These
black holes would be crime-ridden, unrecognisable spots
within an otherwise cohesive nation. Thus a campaign 'to
reclaim Britain for Britain' (ibid.:132) began to take shape:
'Saeed and Nadia heard it said that nativist extremists were
forming their own legions, with a wink and a nod from the
authorities, and the social media chatter was of a coming
night of shattering glass, but all this would probably take
time to organize, and in that time Saeed and Nadia had to
make a decision: whether to stay or to go' (ibid.:132).[8] This
reactionary tension and violence mounted during a time when
there was limited capacity to stop or manage the arrival and
movement of migrants, and these violent forces are still alive
within the cultural climate of Great Britain.

The fear that an ongoing arrival and influx of migrants
would end up fueling nationalist resentment and hostility is
a real concern to which Hamid's narrative is quite attentive.
Even within their communal living space, their sense of comfort and cohesion begins to falter. Saeed for his part starts to
feel 'less comfortable' among the Nigerian men living in their
house, as he senses that 'the other young men would size him
up from time to time' (Hamid 2017:146). Saeed finds this
'disconcerting' not because 'he had not encountered anything
similar in his own country, he had, but because here in this
house he was the only man from his country, and those sizing

him up were from another country, and there were far more
of them, and he was alone' (ibid.). Throughout the story, one
does not develop any illusions about the intercultural, transnational contact and conflict which could immediately arise
once mobile populations can converge into living spaces.
Differing traditions and values would very easily result in
miscommunications, tensions, conflicts, and offenses because
of different histories, languages, and customs. Yet, the narrative notices that, like many social and cultural systems of
meaning, these have to be reshaped according to the present
material conditions. At one point during their stay in London, the immigrant communities attempt to form a council
in handling the militant violence within their city surroundings. However, the inhabitants soon realise that 'divisions of
race or language or nation' hardly 'matter now in a world
full of doors' (ibid.:152). The narrator continues: '[T]he only
divisions that mattered now were between those who sought
the right of passage and those who would deny them passage, and in such a world the religion of the righteous must
defend those who sought passage' (ibid.). Clearly, in a regime
of open borders, constructed by doors and portals that pass
between nations, the standard political boundaries that govern global no longer bear relevance. After all, sustaining a
system of exclusion, division, and (il)legality remains impossible so long as the material forces of managing this system
are unsustainable.

Quickly the world they inhabit in the narrative forces the
residents of London and the communal house to adapt; the
language, identities, and cultural values that had taken for
granted – ideals such as citizenship and political belonging –
soon loses currency when the structure of the world is being
reshaped. Close to the end of their stay in London, before
proceeding onward to Marin County, California, the narrative expounds more broadly on the firmly shifting political
changes that these doors are creating. As such, this global

arrangement of borders, states, and nations starts to change permanently, going on a path that is seemingly without return:

> Without borders nations appeared to be becoming some-what illusory, and people were questioning what role they had to play. Many were arguing that smaller units made more sense, but others argued that smaller units could not defend themselves. Reading the news at that time one was tempted to conclude that the nation was like a person with multiple personalities, some insisting on union and some on disintegration, and that this person with multiple per-sonalities was furthermore a person whose skin appeared to be dissolving as they swam in a soup full of other people whose skins were likewise dissolving. (Hamid 2017:155–6)

In this manner, the narrator is conveying the most explicit articulation of the open-borders regime, questioning firstly what role borders had to play, and then intervening with one perspective (among many) for what an open-bordered world might look like: one in which 'smaller units' would be a more feasible means of managing global affairs. Once the problem of mobility and accessibility seems to be solved, the next part of realising such a world is thinking about the long-term impacts of free movement. However, rather than trying to advocate and argue for an open borders society, the narrative instead compels us to fit such a world within our imagination, redistributing the sensible such that borders and nation-states no longer hold centrality in the way the world operates. Even the 'dissolving' skin that marks peo-ple's difference, as they swim 'in a soup full of other people' suggests a breaking-down of physical boundaries and sepa-rations, creating an entry of relational connectedness that does not abide by the constructs of skin-colour. Differences in race and skin tone, like borders, become 'illusory', and from such a metaphor, readers can question 'what role they had to play'. In other words, the story does not necessarily provide a strong intervention into the open-closed borders debate; it rather attempts to expand our epistemological horizons in order that our intensive and affective relation to an open borders world is made with more ease. In doing so, Hamid juxtaposes this above passage, in which people 'were questioning what role [borders] had to play' (Hamid 2017:155) alongside both the doors as well as the everyday banalities of modernity.

As I stated earlier, the narrative betrays no illusions about several of the problems that may arise: managing migrant populations, cross-cultural conflicts, economic chaos, and nationalist resentment still exist in the world that *Exit West* constructs. Disarming any accusations of utopian, wishful thinking, the story instead provides the otherwise banal truth that the same assumptions and ideologies that undergird our present world are still alive in a world of magical doors; and it is these ideological systems that need to be confronted and reckoned with. Read in light of a destructive kinopoetics, *Exit West* produces two effects. On the one hand, it 're-distributes the sensible', thereby reconstructing the system of 'inclusion and exclusion' (Rancière 2004:85), in the manner Rancière argued for. In this case, the narrative invents and makes the space through which 'those who sought passage' (Hamid 2017:152) are empowered and affirmed. Much like the previous section, one could say that to suggest that 'the righteous must defend those who sought passage' (ibid.) means that there is an affirmative ethics that the nomadic, migrant figure enacts and creates through the force of their desire.[9] In doing so, the narrative then opens up the capacity for the nomadic subject to *intervene* in the distribution of the sensible, thereby realising their pedetic power. The intervention in this case produces a world in which the old divisions on the basis of race, nation, and language are no longer viable, and moves toward one in which mobility and movement is the organising, constitutive force of society. The standard hierarchies that place the nation-state at the centre and migrants at the periphery are now reordered; and in turn, that reordering is made perceptible through the narrative. By 'striking' readers with affective connections and a 'sense of embeddedness' (Massumi 2015:6) in the narrative, there emerges a heightened imaginative capacity to see and understand an open-border society. In other words, the text produces an intensity whereby moving affectively into this new, perceptible reordering of society is made thinkable. The destabilising intervention that portals and magic doors create thereby disturb and undermine the epistemic expectation of a rigidly bordered world.

On the other hand, too, the destructive kinopoetics enacts a 'stereoscopic vision' much like what Deleuze and Guattari envision with minor literatures (see Chapter 1). This feature is still crucial to a destructive kinopoetics and Magic Realism more broadly. By placing the mundaneity of reality and magic side-by-side, the narrative in turn can work to bring this possible future into one field of vision. In the case of *Exit West*, the problems of modernity and migration are important facts that help strengthen, rather than weaken, the cause for an open border world. Knowing that the everyday conflicts, struggles, challenges, and complications would still exist in a world of doors and portals makes it possible to think and imagine a different future, and one would not have to abandon or idealise human behaviour or social relations. So, the destructive kinopoetics of *Exit West* relies on the expanded, relational capacity of Magic Realism to restructure and reorder the socially-constructed, but nevertheless real, hierarchies that pervade our global society. In turn, the text's nomadic power to create affects and intensities, redistributing and rearranging the sensible and perceptible world is ensured in its capacity to be both inventive and destructive: the narrative invents magical features that intervene in the social and political hierarchies, but also destroys the ideological centrality of borders and nation-states. These doors, as stated in the third section of this chapter, are constructs of the migrants' desires and affects, making them the constitutive figures of the text's relational life world, not the other way around. It follows, then, that the resulting open bordered world is also one of their nomadic, pedetic creation.

The Mistress of Spices: *Tilo's Calling Thought*

Juxtaposing conceptions of reality into one field of vision is one generic dimension of Magic Realism. At the same time, in Magic Realist migrant texts, magical elements forge pathways that enable intensive and extensive movement. As this dynamic occurs throughout *Exit West* in the form of doors, one sees this re-emerging in Divakaruni's *The Mistress of Spices*. The protagonist, Tilo, begins her first-person narration – or internal focalisation (Genette 1988:65) – insisting on her magical traits, addressing herself to an abstract, general audience:

> I am a Mistress of Spices. I can work the others too. Mineral, metal, earth and sand and stone. . . But the spices are my love. I know their origins, and what their colours signify, and their smells. I can call each by the true-name it was given at first, when earth split like skin and offered it up to the sky. Their heat runs in blood. . . At a whisper they yield up to me their hidden properties, their magic powers. (Divakaruni 1997: 3)

Already Tilo distinguishes herself from her Oakland, California surroundings, as the 'spices of true power' are from her 'birthland, land of ardent poetry, aquamarine feathers. Sunset skies brilliant as blood' (ibid.). It is here that the complex picture of Tilo begins to crystallise. The novel is set within Tilo's Indian grocery store located in a multicultural, low-income part of Oakland. The customers arrive each day to divulge their various

daily conflicts and complications; and through her identification and sympathy with her community, Tilo meddles and
intervenes in their lives, employing the 'magic powers' of the
spices to ameliorate their troubles. At a basic level, the narrative delineates Tilo's involvement in her community as someone
arriving from India, finding a romantic partner in a Native
American, Raven, and forging bonds with a range of other
characters.[10] Yet, as Gita Rajan insists, '[t]his romantic shell,
worn and curiously static, comes startlingly alive as Tilo begins
to intercede in the lives of the cast of characters around her.
Divakaruni keeps the story simple because she will complicate
the telling of it' (2002:215). From her origin story to the constraints on her movement and her responsibility as a mistress,
Tilo's story embodies a complexity and vitality that exceeds
the bounds of a standard love story or realist narrative. In this
section, I will characterise Tilo more broadly as embodying
the nomad configuration, both conceptually and historically.
Through this perspective, I will insist on the centrality of Tilo's
destructive and productive qualities to the novel's action. In
the next section, I will broaden the scope toward the Magic
Realist narrative technique to insist (as I did with *Exit West*) on
the expanded, stereoscopic vision that this novel creates.

The circumstances that surround Tilo's birth and migration are alone worthy of consideration. She reveals that her
'birthland' of 'ardent poetry' (Divakaruni 1997:3) referenced
on the novel's first page is a village in India; and when she
was born we learn quickly of the complicated racial and gender dynamics of both her family and her surrounding village:
'They named me Nayan Tara, Star of the Eye, but parents'
faces were heavy with fallen hope at another girl-child, and
this one coloured like mud' (ibid.:7). At the time of her
birth, it was a 'dry season' and the day itself was 'when heat
parched the cracked paddy fields' (ibid.). In the days following, villagers had to put out a 'fire in the marketplace'; and
her 'mother lying fevered all the while, and the cows run dry'

(ibid.). Under these conditions, it seemed, Tilo arrives in a milieu beset by hardship and distress.[11] 'Perhaps,' she says, 'that is why the words came to me so soon. And the sight. Or was it the loneliness, the need rising angry in a dark girl left to wander the village unattended, with no one caring enough to tell her Don't' (ibid.:8). Already, Tilo had a keen sense beyond those in her village; she could penetrate mysteries and see deeper and further than her family and community:

> I knew who stole Banku the water-carrier's buffalo, and which servant girl was sleeping with her mater. I sensed where under the earth gold lay buried, and why the weaver's daughter had stopped talking since last full moon. I told the *zamindar* how to find his lost ring. I warned the village headman of the floods before they came.
>
> I, Nayan Tara, the name which also means Star-seer. (ibid.)

Tilo's clairvoyance imparts her with both fame as well as a sense of responsibility. Her need to offer solutions from the time of her birth carries throughout her life, as she later uses these powers to concoct spice-based remedies for her Oakland clients. When Tilo arrives in Oakland, she insists on playing an active role in improving the lives of her customers. Such impulses, though, demonstrate her resistance to domination and exclusion which determined her status both in her home village as well as in Oakland. The systems of exclusion in this novel are predominantly determined through her skin colour. Tilo's consciousness of her own skin colour and appearance in relation to her surroundings become a key part of her self-formation throughout the text. Yet, it is also these various interpellating regimes that create her sense of connectivity and solidarity with the Indian American diasporic community. Her awareness of beauty and the rejection she feels from her parents later come to shape her inventive and pedetic force, even as she strays from her duties as a mistress of spices. It is the basis of her race and appearance, too, that marks her

difference both from the local society, but also within the diaspora. Racial antagonism, in many ways, shapes the discursive
system that she has to confront, as her beauty and authority
are treated in relation to her outward appearance throughout
the text (especially in terms of her romantic partnership).

Based on this experience of racialisation, Tilo assumes a
sense of opposition, guiding her toward responsibility and
stewardship of her community. When a young character, Jagjit, who arrives at the grocery store with his mother, experiences racist violence from his classmates, Tilo immediately
offers him 'crushed clove and cardamom' to make his 'breath
fragrant' (Divakaruni 1997:39). She sees, without being told,
the degree of racist violence and bullying Jagji experiences:
'In the playground they try to pull it off his head, green tur-
ban the colour of a parrot's breast. They dangle the cloth
from their fingertips and laugh at his long, uncut hair. And
push him down. *Asshole*, his second English word. And his
knees bleeding from the gravel' (ibid.:38). Tilo then, through
an apparent internal dialogue with Jagjit (to which he does
not reply) she wonders about his racial trauma:

> Jagjit do they come back when you at last must close your
> eyes because what else can you do. The jeering voices, the
> spitting mouths, the hands. The hands that pull your pants
> down in the playground, and the girls looking.
> 'Chhodo mainu.'
> 'Talk English sonofabitch. Speak up nigger wetback
> asshole.' (ibid.)

Not only does Tilo feel a certain kinship with Jagjit, being as
she is also someone whose racialisation subjected her to rejection from a young age; she also develops a certain responsibility and maternal connection to his life. As Rajan writes, this
'string of abusive names' holds up 'a horrific mirror image to
the racism in popular American culture wherein non-white
peoples are lumped together as the undifferentiated, racialised

other' (Rajan 2002:229). The crucial issue, for Tilo, seems to be
Jagjit's relative invisibility to other authority figures, his mother
as well as his teacher. The crushed cloves and cardamom are
to be scattered in the wind, Tilo reflects, '[n]orth wind carrying them to [Jagjit's] teacher's unseeing' (Divakaruni 1997:39).
She also offers 'sweet pungent clove, *lavang*, spice of compas-
sion', ensuring that Jagjit's mother, 'of a sudden looking up
from the washboard' will hold Jagjit 'in her soapsud arms'
(ibid.). Finally, Tilo offers cinnamon, a 'friend-maker, cinnamon *dalchini* warm-brown as skin, to find you someone who
will take you by the hand, who will run with you and laugh
with you', but also 'destroyer of enemies': 'to give you strength,
strength which grows in your legs and arms and mostly mouth
till one day you shout *no* loud enough to make them, shocked,
stop' (ibid.:40). She offers Jagjit, thus, spices which produce in
him a power of freedom and control, a strength to overcome
aggression and racism. In doing so, he achieves recognition and
acceptance that undermines the regimes of racial exclusion.

Tilo's involvement in Jagjit's life demonstrates one instance
in a much larger pattern throughout the narrative. Tilo's role
as a mistress of spices compels her to strengthen and empower
her community; and through the various smells and sensations
arising from the spices, her customers overcome difficulties
and pains that would otherwise go unresolved. Rajan insists
upon the ways in which Tilo's community involvement signals
intra-racial solidarity and feminist alliance:

> Tilo's intervention emphasizes the activism of women of
> color as they pledge their help to each other. Divakaruni
> interlaces an emerging modernity with minority traditions
> to reshape life's conditions into a free-flowing, rippling,
> equitable, present reality . . . Divakaruni gestures toward
> feminist solidarity by moving Tilo away from the estab-
> lished epistemological apparatus that contrasts tradition
> pejoratively with modernity. (2002:228).

198]   *Poetics of the Migrant*

Tilo's power to 're-shape life's conditions' for both her-self as well as her community constitutes and confirms her nomadism. By way of spices, Tilo imparts upon the other immigrants intensive capacities and affects that create, deter-ritorialise, and produce their social system – a system that is devised and animated through their desires. In the opening pages of the novel, Tilo reflects upon the active and produc-tive nature of her community's desires as they are 'exhaled by those who entered here': 'Of all things in my store, [desires] are the most ancient. For even here in this new land Amer-ica, this city which prides itself on being no older than a heartbeat, it is the same things we want, again and again' (Divakaruni 1997:4). As with Saeed and Nadia in *Exit West*, Tilo's and her fellow immigrants' desires precede and exceed the social milieu in which they dwell. The desires and affects themselves are the forces that produce their political system, not the other way around; they define the relational power, speeds and slownesses through which they form their exis-tence. It is Tilo who deems herself to be 'architect of the immigrant dream' (ibid.:28), fashioning the smooth space through which immigrants can feel liberated. What she calls her 'calling thought' (ibid.:19) even sets in motion the various events around her, including her escape from her homeland, and the methods through which she is able to call upon the spice's powers. She sends out this calling thought in order to then destroy but also invent the world in which she and her community live. Again, we can think of this calling thought as the affective force – a flow that she imposes and imparts upon her milieu, shaping the world into her own image.

Developing her powers as a mistress, we learn that her active capacity to 'reshape life's conditions' is something that Old Mother, the one from whom Tilo and other mistresses receive training, has imparted:

The lessons we learned on the island might surprise you, you who think our Mistress-lives to be full of the exotic,

mystery and drama and danger. Those were there, yes, for
the spice-power we were learning to bend to our purposes
could have destroyed us in a moment if wrongly invoked. . .
Most of all we learned to feel without words the sorrows of
our sisters, and without words to console them. In this way
our lives were not so different from those of the girls we
had left behind in our home villages. (Divakaruni 1997:52)

Tilo's origin as a mistress of spices begins on an island
alongside other women who learn powers from Old Mother,
or First Mother. Old Mother eventually prompts them to
describe their 'foremost duty'; and a mistress answers obe-
diently, that they are to 'aid all who come to her in distress
or seeking' (ibid.:91) and that they must feel '[e]qual love
to all, particular to none' (ibid.). The mistresses' responsi-
bilities require a collective, universal love for, and solidarity
with, the communities of oppressed people who come to seek
help. As we find with Tilo, her keenness to purely serve the
struggling and oppressed members of her community comes
into conflict with her own needs for affection, romance,
and friendship. Maria-Sabina Draga Alexandru underscores
the nomadic subjectivities that Divakaruni's fiction enacts:
'Divakaruni's female protagonists work their initial experiences of dislocation into a nomadic discourse free from
boundaries. . .' (2012:82). In other words, characters like
Tilo carry with them a connectedness and sense of identification that derives from having a shared intensity and mobility.
Similarly, in a rather scathing review of the text, Amitava
Kumar rightfully detects in the character of Tilo a 'preoccupation with the lumpen' that is 'all-consuming' (1998:86).
In either case, the text represents a concern for collectivity,
positioning Tilo as the one leading the expelled and dispossessed into their salvation. As stated above, though, it is
ultimately their desires that constructed and produced her
spice shop; she only needed to act as the nomadic figure
that could properly 'bend them' to her 'purposes' (Divakaruni 1997:52). The spices do not give her customers special

powers; rather they awaken potentials that they can use to free themselves from alienation and racism.

The most visible example of 'feminist solidarity' (Rajan 2002:228) in *The Mistress of Spices* comes in Tilo's developing friendship with Geeta Banerjhee. Iwona Filipczak outlines in detail Geeta's predicament with which Tilo identifies and feels compelled to resolve:

> When Geeta, a young Indian woman raised in the United States, informs her parents that she has already found a man whom she wants to marry, they are shattered to hear that she has decided to go against their will and against the tradition of the arranged marriage. They cling to a hope that the man is at least white, in which case the marriage would not be a transgression but actually a way to move up on the social ladder. Yet, when Geeta reveals that the man is a Chicano, she crushes the family's expectations for an appropriate husband. (2016:52)

Upon learning about Geeta's grievous circumstances with her family and her romantic desires, Tilo reflects to herself, insisting on her relation to Geeta's struggle: 'Geeta, like you I too am learning how love like a rope around glass can snake around your heart and pull you bleeding, away from all you should' (Divakaruni 1997:92). Later in the text after a second visit from Geeta's grandfather who has asked Tilo to go to Geeta and have her return home, Tilo prepares for her 'first foray into America' (ibid.:125). Her goal is not, however, to fulfill Geeta's grandfather's wishes; she rather intends to nurture and support Geeta's 'forbidden love' (ibid.:128). To do so, Tilo needs to free herself from the spiritual and physical constraints placed upon her within the spice shop: 'For as you know, when I woke in this land the store was already around me, its hard, protective shell. The spices too surrounded me, a shell of smells and voices. And that other shell, my aged body, my aged body pressing its wrinkles into me. Shell within shell within shell, and inmost of all my heart beating like a bird' (ibid.:125). Breaking free from this protective shell, Tilo reflects that never before had she 'pitted' her 'strength against a spice's. Never before driven my desire against duty' (ibid.:126). As with Nadia and Saeed, here again we see the use of 'desire' as an outward-directed force to free Tilo and send her down her own, nomadic line of flight. For this transgression and act of, perhaps, revolt, Tilo imagines already what the Old Mother who trained her would say to her: 'Hasn't that always been your trouble Tilo, you who would think you know best, who choose to forget that the highest motives lead fastest to doom. And are your motives so high, or do you help Geeta because you see in her forbidden love an image of your own' (ibid.:128). Tilo, though, in a gesture of self-transformation overcomes these commands and moves through a smooth space of emancipation.[12]

As she then finally meets with Geeta, she tries to offer her words of advice to reconcile her conflict with her grandfather. After Tilo assures her of her family's concern and undying love, Geeta is truculent at first; but Tilo recognises the 'unsaid words of her wish: *The people I love most, make them love each other*' (Divakaruni 1997:138). Before she departs, Tilo hands over spices to Geeta: '[A] bottle of mango pickled in mustard oil into which I've added *methi* for healing breaks and *ada* for the deeper courage which knows when to say no, and also *amchur* for deciding right' (ibid.:137). Again, Tilo assuredly is not giving Geeta powers that she did not already have; she is instead enabling Geeta to channel her own potential and desires. Geeta asks (perhaps sarcastically) if she said 'some magic over it', to which Tilo replies: 'The magic is in your heart' (ibid.). Tilo is enacting toward Geeta what we might consider a nomadic ethics: she forges a connectedness at a molecular level that generates, produces, and expands relational

power and affectivity. Rosi Braidotti writes that this form
of ethics expands affectivity through connectivity:

> [A]n ethically empowering option [of existence] increases
> one's potentia and creates joyful energy in the process. The
> conditions that can encourage such a quest are not only
> historical; they all concern processes of self-transformation
> or self-fashioning in the direction of affirming positivity.
> Because all subjects share in this common nature, there is
> a common ground on which to negotiate the interests and
> the eventual conflicts. (2011:308)

This type of nomadic ethics entails a rejection of Kantian
appeals to a 'transcendent standard or a universal moral
rule', and it goes against the tendencies to deny 'embodiment, matter, and the flesh' (ibid). Instead, Braidotti writes,
'[t]hey stress that moral reasoning locates the constitution
of subjectivity in the interrelation to others, which is a form
of exposure, availability and vulnerability. This recognition
entails the necessity of containing the other, the suffering and
the enjoyment of others in the expression of the intensity of
our affective streams' (ibid.). In other words, a nomadic ethics is not merely an ethics of destruction and 'oppositional
consciousness' (ibid.:285). Nomadism, and particularly the
nomadism that Tilo enacts, is one of creating affectivity,
power, and joy through a connectedness and collectivity.
In her expression of nomadism, Tilo had to depart from
her spice shop and exist in closer physical proximity among
people, if she was to activate Geeta's and her own affectivity. She also had to create conditions of complete openness,
connectivity – a sense of multiple, rhizomatic bonds existing
beyond the law-like restrictions of a transcendent duty (in
her case, the duty handed down to her from Old Mother).
Although her prescribed duty is to show a love for and commitment to the community as merely a giver of spices, Tilo's
nomadic impulse leads her beyond any sense of duty toward

an affirmative ethics of empowerment and joy, that brings into a deeper relation. She no longer connects with people within the strictly mediated confines of the spices shop. She rather fully opens her own vulnerability to Geeta and openly receives the pains of Geeta beyond the strictures of her spice shop and beyond her position as a mistress of spices. What Geeta and Tilo both needed was a mutual recognition of desire that can flourish and thrive, against familial and social pressures.

The origins of Tilo's magic powers and the trajectory of her movement is worth analysing in depth, as it shows the continuous nomadism of her life – a nomadic deterritorialisation that she, in turn, injects into her community. It also shows that her configuration within the narrative aligns her with both a nomadic ethics as well as the historical figure of the nomad. After she narrates the circumstances of her birth, she reveals the curiosity she sparks beyond her immediate setting. In particular, she captures the attention of pirates: 'Meanwhile the travelling *bauls* sang my praises, goldsmiths impressed my likeness on medallions that were worn by thousands for luck, and merchant sailors carried tales of my powers across the harnessed seas to every land. That is how the pirates learned of me' (Divakaruni 1997:9). What transpires later is a horrific pirate invasion in Tilo's home village, culminating in a raid and pillage of the surrounding homes. The pirates then capture Tilo and carry her onto the deck of their ship, taking her away from her homeland. Immediately, though, Tilo's powers enable her to rise from the position of a captive to instead become 'queen of the pirates' (ibid.:19). Her journey upon this pirate ship thus set in motion her trajectory beyond her homeland, constituting a significant part of her life previous to the island: 'For a year – or was it two, or three? Time runs into itself at moments in my tale – I lived as queen, leading my pirates to fame and glory, so that bards sang their fearless exploits' (ibid.). Here her movement has a particular historic and cultural characteristic that is invested

204] *Poetics of the Migrant*

with forms of power; in this case, pirates who in their 'fear-less exploits' orchestrate and carry out raids.

Her escape and subsequent movement is executed in more raids and pillaging, demonstrating the 'pedetic social force' of the nomad. Nail reminds us that nomadism 'produces social kinetic power' against the conditions of 'territorial kinopower in the form of 'the raid" (2015:134). Nail continues, noting the necessity of carrying out raids for the nomad:

> Since the figure of the nomad is the one who has been aban-doned by centripetal force of territorialisation, its point of counterpower or pressure is precisely its attempt to break into the territory via the raid. The nomadic raid thus defines the mountain peoples who come out of nowhere, riding their mounts to take what they need from the territorial peoples of the lowlands. (ibid.)

The key point to understand here is that 'the primary motive of the raid is not violence or war but survival' (ibid.). In Tilo's case, the centripetal forces against which she must apply pressure are those of racialised, internal exclusion. On the days following her birth, as we will recall from above, the disappointment Tilo's parents feel toward her skin colour leave her immediately ostracised. Crucially, though, she is also excluded and malnourished, her 'mother lying fevered all the while, and the cows run dry', and Tilo 'screaming until they fed me milk from a white ass' (Divakaruni 1997:7). This experience of exclusion and neglect, where Tilo is left with-out sufficient resources to survive is, as she says, where 'the words' and 'the sight' (ibid.:8) – that is to say her telepathic capacities – first came to her. They developed from 'the loneliness, the need rising angry in a dark girl left to wan-der the village unattended, with no one caring enough to tell her Don't' (ibid.). For Tilo, her status as a racialised, social outcast left her to fend for herself, seeking resources, nour-ishment, comfort, and survival techniques where none were given to her. This tragic circumstance of neglect produced within her sudden abilities to see what others were unable to see, solving mysteries in her village and gaining their respect. Yet, her powers culminated in her eventual desertion; her powers beckoned the pirates to commit the raid on her village and take her abroad. She knows that it was her 'calling thought' (ibid.:19) that summoned the pirates in the first instance. Her desire to escape and survive conditioned her magical powers, not the other way around. They instilled the adoration of her village and, even, the resentment of her parents. After her powers became known to the wider society, Tilo was given 'the best portions and threw the leavings on the floor' for her brothers and sisters' (ibid.:9). Tilo's 'mother and father dared not voice their anger, for they were afraid' (ibid.:9) of Tilo's power.

The persistent antagonism with her parents and her racial difference from her society generates an even stronger compulsion to desert her village and family. Her thoughts thus open the opportunity: mobilising the pirates in their raid, and then continuing to carry out raids with the pirates. Tilo's movement is consistent with the historic nomad: she was deprived of support, nourishment, and belonging, and thus had to seek it elsewhere. Violence and war were not her initial goals; in fact, Tilo remained plagued with guilt, apologising for having inflicted the pirates upon her village 'in boredom and disappointment' (Divakaruni 1997:19). The signal she sent out, telepathically, was her own desire and affect, activating and enabling her desertion. Her desire called to the pirates and her affects set in motion her extensive movement to the island and eventual settlement in Oakland. Much like Saeed and Nadi, these pathways were invented and produced in and through Tilo's 'calling thoughts'; and these powers continue to structure her maneuverability in the social system throughout the text. As I outlined above, her powers continue to shape her milieu and assemblage such that the capacity for desertion and survival is also imparted upon her community. By coming to her spice shop, Tilo's customers receive the resources, power, and affects that they need to survive, but of which they were previously deprived.[13] Tilo knows the struggles of deprivation from her early childhood and brings with her these powers, such that she makes sure her fellow immigrants are able to share in her power of nomadic desertion. They can, in turn, desert their racism, ennui, familial oppressions, and alienation, thanks to resources Tilo provides.

Tilo is thus a figure in whom both the conceptual and historic figure of the nomad coalesce. On the one hand, she enacts a nomadic ethics and power through her magical abilities. By being able to externalise her thoughts and call upon spirits, she shapes her community and social milieu according to her own desires. She provides a liberating affect that is responsive and open to the various vulnerabilities, pains, and yearnings of her fellow immigrants. In turn, she can also magically destroy the physical and psychic separations and boundaries between her and other people. She imparts a capacity to break down the laws of time and space to ensure that her diasporic community is cared for. Tilo expands and redefines Old Mother's injunction to give '[e]qual love to all, particular to none' (Divakaruni 1997:91) and act as the 'architect of the immigrant dream' (ibid.:28). That is, she expands this ethics to a wider horizon of consideration, using it toward a deeper and broader social commitment unrestricted by duty and the physical walls of the spice shop. On the other hand, she also coincides with the counter-historic figure of the nomad, demonstrating the pedetic force of the raid. She does not wish for violence, war, or destruction; but in her need to survive and achieve support, she first commits raids along with the pirates, and then raids (in a figurative sense) the inner and personal lives of her customers. In this sense, she carries out the 'pedetic social force' (Nail 2015:134) of the nomad.

Tilo's nomadism – in both the conceptual sense and the historic sense – share a resonance that rests upon solidarity. As I noted above, Tilo ingratiates herself in her community in such a way that produces 'feminist solidarity' (Rajan 2002:228). She carries out the nomadic ethics that activates her subjectivity in 'the interrelation to others' (Braidotti 2011:308). In her case, she produces and engages an intensive relation to her community by spiritually and telepathically communicating with their desires and calling upon a spirit realm. Such a relation helps her move, affectively, into their lives and, in turn, activate their relational possibilities and potentials. Historically and politically speaking, though, solidarity is something that nomads often relied upon for survival. 'Soldarity,' writes Nail, 'is, as its root *sol-* indicates, a fluid and undivided, pedetic phenomenon. The social bond of solidarity unites the undivided wave of nomads in a collective and continuous motion without dividing them into territories' (2015:133). Moreover, Nail continues, '[n]omadic groups and their allies share a common social bond or wave in their mutual aterritoriality or transterritorial solidarity' (2015:226). Tilo demonstrates this trait as well: she joins in the pirates 'exploits', joins with other mistresses, and later connects and bonds with her immigrant community, overcoming psychic divisions and boundaries erected through social obligation. In all cases, she supplies or trades resources with them that enable their survival. Without the protection from their homelands, families, or immediate surroundings, these characters call upon Tilo to aid them in their struggle for belonging and recognition.

Solidarity, thus, produces the nexus in which conceptual and historical nomadism come together; and Tilo is the fullest expression of it. In a kinopoetic reading, she destroys divisions both psychically and physically, and offers aid in both an affective and intensive sense, but also in a very real sense of providing resources and guidance. Having outlined

Tilo's nomadism here, in her capacity to administer affects but also in her desertion of her homeland, I will now turn to analysing the narrative form and structure of *The Mistress of Spices*. Much like with *Exit West*, I will insist upon the text's destructive nature which opens up epistemic possibilities. It interacts at the level of content, with Tilo acting as the nomadic figure; yet, through its Magic Realism, *The Mistress of Spices* demonstrates a destructive kinopoetics.

The Mistress of Spices: *Depicting Nomadic Modernity*

In an interview with *MetroActive*, Divakaruni gives an account of her personal experience undergoing a risky, life-threatening pregnancy. Based on this experience, Divakaruni suggests, she was led to consider the necessity to balance between two types of reality:

> First, I believe a writer should push boundaries, and I wanted to try something new, take risks . . . But more to the point, the risk-taking came out of a near-death experience I had two and a half years ago with the birth of my second child, Abhay, who was born of a Caesarean operation that went wrong. My incisions became infected and I had to have another surgery. I was in the hospital for a month and only half-conscious most of the time. I had the sense that I was hovering between life and death. It was a strange sensation – not frightening but dreamlike, and I felt at that point that we could move back and forth between these two states, and that this is something we don't comprehend when we're living our daily lives; that, really, we are always moving between life and death and new life. I think that experience gave birth to the main character of the book, Tilo, the mistress of spices, who moves back and forth between one existence and another. (Marcus 1997)

Such a traumatic experience, it seems, made it necessary to conjure up Tilo's magical life, negotiating between two forms of reality. The sense of 'hovering between life and death' – an experience that is 'frightening but dreamlike' – helps Divakaruni come to terms with 'always existing between life and death and new life'. In the case of *The Mistress of Spices*, the birth, death, and rebirth of Tilo has her travelling spatially from her home village, to The Island, and then to Oakland. Yet, it also has her inhabiting different lifeworlds, where she is forced to enter into a mystical relation with Old Mother on the island, but then pushed into a fire that eventually ages her dramatically. As a text of Magic Realism, the narrative plays with and makes visible the tension between two existences, thereby activating the nonterritoriality of Tilo's migrancy. The text's focus upon her through first-person narration – internal focalisation (Genette 1988:65) – makes her character the agent through which we as readers access these contradictions in her life and in society more generally. Her reach that extends telepathically and across spiritual realms also empowers the solidarity established in the previous section. Tilo reflects on her conflicting feelings toward her lived reality: 'Sometimes I wonder if there is such a thing as reality, an objective and untouched nature of being. Or if all that we encounter has already been changed by what we imagined it to be. If we have dreamed it into being' (Divakaruni 1997:16). This rumination on Tilo's part parallels Divakaruni's own complicated relationship to reality that is constitutive of a life of trauma; yet it is also one in which reality itself is nomadic and destructive.

Rajan analyses the broader structure of the novel in relation to theories of modernity, flux, and diasporic subjectivities:

> Divakaruni's agenda spotlights a fluid space in modern culture wherein Tilo imagines and makes real her potential to become an agent of change for herself and for the rest of the characters worlding the narrative. In fact, the marginalised cast of characters in the novel, be they indigenous, exilic, hybrid, immigrant, diasporic, ethnic, or border subjects are

pulled and pushed into engaging in a facet of communitarian ethics that remains a little ambivalent at the end of the novel. Thus, the mystical component is constantly under pressure to perform viably in the real world. If Tilo decides to take responsibility, as the premier subject, to seek ethical and accountable alternatives to serve the interests of a greater, common good and create an equitable society, she has to 'flow' to that anticipated end of mysticism by adapting to real situations as the agent of change. (2002:224)

Highlighting the flipside of the nomadic metaphysics, Rajan's argument brings *The Mistress of Spices* into a broader discourse on modernity. This intervention opens up and makes visible a commentary on advanced capitalism's coercive patterns of mobility and displacement resulting from accelerated, globalised accumulation. The novel delineates the interaction between the local and the global when, as Rajan points out, First Mother 'shows Tilo the world by literally conjuring up scenes and peoples from all over the world'; yet, in the way these scenes are presented, one rather sees an 'itinerary of the random migration of decolonised peoples in a fluid modernity' (ibid.:231):

> 'Toronto', said the Old One. 'Calcutta Rawalpindi Kuala Lumpur Dar es Salaam'. . .
>
> Garment factories smelling of starch and sweat and immigration raids, women hand-cuffed and piled crying into vans. Children coughing and struggling blind out of sleep into lung-burning gas. *Bloody bugger Hindoostani. Fucking Dothead. Paki go home* . . .'London Dhaka Hasnapur Bhopal Bombay Lagos' . . . (Divakaruni 1997:52).

Immediately one sees here that movement and mobility coincide with the realities of exploitative labour, criminalisation, racism and illness that constitute the life of the immigrant under modernity. The ever-expanding network of global flows and junctions comes alive in listing the various places to which mistresses are sent, dramatising the multi-directional movement and coercive displacement character-istic of the present era.

In the context of transnational free trade agreements, whereby corporate power deterritorialises state and national sovereignty, the resulting impact is further displacement and dispossession, leading to massive flows of migrants through-out the globe. Coupling this process with climate change and military intervention, and we come to recognise the nomad-ism that characterises the twenty-first century. This present era culminates in what Jodi Dean (following Perry Anderson and Ellen Meiksins Wood) calls 'parcelised sovereignty':

> Under neofeudalism, the directly political character of soci-ety reasserts itself. Global financial institutions and digital technology platforms use debt to redistribute wealth from the world's poorest to the richest. Nation-states promote and protect specific private corporations. Political power is exercised with and as economic power, not only taxes but fines, liens, asset seizures, licenses, patents, jurisdictions, and borders. At the same time, economic power shields those who wield it from the reach of state law. (Dean 2020)

Dean's claim here updates and confirms the modality of nomadism that is available to the state and imperial order. These systems of power are able to shift the political sta-tus of sovereignty and exceed its boundaries and borders. Nomadism, here, is not a potential that exclusively acti-vates the stateless, nonterritorial, and revolutionary subject; nomadism is also a constellation of deterritorialising forces that state and imperial power employ to their own ends. Hardt and Negri write that '[c]apital operates on the plane of immanence, through relays and networks of relationships of domination, without reliance on a transcendent centre of power. It tends historically to destroy traditional social boundaries, expanding across territories and enveloping always new populations within its processes' (2000:326). Thus, they add,

> in the passage of sovereignty toward the plane of imma-
> nence, the collapse of boundaries has taken place both
> within each national context and on a global scale . . . The
> global society of control that smooths over the striae of
> national boundaries goes hand in hand with the realisation
> of the world market and the real subsumption of global
> society under capital (ibid.:332).

Through the state's authorisation of financial deterritorialisation (in other words: where 'political power is exercised with
and as economic power' [Dean 2020]), capital need not abide
by the constraints of sovereignty. Instead it relegates and
eclipses striations beneath its all-consuming power. As a result,
imperial organs of power – particularly state-backed corporate
entities – have their own nomadic capacity to consume public
space, exceed boundaries, and produce conditions for profit
on its own terms, against any bulwarks of sovereignty and
protection. This is the as-yet-unacknowledged dark side of
nomadism: that it is not, by itself, intrinsically liberating and
revolutionary; it can also empower the reach and strength of
coercive state forces, surveillance, and institutions of financial
extraction (such as the IMF) from which the migrant subject
is alienated, but in whose web of power they are nevertheless
caught. In this case, it is a social machine of domination and
displacement, a social drive toward expanding kinopower.

Returning to *The Mistress of Spices*, Rajan rightfully sees
Tito as a character emblematic of the contradictions inherent
in modernity. Rajan writes:

> [T]he increasing number of disenfranchised people all over the
> world is a fact. Divakaruni . . . illustrates this gap by showing
> that while Tilo and her spices are potent presences, the cast of

characters is really disenfranchised – ranging from immigrant Indians (Hindus, Muslims, Sikhs) and Bangladeshis to the disempowered, hyphenated American citizens. The inclusion of Kwesi, the African-American, Juan, the Mexican-American, Raven, the Native-American, makes the novel a theater of global culture. Thus as Tilo senses the pain of those around her at a local level, and unleashes the mystical power of her spices for the greater common good, she works for the global citizen. (2002:222)

Tilo, as a result, hears men's thoughts in the shop that 'give off the smell of parched earth in a year of failed monsoons' (Divakaruni 1997:62). The men's reflections thus enter Tilo's mind:

> No one told us it would be so hard here in Amreekah, all day scrubbing greasy floors, lying under engines that drip black oil, driving the belching monster trucks that coat our lungs with tar … Yes, always smile, even when people say 'Bastard foreigner taking over the country stealing our jobs'. Even when cops pull us over because we're in the wrong part the rich part of town. (ibid.).

These intrusive thoughts co-mingle with Tilo's mystical powers in a way that informs her of the general plight of immigrants around her – the poverty, disenfranchisement, exploitation, and racial hostility; while, at the same time, she takes it as her responsibility to mitigate their struggles and alienation. With Haroun, for example, whom we meet in the second chapter, Tilo gains his trust early when he asks for a palm reading. Yet, throughout the text, Tilo is burdened with the knowledge of Haroun's difficulties, making him the most visible example of migrant precarity and desperation. He quits his job driving 'a Rolls for Mrs Kapadia' (ibid.:25) and instead purchases his own taxi. From here, however, thanks to Tilo's premonition we are immediately alerted to the violence that awaits him, as he is tragically assaulted early on in the novel. In the course of his recovery, Tilo feels a responsibility to him (perhaps out of guilt), and is exposed to the hardships of his existence. Attempting to locate him, she first calls upon his friend who can lead her to him. Inquiring into his whereabouts, she immediately realises the gulf between herself and those in Haroun's situation. After saying that she's looking for Haroun, she comes to recognise how such a question would seem to most immigrants: 'As soon as I say the sentences I know their wrongness. I feel her suspicion course like electricity through the wires. Her fear. *Immigration? Creditors? Old-country enemies following his ocean trail?*' (ibid.:184). It is at this moment where several constellations of migrancy come into view. First, her separation from her community as still a mere stranger in their presence makes her someone untrustworthy. Second, the context that led her to seeking Haroun's location was an outcome of both his unstable labour conditions, combined with horrifically racist violence. And, finally, she sees here an aspect of migrant existence that often goes unacknowledged: that immigrants live in a state of constant fear from deportation officials and manipulative creditors. All of these facets of migrant life result, again, from the parcelisation of sovereignty, whereby organs of state and financial power wield disproportionate control over immigrants' lives, and wherein they are subject to hostility, racism, and alienation. Such moments increase fragmentation and separation, splintering communities into antagonistic and mutually-suspicious groups.

The pains and hardships immigrants endure, though, arise in and through the nomadic conditions of (post)modernity. Because trade agreements enable the flow of capital across borders, while circumventing tax, wage, and welfare protections, immigrants (particularly in the United States) are perpetually forced into precarious, unstable labour conditions. They become the 'light infantry of capital' (Marx

[1867] 1990:818) upon which neoliberal capitalism relies (Walia 2021:91; Mezzadra and Neilson 2013:52–53). Through Tilo's telepathic and mystical capacity, the narrative thus makes visible these economic struggles that are around her at all times. In other words, it is because she can receive their intrusive thoughts that the consequences of parcelised sovereignty and migrant disenfranchisement are made visible. 'Tilo's purpose in the narrative', writes Rajan, 'is to ease the pain of those around her with a potpourri of hope and, indeed, to attempt to alter external reality through her own subjective mechanisms of belief' (2002:219). Tilo's power not only offers her community reprieve from the otherwise hostile economic and political environment; she also exposes the underlying conditions of modernity. Immigrant alienation, precarity, and disenfranchisement are illuminated only through Tilo's telepathy and mystical powers. As a result, the added magical aspects of the narrative make visible and knowable the nomadism of modernity; through affective and intensive intervention, the novel renders accessible the crushing consequences of globalised, neoliberal capitalism.

Through *The Mistress of Spices*, we plainly see the human costs of a nomadic state and imperial power, forcing migrants into ever more difficult precarity, insecurity, and displacement. Luckily, however, as outlined in the previous section, Tilo is able to reconcile and activate a revolutionary nomadism on her own terms, allying with her diasporic community and empowering them toward a sense of belonging and stability. In *The Mistress of Spices*, thus, two forms of nomadism coexist: the nomadic state power (that is, centripetal force) and the nomadic pedetic force (like raids and solidarity). In both cases, the Magic Realism of the novel leads from Tilo's mystical power to shape migrant existence – first by making it thinkable and knowable through a destructive kinopoetics, and second by activating pedetic counterpower. The epistemic possibility, here, is to recognise two side-by-side forces which coalesce and converge throughout the present era: deterritorialising capitalism and deterritorialising affects. As a result, we see the two types of nomadism that come into conflict, making clearer how it exists as a double-edged sword. In many ways, the novel illustrates how these two can coexist within the era of neoliberal capitalism; yet it also leaves us with the hope for solidarity as an ultimately liberating and necessary force to overcome the hardships modernity inflicts upon immigrants. After all, it is Tilo's recognition of, and exposure to, the nomadism of life that makes possible her capacity for supporting and aiding her community.

Chapter Conclusion

Magic Realist texts produce what we might (following Fredric Jameson) call 'registers' (Jameson 1983:90) of nomadic power; they produce at the level of form a perceptible shift toward a wider epistemic horizon – one in which two realities converge. As a result, texts challenge the liberal humanist notions of rationality, objectivity, and progress that constitute the thematic preoccupations of Enlightenment discourse. Broadly speaking, Magic Realist texts enact a process of overcoming the constraints of modernity by imagining a reality that coincides with and, in some senses, modifies the present. They also, though, make visible political circumstances and possibilities which may be beyond our immediate grasp. In *Exit West* and *The Mistress of Spices*, we have two sides of nomadic existence made visible and thinkable. In the former case, through the magical portals carrying Saeed and Nadia to other countries, the text illuminates the possibilities of an open-bordered regime. In particular, *Exit West* demonstrates a world in a future that can be conceptualised and understood based on its similarities with the present; the only addition beyond belief being the magical doors. With these doors, the text sheds light on the open-borders ideal within migration justice movements and makes it a regime that is both plausible and attractive. The open borders world imagined in *Exit West* deterritorialises the regimes of sovereignty, statehood, and protectionism, enabling the free passage of migrants; and such a world (as I outline above) is produced by the migrant's desires. The migrants in the novel, in other words, animate and actively shape, produce, and invent the open borders regime on their own terms – intensively pushing the borders of modernity and forcing the world to comply with their movement. In *The Mistress of Spices*, by contrast, we recognise a powerful reflection on the nomadic force that is not necessarily liberating, but instead maps the unending expansion of imperial domination and control. The text highlights the human impact of neoliberal capitalism and the attending poverty, desperation, agony, and instability it creates on a global scale. Yet, through Tilo's magical powers, these effects of modernity are brought into view in such a way that allows her to enact a counter-force against its most dramatic consequences. In doing so, she shows us the beauty and power found in collective struggle and solidarity – a power that constitutes the nomad's pedetic counterpower. In this text, therefore, we have two types of nomadism that coincide and confront one another: the nomadism of capitalism, on the one hand, and the oppositional, nomadic subject of resistance, on the other. The novel thus clarifies that nomadism is a double-edged sword, both liberating but also damaging. Through this lens, we realise and expand our capacities to see and understand forms of deterritorialisation both at the level of state, imperial power and at the level of collective struggle. It is in this latter assemblage where we find a hopeful capacity for the characters' salvation and liberation.

Carrying out a destructive kinopoetics, these texts thus utilise a narrative genre (Magic Realism) that offers a corrective to the scope of social and political imagination. They both open up and redistribute the regime of what is think-able and knowable, making it possible to imagine worlds that are often obscured within the dominant discourse. Such aspects are revealed to us, or offered, through the internal thoughts of the migrant figures; thanks in part to the formal perspective of internal focalisation (Genette 1988:65), the narrative point of view makes the various systems of mobility and converging regimes of power possible. Coinciding with and constructed through the figure of the nomad, these novels and the lifeworlds disrupt and destroy the common-sense categories of political sovereignty, history, migration, settlement, and alienation, and assert instead a world of flows, movements, connections, and collectivity. Such a world appraises the nomadic desire for autonomy and solidarity, and considers a political system beyond psychic, political, and social borders. Such a political system seems best ren-dered and made legible through the narrative techniques of Magic Realism and a destructive kinopoetics, overcoming the constraints of time, history, space and movement.

Notes

1. I have chosen to use this term 'Magic Realism' as opposed to Faris's use of 'Magical Realism' for no real reason other than finding it the more common construction within critical literature. Reading through Zamora and Paris's edited collec-tion, *Magical Realism: Theory, History, and Community*, one finds both renderings used interchangeably and, seemingly, arbitrarily, with the former one being the most frequent.

2. See Chapter 2, section headed Poetics of Migration: A Typology, for a previous discussion of this concept. This aspect of 'minor literature' is worth holding onto for destructive kinopoetics, as I will show.

3. See Chapter 1, section headed Kinopolitics: Expansion by Expulsion.

4. The Deleuzo-Guattarian concept of 'nomadism' has produced varying responses in the decades following its publication. Probably the most famous application of this concept is through Rosi Braidotti's work on nomadic subjects and nomadic citizenship. Furthermore, Jeremy Gilbert has noted the capacity for the nomadism concept to provide a useful praxis for radical democracy and collective politics in his book *Anticapitalism and Culture*. This concept has also been subject to ridicule and criticism, most notably in James Clifford's book *Routes* in which he accuses Deleuze and Guattari of 'postmodern primitivism'. These criticisms of Deleuze and Guattari are worth taking seriously; and readers can hardly deny, especially reading the chapter on the 'Rhizome' in *A Thousand Plateaus*, an implied Orientalism, particularly in how they separate out the distinction between 'figures of the East' and 'figures of the West'. Again, though, this problem can perhaps solve itself by directing our attention toward the conceptual notions of nomadism, rather than idealising or fetishising an historic figure as a model for liberation.

5. In a co-interview with Elias Sanbar, Deleuze reflects on the nomadic forces deployed within the occupied territories of Palestine: '[T]he Palestinians are not in the situation of a colonised peoples but of evacuees, of people driven out. . . [I]t is a matter of emptying a territory of its people in order to make a leap forward even if it means making them into a workforce elsewhere. The history of Zionism and Israel, like that of America, happened that way: how to make an empty space, how to throw out a people?' (Deleuze and Sanbar 1998:26). Rather remarkably and alarmingly, brigadier-generals within the Israeli Defense Forces (IDF) have admitted to in fact deriving inspiration from Deleuze and Guattari to carry out displacing operations against Palestinians (Weizman 2006).

6. More about this in the next section headed *Exit West*: Making the Open Bordered World Thinkable.

7. Shazia Sadaf writes: '[Saeed] starts praying whereas he never did before, and he desperately seeks people who speak his language, and belong to his birth city. Nadia, on the other

hand, wants to look to the future, even as she staunchly and stubbornly wears her black robe throughout the geographical journey, a robe that disrupts all the stereotypical symbolism attached to the covering as an identity marker. Having it on and keeping it on as a sign of her agency, Nadia finds a new confidence in her identity and refuses to be labelled immutably by her choice of clothing. In other words, she keeps her robe on, but liberates her identity to new experiences. Unlike Saeed, who is still nostalgic about the physical location in which his identity is anchored, her journey is not through' representations on maps, but through a process of invention and creativity. (2020:643).

8. The clear reference to 'Kristallnacht' in the phrase a 'night of shattering glass' (Hamid 2017:132) seems an overt (and perhaps heavy-handed) way of Hamid signalling the continuities between anti-immigrant paranoia, reactionary violence, the historical manifestations of fascism.

9. The use of the term 'righteous' here seems to ironically subvert the connotation of religious and, specifically, patriotic duty. Here instead of the typical rendering of a crusading patriot defending the homeland, the righteous feels an obligation to justice and migrant liberation.

10. The fact that Tilo forms a romantic relationship with a Native American is by no means incidental, considering he is part of a group previously interpellated as 'Indian'. Several times throughout the text, Tilo's identification with Raven shifts, increasing and decreasing in intensity. By and large, we learn that she knows far more about his existence than he does about hers, and not merely by virtue of her magical powers, but a general exoticisation upheld toward people from India.

11. See also: Filipczak 2016, 50–51.

12. Tilo's disobedience is not always positive, however. As punishment for getting to actively involved in Jagjit's life, for example, her efforts back-fire; Jagjit later on turns into an overpowering bully and delinquent.

13. One can compare Tilo's community aid to the migrant aid groups that Nail analyses, such as the Border Angels,

Humane Borders, and the Electronic Disturbance Theater (EDT): 'These groups are composed of volunteers dedicated to helping migrants survive the seasonal hazards of crossing the Mexico-US border by providing them with food, water, maps of water stations, cell-phone coverage, emergency telephone numbers, clothing, supplies, free legal advice, directions – key items for survival' (2015:225). These groups express, according to Nail, the 'kinetic counterpower of the raid' (ibid.).

CHAPTER 4

WANDERING KINOPOETICS

The Migrant and the City

Literary representations of city and urban life recur throughout modernity. Going back to the Victorian era, especially
following the Industrial Revolution, depicting crowded cities, multiculturalism, violence, and contrasting wealth and
economic circumstances became a common narrative feature
(Warwick 2008:37; Lehan 1998:4; Berman 1982:132). As a
narrative setting, urban cities offer novelists useful devices to
present a range of social conditions and conflicts converging
in one place. Cities, after all, offer fast-paced, circuitous communication and travel networks through which people have
to navigate professional and social encounters, but within
which class contrasts and wealth disparities become readily
apparent. Especially in large metropolitan cities, one will find
'divisive architectures of power' (McLeod 2004:11) that regulate the relational and spatial capacities of their inhabitants.
How one is able to use public transportation, avoid police
harassment and profiling, or disarm suspicion from passersby are all everyday situations shaped through differences in
gender, race, power, and wealth. Moreover, capital-intensive
places are increasingly competitive for employment and living,
further intensifying alienation and fragmentation. Friedrich

Engels, writing about the density of habitation of London in 1847, detected early on the harm that city life presents for the working class: 'The centralisation of population in great cities exercises of itself an unfavourable influence; the atmosphere of London can never be so pure, so rich in oxygen, as the air of the country; . . . and the consequence is mental and physical lassitude and low vitality' (Engels 1845). This 'centralisation', however, is a necessary feature of modernity, ensuring 'physical security and social continuity' (Mumford 1956). Lewis Mumford, in his 1956 essay, 'Natural History of Urbanisation' writes that the urban city has always functioned as 'a secure base of operations, a seat of law and government, a repository of deeds and contracts, and a marshaling yard for manpower'. Urban cities in their modern form grew out of factory and manufacturing centres where there was a higher demand of labour, a concentration of finance, and faster commodity transport and exchange. For the average person, cities are therefore crowded spaces of both concentrated wealth and influence, on the one hand, and pollution, desperation, insecurity, and illness, on the other. Richard Lehan writes that 'the city becomes more complex as a physical structure' (1998:8):

> [T]he ways of seeing it become more difficult and the individual more passive in relationship to it. The city came into being when a surplus of food allowed a diversity of tasks. Diversity is a key to urban beginnings and continuities, and diversity is also the snake in the urban garden, challenging systems of order and encouraging disorder and chaos. And as the city reached out into the hinterland and eventually beyond itself in the name of empire, more was demanded of the urban center. The industrial city brought with it urban pollution and slums: smokestacks became a way of life. The urban crowd, unstable and volatile, made city life increasingly unpredictable (ibid.)

In the literary representation of cities, one finds that this 'unstable', 'volatile', and 'unpredictable' (ibid.:8) dynamic creates differing subjectivities and connections to power, all of which are intensified with class, gender, and race. Using these settings of centralisation and modernity, texts enliven the structures of difference and resistance that occur within urban spaces. In the postcolonial migrant tradition in particular, one finds that, as John McLeod notes, 'these texts primarily give expression to the improvisational, creative and resistant tactics of those who make possible new subaltern spaces in the city' (2004:9–10). Carrying on in the same way that McLeod does in *Postcolonial London*, this present chapter also 'emphasizes the agency of the imagination in mediating and shaping urban reality', while being careful not to collapse 'material forces into the two-dimensional weightlessness of Post-modernist representation where issues of power and authority conveniently evaporate' (ibid.:10). To retain the emphasis on 'material forces' as well as the 'agency of the imagination' (ibid.), it helps to remember that affect and intensity shape and determine subjectivity and relational power. As this chapter will show, another migrant subject, the vagabond, instantiates a wandering form of movement and pedetic force to confront and challenge the pre-established coordinates of permissibility and access within the urban city. Analysing speeds and maneuverability of the migrant subject within the city – as well as her ways of recomposing space – helps make agency and material forces legible. These affective and relational forces of movement, power, and subjectivity are still integral, ontological features of this kinopoetics that I shall call a 'wandering kinopoetics.' How these power-relations interpellate and constitute the migrant subject – in this case the vagabond – will be expanded in the next section. First, I shall develop further an overview of critical and theoretical approaches to the city, and how this setting fits broadly within the migrant literary tradition.

Sustained critical treatments of city life have come to terms with the ways in which quotidian, everyday conditions are intimately bound up with political subjectivity and affect. One famous example of this arises in Michel de Certeau's *The Practice of Everyday Life*. In the chapter titled 'Walking in the City,' de Certeau argues that the city is a place where '[a]dministration is combined with a process of elimination' (1984:94). He writes:

> On the one hand, there is a differentiation and redistribution of the parts and functions of the city, as a result of inversions, displacements, accumulations, etc.; on the other there is a rejection of everything that is not capable of being dealt with in this way and so constitutes the 'waste products' of a functionalist administration (abnormality, deviance, illness, death, etc.). (ibid.:94).

According to McLeod, de Certeau's text 'crucially recognises that cities are crucibles of power, and that city dwellers are constantly in negotiation with factors which attempt to regulate and police their lives' (2004:9). De Certeau argues that 'walking' in a city functions as a 'practice' for analysing and 'writing' the city, 'without being able to read it' (1984:93). That is, the '*Wandersmänner*' (ibid.) compose a 'manifold story that has neither author nor spectator, shaped out of fragments of trajectories and alterations of spaces' (ibid.). Their immersion within the city spaces is localised and partially subdued from the limited observations of the walker, whereby modern 'society' and its contradictions only are 'expressed in mutilated, fragmented, singular ways' (Lefebvre 2014:94). Yet, on the other hand, the walking subject is actively capable of shaping their apprehension of the city, reimagining its boundaries and textures through their own mental geography. As such, walking exist as a 'space of enunciation' (de Certeau 1984:94). This means that the walker not only retains the capacity to write the city and make it legible; the walker can also transform the city, reconstructing its fixed order and spatial arrangement:

> [I]f it is true that a spatial order organises an ensemble of possibilities (e.g. by a place in which one can move) and interdictions (e.g. by a wall that prevents them from going even further), then the walker actualises some of these possibilities. In that way, he makes them exist as well as emerge. But he also moves them about and invents others, since the crossing, drifting away, or improvisation of walking privilege, transform or abandon spatial elements. . . [T]he walker transforms each spatial signifier into something else. And if on the one hand he actualises only a few of the possibilities fixed by the constructed order. . ., on the other he increases the number of possibilities . . . and prohibitions (ibid.: 98)

To return this to the 'affect-sensation continuum' outlined in Chapter One, the walker in the city maintains an active power to change the affective, relational assemblage of the city – to transform 'relations of speeds and slownesses' (Deleuze 1988:125) that constitute political subjectivity. This intervention then redistributes the sensible, making new social arrangements legible and thinkable.

The 'ensemble of possibilities and interdictions' (de Certeau 1984:98) that de Certeau writes about thus makes the city a powerful setting for literary representation. '[T]he city and its literature,' writes Lehan, 'share textuality' (1998:8). In other words, 'the ways of reading literary texts are analogous to the ways urban historians read the city . . . buil[ding] on assumptions about the mechanistic, the organic, the historical, the indeterminate, and the discontinuous' (ibid.). In literary fiction what we find are shifts in mobility, relationships, national identity, and stability. Many writers, especially those in the Modernist tradition, who looked toward the urban 'imperial, totalitarian city' (ibid.:107), provide a literary perspective on urban life compatible with 'what Marx and Engels had taken up in economic terms' (ibid.):

> [T]he land question; the displacement of a peasant class; the entrapment of a commercial class in a new kind of city controlled by money and commodity relationships; the breakdown of the family as the young leave the land; the effect of this transformation on women; the rise of the criminal as an urban type; the rise of urban institutions like the boardinghouse, which in the city substitutes for the nuclear family; the effect on human consciousness of the expanding city; the city as maze, seemingly beyond human scale. (ibid.).

The persistence of the city and urban setting in literature supplies a verisimilitude for the age of industrial capitalism, thereby accurately reflecting the everyday life of any reader living through (post)modernity.[1] Furthermore, in terms of providing the textures and signifiers of political power, the city and urban setting consolidates social and cultural encounters into one locale, ensuring that any given day in the life of its inhabitants can easily demonstrate material conditions of alienation, immobility, and exclusion. Such a condition produces what Iris Marion Young calls a 'being together of strangers', whereby 'persons and groups interact within spaces and institutions they experience themselves belonging to, but without those institutions dissolving into unity or commonness' (1990:237). Such a setting resembles, furthermore, what Jacques Derrida describes as a 'copresence of citizens' (1997:137). In other words, such a setting presents a coinciding and incidentally collective relationship that is attentive to and aware of differences.

'The city development of the last forty years', writes Marshall Berman, in 1982, 'in capitalist and socialist countries alike, has systematically attacked, and often successfully obliterated, the "moving chaos" of nineteenth-century urban

life' (168). Berman continues: '[T]he new urban environment
. . . is sorted out and split up into separate compartments,
with entrances and exits strictly monitored and controlled'
(ibid.). With these structures of control and surveillance, city-
dwellers (tourists, residents, police, etc.) are sifted, managed,
and brought into systematically-enforced relations with one
another. Commuters without access to automobiles are cor-
ralled into public transportation, while pedestrians follow
rules of order and motion to protect the flow of traffic, avoid
collision, and maintain distance from private property. So
while these partitions and controls are recent manifestations,
they also have the effect of further concentrating people into
tightly-regulated spaces and temporalities (following strict
bus schedules, for example). Berman's suggestion here anticipates the 'divisive architectures of power' (McLeod 2004:11)
mentioned earlier: these are various divisions, borders, checkpoints, and restrictions that proliferated throughout modernity and which characterise large metropolitan spaces. As a
setting for depicting migrancy, it provides a perfect milieu
and assemblage. The city, after all, furnishes literary texts
with all of the available vicissitudes of twentieth and twenty-
first century cultural life. How these structures reinforce and
intensify a criminalised underclass will be the topic of the
next section.

Migrancy plays into the writing and transformation of
the city, as the migrant's movement draws out the varying
degrees of power, displacement, discrimination, and permissibility that the city creates. The migrant subject is broadly
prohibited from access to the job market, housing, juridical
representation, and civic participation; they are also limited
in their linguistic capacities and familiarity to local cultural
customs, and are subject to suspicion and discrimination
from employers, landlords, police, and other residents. The
convergence and overlap of these forces of power and systems of exclusion preclude the migrant from the comforts

and safety enjoyed by citizens – many of whom just as well experience alienation and dispossession through the contradictions of modernity (such as gentrification, austerity and violence). Nevertheless, as Rushdie writes, '[a] gulf in reality is created' between the citizen and the immigrant: 'White and black perceptions of everyday life have moved so far apart as to be incompatible. And the rift isn't narrowing; it's getting wider' (1992:134). Patterns of discrimination, hostility, and alienation are a daily occurrence among non-white immigrants, and the persistence of these elements create an ongoing system of disempowerment and dispossession.

Yet, at the same time, the migrant navigates everyday life with their own language, history, and perception, and they thus bring these internal qualities to bear on their awareness of their material position. On the one hand, migrant subjectivities are bound up in affective and relational power, according to which someone apprehends not only reality, but their sense of autonomy within the political and economic system. In a city space, in which one often has no choice but to encounter hostility, and in which one's difference is often a source of surveillance, paranoia, and embarrassment, these dynamics are especially pronounced. The partitions and intensified controls keep space and time regulated. In other words, as the city's networks force people into physical proximity, more interactions and encounters take place within tighter spaces and shorter blocks of time. The constant awareness of difference from their fellow residents helps solidify and naturalise one's distance and alienation from sovereignty. On the other hand, actively reading everyday life through the lens of one's own migrancy produces the capacity to transform space. 'Despite the cruelty of urban life experienced by newcomers', McLeod writes, cities like 'London [are] also daringly imagined as making possible a utopian social blueprint where the prejudices and hostilities encountered on the street might be conquered' (2004:27).

Such possibilities are especially enacted through the writings of several diasporic and migrant authors, especially in post-colonial England.

Urban theorists and social anthropologists are deeply aware of the impact city life has on the material circumstances and agency of immigrants. In their book *Migrants and City-Making*, Ayşe Çağlar and Nina Glick Schiller take an approach to the city that highlights 'the migrants whose lives. . .form multiple new social relations and maintain others as they settle in specific places' (2018:9). Çağlar and Glick Schiller pay close 'attention to migrants' agency' (ibid.:13). They not only recognise migrants' place 'within . . . multiple institutional social fields of uneven power of globe-spanning, national, regional, urban, and local institutions' (ibid.:12); they are also keen to highlight the 'claim-making practices, situations, sites, institutions, and social relations in which displaced people, migrant and non-migrant, build sociabilities that can form the basis for new kinds of political action' (ibid.:13). The complex interaction of these institutional and social networks produce a sharp analysis of city-making and migrant agency that has been hitherto neglected. This chapter will supplement such a project through migrant fiction, particularly those within the tradition that depict the daily encounters that the migrant has while wandering through and navigating variegated urban city spaces. How everyday life within the bustling, crowded modern city interacts with class, race, and language will provide an important dimension to this kinopoetics. As such, this approach adopts a critical and cultural tradition of spatial theory that interprets the processes of everyday, city life (de Certeau and Henri Lefebvre). Furthermore, the literary representations of the migrant, vagabond figures will provide the foundations upon which this kinopoetics can build. The vagabond, as I will show, is another kinopolitical figure generated within regimes of criminality and rebellious pedetic force.

Making the everyday encounters visible and thinkable, this kinopoetics will consider two major works of fiction – Teju Cole's *Open City* and Monica Ali's *Brick Lane* – that will produce what I call a 'wandering kinopoetics'. Both of these texts create uniquely textured representations of city life, whereby the focalised migrant figure rewrites and reconstructs the geography of urban spaces on their own terms; and these texts fit within a broader trend of migrant texts making productive use of urban, metropolitan settings (other famous examples include Sam Selvon's *The Lonely Londoners* and Marjane Satrapi's graphic memoir, *Persepolis*). Wandering kinopoetics, in turn, makes the vagabond's challenging, maze-like wanderings within the city legible. The exclusions, encounters, settlements, and connections that constitute the migrant's life within a large city will forge a lucid commentary on the everyday world that may otherwise go unnoticed. As a result, the structures of power and systemic racial exclusion – especially those of criminality and suspicion – will constitute the major features of migrant subjectivity and relational power. Furthermore, the inventive and transformational capacity of the migrant figure to reimagine their social setting and liberate themselves from its hostile, exclusionary construction will further demonstrate their pedetic force. In *Open City*, the narrative protagonist, Julius, a Nigerian immigrant and aspiring psychiatrist living in New York City, is focalised in a way that invites us to inhabit and read the textures of the city – complete with the various noises, sensations, and connections that Julius wades through. In particular, his outsider status and alienation are not less, but more illuminating in terms of the detailed, everyday intensities of urban existence. Julius's pattern of movement throughout the city both inhabits it while also creating it; he blends into the everyday life, while at the same time reconstituting and transforming the social milieu. In *Brick Lane*, the narrative conveys the life of Nazneen, whose turbulent and challenging life as a Bangladeshi woman in London provides a meaningful portrait of fragmented belonging. In particular, she takes up residence among other immigrants of Brick Lane, balancing her identities, as well as the obligations, of her past and her present. As a result, she is subject to both discrete and overt regimes of surveillance from her community, reinforcing her criminalised subjectivity. On the other hand, though, her various interactions and movements – both small and large, extensive and intensive – help connect her to her desires, and affirm her selfhood. Such a selfhood in turn reaches beyond her atomised self, helping her access her prefigurative becomings.

Both protagonists upon whom this chapter will focus constitute a migrant configuration known as the 'vagabond' – the wandering, city-dwelling kinopolitical figure who experiences varying forces of mobility and immobility within an urban space. Before looking into both novels in detail, the next section will situate, analyse, and further clarify this figure. In particular, this section will distinguish the vagabond's political position throughout social history as one governed by forces of alienation and, specifically, criminality. As a result, I will then define what I call a 'micro-politics of suspicion' which will be the basis under which I analyse the vagabond figure.

The Vagabond, Criminality and Suspicion

Like the nomad, the vagabond is another migrant figure who retains a unique position throughout social history. Rather than emerging from the Neolithic period (see Chapter 2), the vagabond figure is largely identified with the Middle Ages. They gained political and social significance in the ensuing revolts against enclosure, improverishment, land privatisation and dispossession (Federici 2014:82). Around the sixteenth century, 'enclosure' factors as one form of land expropriation, 'indicating a set of strategies the English lords and rich farmers used to eliminate communal land property and expand their holdings' (ibid.:69). This process – arguably marking the 'beginning of capitalism' (ibid.:68) – entailed privatisation and, in turn, the dispossession of the peasantry. Now entry, access, prices, and commodities were in the exclusive control of the capitalist class. Moving from a communal and collective yielding to instead granting access to land on the basis of purchase or through the coercion of wage-labour, such a process created the basis for 'primitive accumulation' discussed in Chapter 1. Recall, too, that this historic moment coincided broadly with the rise of a bourgeois ruling class whose (often violent) process of global differentiation and dispossession ensured their control over much of the Earth's resources and labour. In both the case of colonial projects and domestic land expropriation, one finds the 'appropriation and co-optation of pre-existing social achievements as well as confrontation and supersession' (Harvey 2003:146). Because land expropriation, enclosure, and privatisation were permitted through the legal sanctions of deeds and contracts, there emerged as a result a permanent criminal class composed of those who revolted against this deprivation. As a result of these ongoing struggles, there arose a regime of criminalisation that determined idleness and disregard for property as criminal acts; and, as a consequence, this regime of criminality was produced and secured by the structural conditions of capital accumulation.

'The vagabond', writes Nail 'is both the figure that allows juridical kinopower to expand and legitimate its apparatus of enforcement and also serves as a counterpower to it' (2015:145). To start with the first characteristic, the vagabond is a criminalised figure whose identity ensured the expansion of a juridical apparatus meant to enforce enclosure and land expropriation. Thus their ongoing repression, arrest, criminalisation, and social ostracism helped naturalise a system of dispossession and establish hegemonic control over not only land and capital, but also over juridical power. This form of power creates what Nail describes as 'tensional force' (ibid.:64–5). The need to establish a political order on the basis of rights and legal protections required, thus, an excluded, criminalised figure against whom this kind of power could be consolidated. Historically, the vagabond was identified with social deviants and heretics (ibid.:145). A series of 'anti-Vagabond Laws' were enshrined in the Early Modern period to replicate this social hierarchisation and differentiation. 'Starting with England,' writes Federici, 'always a pioneer in these matters, the state passed new, harsher anti-vagabond laws prescribing enslavement and capital punishment in cases of recidivism' (2014:82). Vagabonds were looked upon and condemned as social parasites, lazy idlers, thieves and heretics who did not consent to wage-dependence or the rules of capital, but who were also suspected of corrupting the population (such as witches).[2] It is thus during this period that intensified forms of incarceration and punishment began to crystallise and which began to function according to 'abstract quantification' and 'computability' (Davis 2003: 44) that were manageable according to a logic of capitalism and labour. Criminalising institutions could easily quantify the lost value of commodities in terms of labour hours and a loss in profits; and to ensure that the penalty is commensurate with that lost value, the punishments were given in terms of time that one is meant to serve.

As Foucault extensively documented, the disciplining technology of 'confinement' was uniquely suited to the vagabonds and paupers, seeing as 'looting and violence [had to] be prevented' (1977:142). As I will detail below, these institutional dynamics of confinement act as reactive forces against the ongoing movement and mobility enacted through vagabond rebellion. The relationship between criminality and forms of quantifiable punishment, on the one hand, and capitalism, wage, and property, on the other, is the basis upon which the modern form of incarceration developed. The form that incarceration and imprisonment took in terms of making punishment a quantifiable and computable system made it a system that could be measured according to the same logic as property, wages, and labour-time.[3] The vagabond was a figure largely recognised as being 'masterless' (Bauman 1996:28) 'lazy' (Foucault 1977:106), 'heretical' and 'homeless' (Nail 2015:145), and as threats to 'property' (Federici 2014:82), making the 'wipp[ing], brand[ing], and torture' (Marx [1867]1990:899) of vagabonds compatible with the damages to, and disruption of, the flow of commerce. The state and the ruling class, therefore, responded to the vagabond's criminal rejection of land privatisation and the law of capital by intensifying repressive force, including a widespread campaign of social condemnation, suspicion, and paranoia. The vagabond's apparent rootlessness, along with their apparent disobedience to the dictates of labour-time, are curtailed through regimes of quantification that keep them ordered and managed.

The second characteristic that Nail mentions, though, in which the vagabond serves as a 'counterpower' to 'juridical kinopower' (Nail 2015:145), makes the vagabond another suitable migrant figure for kinopolitics. After all, their counterpower, or 'pedetic force' is, just as it is with the nomad, enacted through movement. Nail writes: 'The vagabond, from the Latin *vagus*, meaning 'to wander', and the Latin *proprius*, meaning 'one's own way', is also the name of the migrant whose free wandering has its own techniques of pedetic force' (ibid.). Such free wandering produced in fact the same trait or characteristic that tensional kinopower was attempting to manage through criminal and juridical force: the vagabond's ability to *rebel* and 'confront authority form within' (ibid.:146). The vagabond's wandering, then, makes them a suitably expelled migrant figure to enable the expansion of a juridical apparatus. Instead of a potential destruction from without, the vagabond compromises security and kinopower from within. As a pedetic force, wandering is a seemingly rebellious act, associated with trespassing, sabotage, theft, disobedience (especially in the workplace), and loitering. As mentioned previously, anti-vagrancy and -vagabond laws emerged precisely as the dominance of capitalist power through private property took shape; they were a necessary consequence of the state's legitimisation and enforcement of property law. So the (seemingly) rebellious activities of wandering were treated as such thanks to the entrenchment of capitalist power. Even today, vagabond actions are carried out in the contemporary United States: 'In the United States, vagabond counterpower takes the similarly direct form of rebellion in the open rejection of immigration authorities and the illegal seizure of necessary services [such as education, political protest, labour, and unionisation]' (ibid.:230). Existing from within a territory but openly rejecting its authority or acquiring provisions unavailable to them are expressions of the vagabond's rebelliousness. But even broader, their pedetic counterpower is one that de-stabilises power from within, either by disobedience or by heretically challenging church or state authority. Silvia Frederici writes:

> Everywhere masses of people resisted the destruction of their former ways of existence, fighting against land privatization, the abolition of customary rights, the imposition of new taxes, wage-dependence, and the continuous presence of armies in their neighborhoods, which was so hated that people rushed to close the gates of their towns to prevent soldiers from settling among them (2014:33).

Thus, wandering entails both a literal and physical wandering – such as onto prohibited land or property – but also a figurative, mental or spiritual wandering – moving away from state, religious, or political orthodoxy.

The pedetic force of 'wandering' makes this migrant configuration suitable to the urban city. The vagabond is a product of the intensified concentration of capital and the 'immiseration of the working class' (Federici 2014:68) that characterises urbanisation; and their rebelliousness is considered such because the state has enforced private property and coerced wage labour. As mentioned above, cities are spaces in which a network of material relations and economic strata converge. Because of this structure, a wide range of exclusionary patterns and differentiations occur within urban life, leading to intensified policing and surveillance. Hall et al. state in *Policing the Crisis* that, 'in a class society, based on the needs of capital and the protection of private property, the poor and propertyless are always in some sense on 'the wrong side of the law', whether actually they transgress it or not' (Hall, Critcher and Jefferson 2013[1978]:188). One result of this is a range of social panics and ideologies. Such affects comport with efforts to shape public opinion, coinciding with and reinforcing these policing tactics. They help generate a social perception of criminality. These practices become especially pronounced across racial and class lines, whereby media forces identify violence and criminality with the converging ethnic and racial groups within a large urban space. Immigrants and non-citizens are thus more easily targeted within such a regime, as they are likely to be looked upon with fear and suspicion (ibid.:48). Yet, on the other hand, another result is the pre-emptive and active vigilance toward non-violent 'crimes', or crimes which are merely against property: jaywalking, trespassing, vagrancy, loitering, panhandling, and vandalism. As a result, these acts which may appear condemnable and destructive, are in fact produced within the context of private property, and are largely therefore suited to police, exclude, and disempower the masterless, propertyless, and rebellious vagabond.

As a migrant figure, then, the vagabond falls right within this system of converging socio-economic forces of policing and surveillance. As a wandering figure whose pedetic forces involve 'heresy and rebellion' (Nail 2015:145), and whose existence is characterised by criminality and suspicion, this migrant figure has a unique position within the urban setting. As mentioned above, 'walking' and wandering can be considered a form of 'enunciation', a practice that 'actualizes' a city's 'possibilities' (de Certeau 1984:98) with all of the various relations of affective and social power. As a kinopoetics, therefore, a wandering kinopoetics pays particularly close attention to this type of enunciation enacted by the focalised migrant figure within an urban space; and in particular, wandering kinopoetics formally draws out the various meanings, sensations, and possibilities that the vagabond figure realises. These myriad forces will constitute the object of study for a wandering kinopoetics. This section will consider how the (im)migrant figure in these novels understands the urban landscape in terms of its various structures of exclusion, differentiation, and surveillance, but also how they produce their own discourses that are sometimes heretical and rebellious. One way of looking at these forces will be to consider a 'micro-politics of suspicion'. What this means is the individual, daily occurrences of paranoia, surveillance, discipline, and control that happen in many interpersonal encounters, especially in a setting of strangers and newcomers. These are the instances whereby everyday personal situations result in being subject to stereotyping, watchful surveillance, or profiling from citizens and other residents. Yet, there is also the immigrant's own suspicion of the society in which they have arrived and the one from which they left, leading them to reject or rebel against social norms – either norms from the junction of 'origin' or from the junction of 'arrival'. These moments create an assemblage of multiple suspicions from and toward the wandering, vagabond figure. This situation, as I will detail below, plays a large thematic role in migrant literatures set in urban city settings, as many situations require one to navigate and overcome these various acts of suspicion and surveillance. In turn, the micro-politics of suspicion is not only represented, but made visible and knowable – it is produced in and through the wandering of the vagabond figure, and it is their pedetic power to use their suspicion to then enact a 'personal transformation' (Nail 2015:154) through rebellion. Throughout this chapter, therefore, the manner by which the migrant figure creates and produces space in a rebellious, heretical, or unorthodox manner will solidify this type of kinopoetics as its own within the migrant literature tradition. Their empowerment through movement, walking, and wandering thus engenders a new migrant poetics for making visible and thinkable various affective networks of surveillance, criminality and suspicion, but also transformation, rebellion, and heresy. In turn, the sensible regime of the urban space is reorganised and redistributed to change the orderings and priorities of the city, on the migrant's terms. The pedetic force of the vagabond thus renders this space *their* space as they reject its commands, structures, and rules.

Open City: *Julius Revises the City*

Throughout the narrative of *Open City*, Julius's subjectivity as a Nigerian immigrant in the United States is intensified in his wandering, first in his place of residence, New York City, and later as a tourist in Brussels, before returning to New York. Through these spaces, he internalises his own sense of difference, but also constructs his own psychological profile as it is produced by and through his spatial awareness and sense of alienation. He is, after all, a psychiatry student, and thus maps his own understanding of various neuroses onto his own mental geography. It is the walks in the city that enable him to not only process, but to enunciate his subjectivity. 'The walks met a need', he says: 'they were a release from the tightly regulated mental environment of work, and once I discovered them as therapy, they became the normal thing, and I forgot what life had been like before I started walking' (Cole 2011:7). The streets of the city opposed 'a regimen of perfection and competence': 'Every decision . . . was inconsequential, and was for that reason a reminder of freedom' (ibid.). Many of the available commentaries on Cole's *Open City*, emphasise the novel's depiction of, on the one hand, cosmopolitan encounters (Fongang 2017:142; Varvogli 2017:237), and, on the other hand, diasporic alienation (Vermeulen 2013:41; Krishnan 2015:682); and critics are often at a disagreement regarding which of these categories better describes the protagonist, Julius. To engage these scholarly analyses in a wandering kinopoetics, I will argue that both cosmopolitanism and alienation are present in the novel in productive, yet ambiguous ways, and they are precisely what define Julius's vagabondage. In this section, I will reframe the novel's cosmopolitanism, but rather suggest that these elements exist as a potential: the cosmopolitanism is thoroughly limited in Julius's life, but elements of it are also invoked to chart out a desire for universal belonging. In his observation of and immersion within the New York City landscape, Julius specifically notes the presence of several diasporic identities converging around him. Although this experience is, for him, hardly something that confirms the existence of a liberal, multicultural and tolerant society, it does illustrate his appetite for belonging. In a much deeper sense, his distaste for the city's structures of class and race divisions suggests that Julius wants more than cultural pluralism; he asserts his pedetic counterpower in inventing the metropolitan space on his own terms. In a sense, this suggests an affective opposition to the systems of criminality and privatisation that materially inhibit cosmopolitanism and perpetuate racial antagonisms. Throughout the rest of this section, I will therefore reassess the critical consensus on cosmopolitanism in the novel, in light of Julius's vagabond configuration. In the next section, I will comment on alienation and redefine this rather as a mode of 'active disidentification', thereby bringing this again alongside the micro-politics of suspicion.

In the opening chapter of the novel, Julius reflects on a common feature of major financial centers: the rapid gentrification of low-income neighborhoods, coinciding with the rise and fall of corporate businesses. As he is purchasing food from a grocery store and a Jamaican shop, he notices on the far side of the grocery store a Blockbuster store with a notice that it is going out of business. The association with the bygone video rental company reminds him of Tower Records, another corporation long swallowed up by digital streaming programs. He reflects:

> [B]oth companies [Tower and Blockbuster] had for a long time dominated their respective industries. It wasn't that I felt sorry for these faceless national corporations; far from it. They had made their profits and their names by destroying smaller, earlier local businesses. But I was touched not only at the passage of these fixtures in my mental landscape, but also at the swiftness and dispassion with which the market swallowed even the most resilient enterprises. Businesses that had seemed unshakable a few years previously had disappeared in the span, seemingly, of a few weeks. Whatever role they played passed on to other hands, hands that would feel briefly invincible and would, in their turn, be defeated by unforeseen changes. These survivors would also come to be forgotten. (Cole 2011:19)

Juxtaposing two corporations that signify a previous era of media consumption alongside a Jamaican store allows Julius to recognise the well-recognised impact of gentrification and finance capital. Corporate behemoths such as these can easily render low-income neighborhoods, largely inhabited by immigrants, cost-prohibitive thanks to property speculations deeming them better suited to commercial interests. That Blockbuster is soon disappearing anticipates that businesses much smaller than Blockbuster will also succumb to 'unforeseen changes' (ibid.). The promise, too, of available cosmopolitan cultural institutions, including the existence of Jamaican cuisine, will also soon 'come to be forgotten' (ibid.) once high-end restaurants and wealthy residents take over the area. The communities most affected by these trends are immigrant and ethnic minority groups who formed diasporic enclaves within large metropolitan centers. It is these commercialising and gentrifying forces that continuously displace people and deprive the inhabitants of genuine cosmopolitan capacities. Cosmopolitanism signifies both an ideal moral system (universal tolerance) and, at the same time, a system of political inclusiveness (such as multicultural policies and anti-nationalism). In *Open City*, as many critics have noted, one finds both of these senses converge in the inner monologues and reveries of Julius. Yet, as the above reflection shows, the narrative distances itself from the consensus that metropolitan cities, replete with 'divisive architectures of power' (McLeod 2004:11), could ever truly facilitate a genuine 'world-city' where all cultures can equally belong and coincide (Žižek 1997:43). Thematising diasporic and migrant subjectivity, naturally the text gestures toward, or attempts to signal, a moral and political constellation that welcomes all identities and rejects exclusivity on the basis of nationality. However, cosmopolitanism is treated as a mere fantasy, given it would require 'independent means, high-tech tastes, and globe-trotting mobility' (Robbins 2009:312). With the existence of material limitations and immobilising forces, such cosmopolitan ideals are utopian.

Later in the text, Julius reflects on New York City as a 'palimpsest': 'written, erased, rewritten' (Cole 2011: 59). As a metaphor, this helps articulate the continuously changing features of a society that covers over its historic patterns of displacement and settlement: 'Generations rushed through the eye of the needle, and I, one of the still legible crowd, entered the subway. I wanted to find the line that connected me to my own part of these stories' (ibid.). Instead of hastily celebrating plurality and difference, *Open City* demonstrates that 'this celebratory gesture . . . is a ruse' (Krishnan 2015:679). Madhu Krishnan writes: 'Instead, postcolonial space takes on the mask of difference as a means of disguising its reconfigured brand of violence, which seeks to exploit and enlarge divisions through a cleaving of memory' (ibid.). Therefore, adds Krishnan, 'the novel's performance of space self-consciously presents a celebration of cosmopolitan diversity which serves to distract from what it seeks to cover' (ibid.:680). It is clear, then, that as Julius wanders through and absorbs his urban surroundings, he is skeptical of and reluctant to assume that he is dwelling within a truly multicultural, heterogeneous, and pluralistic society. Even when he is 'standing close to strangers, jostling them and being jostled by them for space', the 'solitude intensifie[s]' (Cole 2011:7). At first glance, we might note that the novel emphasises Julius's interactions with several cultural backgrounds, more specifically African diasporic subjects; yet, it is also clear that the novel distances itself from hastily celebrating New York City and Brussels as though they are environments compatible with cosmopolitan ideals. Instead, the text carefully shows that toward, within, and among diasporic groups, there still exist antagonisms and divisive structures that prevent a genuine plurality and coexistence from emerging. Competitive job markets combined with ethnic tensions preclude the multicultural dream from coming about.

For example, when Julius eventually takes a trip to Brussels, he observes there a similarly hostile social milieu. Visiting Brussels to find his grandmother, Julius eventually befriends Farouq, a Moroccan clerk at a telephone shop. Although Julius designates Brussels an 'open city', in that it surrendered to the 'invading powers' in the Second World War (Cole 2011:97), it is also one in which anti-immigrant sentiment is readily apparent. Julius begins to reflect upon Farouq's claim to 'victimised Other[ness]' that he asserts in the midst of conversation:

> What Farouq got on the trams wasn't a quick suspicious glance. It was a simmering, barely contained fear. The classic anti-immigrant view which saw them as enemies competing for scarce resources, was converging with a renewed fear of Islam. . . But the stranger had remained strange, and had become a foil for new discontents. It occurred to me, too, that I was in a situation not so radically different from Farouq's. (ibid.:106)

As Julius comes to terms with his status as a stranger, he becomes more sensitive to it when his difference intensifies in a country where he is merely a tourist. Yet, he finds in some ways a deep connection with immigrants in other countries. 'Irrespective of cultural background,' writes Delphine Fongang, 'it is evident that immigrants in various parts of the world continue to feel a sense of cultural alienation in diasporic communities. . . Farouq, like Julius, shares a sense of emptiness, and the idea of the diaspora being a safe haven is only an illusion' (2017:146). These instances of alienation will be highlighted in more detail in the next section; however, for purposes of this discussion, I use these moments to highlight the narrative's pessimistic orientation toward the cosmopolitan promises of metropolitan cities. '[T]he titular open city' – that is, Brussels – thus hearkens 'to the mobility of the cosmopolitan subject in the flux of the global or the city open as a space of refuge' (Krishnan 2015:676). It complicates the constructed identity of a spatiality that is considered welcoming to and open for immigration.

Julius's own desires, though, direct his flow toward a cosmopolitan potential. That is, even though he is realistic about the city's actually-existing conditions for alienation and bifurcation, he nevertheless yearns for a cosmopolitan society in which he and other immigrants can belong, envisioning 'a world where all humans can live freely and amicably, void of racial discrimination and structural inequalities that thwart progress for most immigrants' (Fongang 2017:146). Julius's wandering is not only an occasion for him to come to terms with the structures of the city and its various rhythms and vicissitudes; rather, he 'appears to create a counter-discourse to this imperative to order, rehearsed anew each evening' (Krishnan 2015:683) in his habitual nighttime walks. Such a 'counter-discourse' is in fact the precise content of the wandering kinopoetics. His enunciation of resistance – resistance toward the spatiality of the city and the forms of discrimination that emerge – is the rebellion he enacts as a vagabond figure, confronting and challenging the regimes of kinopower that restrict mobility within urban society. His wandering is a pedetic force that rebels against the ordering divisions of city life – divisions intensified through systems of class and criminality. Here I update Pieter Vermeulen's assertion that Julius exists as a *fuguer*, a character exhibiting patterns of dissociation and amnesia – thought of here as a 'dark counterpart to the *flâneur*' (2013:54). I agree that Julius's character retains dark and forgetful tendencies, and therefore he cannot simply be a *flâneur* figure; he is not simply a 'leisurely wanderer . . . acutely attentive to the spectacle provided by the processes of commodification and urbanisation that surrounded him' (Vermeulen 2013:41). Yet, the more precise 'dark counterpart' is not one whose manner can merely be described as a psychiatric disorder. Rather, his vagabond orientation and wandering mind come from a rebellious affect, a recalcitrance toward systems of discrimination that pervade modernity. In doing so, Julius is actually able to make thinkable and knowable the pluralistic world that, although does not exist in fact, exists through him as a potential.

At one point early in the text, Julius walks 'up to a second overpass, the one that once connected the World Financial Centre to the buildings that stood on the site' (Cole 2011:57). Before that point, Julius perceived himself existing in isolation, atomised from the social milieu. But, before long crowds begin ambling out of the World Financial Center:

> [M]en and women in dark suits including a group of young Japanese professionals who, tailed by the rapid stream of their conversation, hurried by me. Above them, for the third time that evening, I saw the bright lights of an exercise facility with the rows of bicycles, in this case looking out onto the construction site. What, I wondered, went through the minds of the exercisers as they pedaled and strained and looked out there? When I came up to the overpass, I was able *to share their view*: a long ramp that extended into the site, and the three or four tractors scattered around inside it that, dwarfed by the size of the pit, looked like toys. (ibid.:57; emphasis added)

From his point of view, Julius overcomes his isolation from the crowd, and immediately asserts himself into identifying with them. He 'shares their view' (ibid.), not just in the literal sense as being able to look from the same spatial vantage point; he can also gain insight into and identify with their affective, internal lives. Continuing his walk along the overpass, Julius begins to blend in with the pedestrians: 'The commuters with me marched along, shoulders up, heads low, all in black and gray. I felt conspicuous, the only person among the crowd who stopped to look out from the overpass at the site. Everyone else went straight ahead, and nothing separated them, nothing separated us, from the people who had worked directly across the street' (ibid.:58). From his standpoint, Julius finds himself lost in a crowd, immersed in an onflow of people and entering into relation with strangers.

Another juxtaposition occurs here, as the contrasting intensities between, on the one hand, a crowd of people in which 'nothing separated them' from the people working in the Financial Center, and, on the other hand, the regulations and bifurcations of sociality and conviviality that financialisation and neoliberalism produces. In other words, the presence of the financial center, with its commanding, fast-paced, twenty-four-hour production stands in opposition to a sense of collectivity that Julius feels among the people on the overpass. In a much deeper sense, the World Financial Center bespeaks what Neil Smith has aptly called 'neoliberal urbanism', where the presence of financial centres results in a permanent restructuring and 'rescaling' of urban activities, relations, and functions (Smith 2002:435; Krishnan 2015:683). A resulting outcome of this system is an increased fragmentation of individuals and communities: '[T]here is a fundamental geographical contradiction between the dramatically increased land values that accompany the centralisation of capital in the core of these metropolises and the marginal, exurban locations where workers are forced to live due to the pitiful wages on which that capital centralisation is built' (Smith 2002:435–6). In other words, with the existence of large financial centers, such as the World Financial Center, the property values increase exponentially, along with the monopolisation and privatisation of space, therefore displacing the surrounding (largely immigrant and ethnic minority) communities who cannot afford the rising prices (Harvey 2007:10; Sassen 2001:261). Such a system prevents or inhibits the ability for convivial relations to exist among various communities, seeing as more and more people are having to commute long distances from the outer reaches of the city. Furthermore, Julius is aptly recognising that this building signifies globalisation *par excellence*, which has meant historically restricting the flow of people and opening the flow of capital, even though it has been sometimes celebrated for its cosmopolitan triumphs. Bauman writes of the inverse relationship between migration and capital: '[T]he pressure to pull down the last remaining barriers to the free movement of money and money-making commodities and information goes hand in hand with the pressure to dig new moats and erect new walls' (2005:154). Such a system invariably inhibits a genuine cosmopolitanism from emerging, as immigrant communities are forced ever further into precarity.

Yet, Julius's wandering maps a different world onto the existing neoliberal urbanism; he forges a different mental geography, in which people are not continuously barred from each other, atomised, splintered, and fragmented. Rather, he is able to see past the World Financial Center, with its forces of displacement, and instead see a world where 'nothing separated them, nothing separated us' (Cole 2011:58). This form of coexistence and sociality runs completely afoul of the monopoly privatisation of space and property that is symptomatic of neoliberal urbanism. The world that Julius is imagining is his way of rewriting the urban space. As de Certeau insists that walking in a city functions as a practice of writing and analysing the city (1984:94), so Julius re-analyses the city anew, against the enforced power relations of finance capital – the power relations that would rather prevent people from trespassing and wandering together upon private property. The point that Julius makes is that, although this centre has separated people physically – particularly those who work in the financial centre and those who do not – he can nevertheless reimagine this situation with people freely mingling. He, in other words, imaginatively and intensively rebels against the conditions of private property and financialisation, 're-distributing the sensible', such that conviviality and community are made visible, and the restrictions on inclusion and exclusion are reconfigured (Rancière 2004:85). Since neoliberal urbanism would rather hide these qualities, Julius's vagabondage interferes in the privatising capture and instead opens up space for him to dwell alongside the other New York City commuters and residents. Such spaces are no longer the exclusive privilege of the capitalist owners, but they can be imaginatively and intensively opened and deterritorialised for everyone. His cosmopolitan desires and intensities go against the 'tensional force' (Nail 2015:64) that enforce displacement through privatised and monopolised space. Julius's vagabondage writes against this system, rebelling and, perhaps even, trespassing against this form of kinopower. His wandering adds another layer to the palimpsest, once again rewriting it, covering the existing layers of gentrification with a new layer of togetherness. The narrative point of view of internal focalisation enables and conditions the spatial circumstances and how they are apprehended; and it also allows the vagueness of free-indirect discourse to shape movement between discourses.

There remains another aspect of *Open City* that enunciates a pedetic power against the forces of fragmentation, and it relates to the novel's form. In particular, the narrative makes clever use of free-indirect discourse, whereby the dialogue and framing narrative blend into one, without marking different speakers through quotation marks or leading dialogue verbs. Such a technique, Vermeulen argues,

> allows the different conjured voices to dissolve into a continuous discourse in which the lack of distinction between free indirect speech, interior monologue, and reported speech robs these voices of their dialogic, agonistic, or contrapuntal potential. The decision not to use quotation marks leads to passages in which it is unclear whether we are reading the interior monologue of the narrator, his own speech, or the reported speech of one of his interlocutors. (2013:48)

Having 'rob[bed] these voices of their dialogic, agonistic, or contrapuntal potential', says Vermeulen, is 'a far cry from the cosmopolitan mobility that *Open City* may on a superficial reading seem to deliver' (ibid.). Yet, I diverge here from

Vermeulen. The assimilation of all voices into one is a way of inserting Julius into a collectivity of intensities and affects. The interaction between the characters adds more to the chaotic noise that surrounds them in the city. There is, here, a kind of *vagueness* (sharing the same etymological root as 'vagabond': *vagus*, meaning 'to wander'), where the precise narrative point of view eludes the reader. Instead there is a heightened ambiguity between speaker and listener, breaking down artificial boundaries between them, as it actually would feel when we overhear a conversation happening in a crowded city. This narrative vagueness *performs* a wandering kinopoetics. It is the sensation, then, of viewing the world from the vagabond's (internally focalised) point of view, rather than from 'above', where Julius joins the noisy, chaotic rabble beneath.

One rather intriguing moment of vagueness and ambiguity occurs while Julius is in Brussels. As Julius is conversing with Farouq his friend Khalil, their conversation turns quickly toward post-9/11 US Foreign policy, rehearsing 'uninspired clichés about . . . Israel, Hamas, and so on' (Vermeulen 2013:48). As if attempting to provoke Julius, Khalil moves toward acknowledging Al-Qaeda alongside others whom he thinks 'are doing the work of resistance' (Cole 2011:120):

> I looked at Farouq. He looked at me levelly and said, It's the same for me. It is resistance. And what about Al-Qaeda? I said. Khalil said, True, it was a terrible day, the twin towers. Terrible. What they did was very bad. But I understand why they did it. This man is an extremist, I said, you hear me, Farouq? Your friend is an extremist. But I was pretending to an outrage greater than I actually felt. In the game, if it was a game, *I was meant to be the outraged American*, though what I felt was more sorrow and less anger. Anger, and the semiserious use of a word like *extremist*, was easier

to handle than sorrow. This is how Americans think Arabs think, I said to them both. It really saddens me. And you, what about you, Farouq? Do you support Al-Qaeda too? (ibid.; emphasis added)

At first read, there is some deliberate ambiguity around the sentence with respect to which of the characters says 'What they did was very bad' and 'But I understand why they did it' (ibid.). As one proceeds further through the passage, it is clear that Khalil is the one speaking, and Julius is simply attempting to maintain composure within this social setting, lest he confirm the 'outraged American' (ibid.) stereotype. Vermeulen asserts here that the 'point of the confusion . . . is that the difference [between Khalil and Julius] is disconcertingly immaterial' (2013:48). Yet, I would argue this vagueness is absolutely deliberate; and the vagueness is meant to challenge the social and ideological construct of 'extremist' that is weaponised to criminalise immigrants. Because of US global hegemony, such a term has had widespread purchase in stoking anti-immigrant panic and paranoia. The narrative's deliberate vagueness here acts as a metafictional commentary on the poetics of 'extremism'; the term offers a shibboleth to divide a criminalised underclass from the rest of society (along with the culturally-constructed dichotomy of 'good' and 'bad' immigrant). Yet, wandering between different voices, allowing the narrative point of view to temporarily blend voices into one, performs a rejection of this regime. Julius is not afraid of being thought of as an extremist, and the dialogue technique of free indirect discourse shows that the text temporarily, but deliberately, obscures his opinion and position. Of course, even later in the above-quoted passage, when it is clear that Julius is the listener, he also nevertheless confirms his rejection of this ideological system. When he notes that '[t]his is how Americans think Arabs think' (Cole 2011:120) he is commenting on the way that, following the September 11 attacks, 'extremist' and 'terrorist' functioned as a poetics, weaponised to define and produce a criminalised subject.

As many have argued, labels like 'terrorist' and 'extremist' have taken up a position in the cultural imaginary to reinforce anti-immigrant sentiment and nativist paranoia (Abbas 2004:26; Zedner 2019:320). In turn, these terms have also led immigrants themselves to forcefully distance themselves from identifying or associating with extremist views. So, the fact that this vagueness exists between Julius's point of view and that of Khalil suggests that the system of meaning wanders into forbidden cultural and discursive territory. He is committing a form of 'heresy' (Nail 2015:145), going against political and social orthodoxies. Furthermore, as he ironically employs the 'semiserious word extremist' (Cole 2011:120), he is acting deliberately reluctant about betraying his actual feelings. Yet, he reveals in later sentences that he retains more 'sorrow' at the fact that such a conversation would allow the society at large to identify him, Farouq and Khalil as 'extremists'. This conversational framing is particularly useful when considering the soundscape of urban environments, where eavesdropping passersby may easily misconstrue this conversation, projecting anti-immigrant paranoia upon a group of dark-skinned men discussing global terrorist organisations. Instead of distancing himself from such suspicion and accusation, Julius in fact willingly invites this perception, knowing full well that such a concept only entrenches divisions between and among immigrants. The vagueness of this passage and Julius's own moral ambiguity acts, then, as a wandering kinopoetics: he is happy to leave the ambiguity about his own position hang in the conversation, thereby ridiculing and mocking the panic over extremism. He enters into a heretical discourse, rebelling against attempts to control, manage, and discipline acceptable speech. It is the narrative itself, through free indirect discourse, that moves into, and rebels against, restricted territory, allowing the meaning and point of view to wander from subject to subject, moral system to moral system.

The vagueness of free-indirect discourse brings various, often incompatible meanings into contact with one another, adding a chaotic experience similar to a crowded city. From here, Julius's vague wanderings, both physical and discursive, are ways of rewriting the spatial and mental geography he occupies. Throughout *Open City*, Julius writes and rewrites his urban environment; and the formal structure of internal focalisation produces a 'vision with' (Genette 1988:65) Julius that grants access to the city's rhythms and (im)mobilities. Even when he is home lying in bed he rehearses 'in the dark the numerous incidents and sights [he] had encountered while roaming, sorting each encounter like a child playing with wooden blocks, trying to figure out which belonged where, which responded to which' (Cole 2011:6). He overlays the city's structures with his own conceptions of togetherness and belonging, enabling him to overcome the confining systems of modernity. His movement through the city, as he walks and absorbs its patterns of motion and territoriality, allows him to invent, construct, and reconfigure the relational and affective structures on his own terms. As a vagabond figure, Julius does not merely wander where he is not supposed to; he takes us one step further and reinvents the city's power of arrangement, stratification, and exclusion. His challenge to finance capitalism, with its coercive and compulsory forces of endless privatisation and expansion, alongside his own acerbic mocking of anti-terrorist panics, are rebellious acts of pedetic (and poetic) power. He extensively moves as a wanderer in the 'open city'; but he also intensively moves the boundaries of what is visible and thinkable. As this section considered Julius's revision of the city-space, and his capacity to assert his own belonging and identify with others, the next section will discuss Julius as also someone willing to dis-identify and isolate. These tendencies reflect Julius's ambiguity as a character, but also draw out the novel's overall vagueness. So, in the following section, I will analyse his supposed alienation, not as someone rejected from a system, but rather as someone deliberately estranging himself. From here, I will delineate where this fits into a micro-politics of suspicion.

Open City: *Julius, Dis-identification and Suspicion*

In a celebratory review of *Open City* for *The New Yorker*, James Woods emphasises the features of the novel which make it 'as close to a diary as a novel can get, with room for reflection, autobiography, stasis, and repetition' (2011). Woods then adds that, 'throughout *Open City*, one has the sense of a *productive alienation*, whereby Cole (or Julius) is able to see, with an outsider's eyes, a slightly different, or somewhat transfigured, city' (ibid.; emphasis added). The term 'productive alienation' here highlights an important dimension of *Open City*. The novel does not simply represent a figure whose alienation is an outcome of his displaced, outsider status. Rather it is productive in the sense that Julius enacts and carries out his own alienation. He enacts, invents, and mobilises a practice of alienation in his deliberate wandering and vagrancy. Fongang writes: '[Julius's] otherness is juxtaposed with the heavily normative, dominant population. Subjects from different backgrounds occupy the same space, but navigate the world within them differently. And for a postcolonial subject like Julius, the navigation of the metropolis is a long, lonely walk across spaces that seem familiar but strange at the same time' (Fongang 2017:142). Yet, rather than seeing, as Fongang does, Julius's identity as something that works 'negatively to cement the cultural isolation and estrangement he faces in the metropolis' (ibid.:141),

I will demonstrate how it functions as an affirmative strategy of rebellion and pedetic force.

After a long passage reflecting on the Dutch influence on New York City history and architecture, he begins to think about his own walking and direction: 'When I crossed the street and entered the small alley opposite, it was as though the entire world had fallen away. I was strangely comforted to find myself alone in this way in the heart of the city. The alley, no one's preferred route to any destination, was all brick walls and shut-up doors, across which shadows fell as crisply as an engraving' (Cole 2011:52). In this instance, Julius is not merely alone, but is comforted in his isolation; he takes 'no one's preferred route' (ibid.), indicating a readiness to abandon the presumed comforts of routine, crowds, and ease of access, rather taking paths that might seem dangerous and leave one overly exposed. At the end of this passage, a rather startling omission enters into Julius's reflection: 'Where that narrow, quiet street met Washington, I saw to my right, about a block north of where I stood, a great empty space. I immediately thought of the obvious but, equally quickly, put the idea out of my head' (ibid.). Although we do not know it yet until the following paragraph, Julius is thinking of the site of the 9/11 attacks. So, '[t]hinking of 'the obvious' would require that Julius confront the enormity of violence marking the site, both in the events of 9/11 and in the site's position within a global system of inequity' (Krishnan 2015: 683). In this passage, therefore, he deliberately obscures from the reader what is nevertheless right in front of him. This shift deprives us of our capacity to recognise and identify with his perspective. This moment stands in stark contrast to the previous section, where I outlined Julius's capacity to bridge the fragmenting structures of division. Now, instead of bringing people together, he actively estranges himself from social connection. He moves away from the reader, forcing us to chase after his perspective and speculate on our own what 'the obvious' (Cole 2011:52) entails. Here, too, we have a micro-politics of suspicion. Julius reveals himself to be an unreliable narrator; yet, simultaneously, we rely on being able to follow his wandering, revealing the cityscape to us through his focalised point of view. Instead, he enacts a suspicious manner of wandering that, in turn, reduces our affective relation to him. This deliberate distancing makes Julius suspicious of the reader while we are simultaneously suspicious of him. As mentioned earlier in this chapter, this contributes to the overall wandering, narrative vagueness that characterises this novel.

Despite Julius's capacity to engender camaraderie with some diasporic subjects – especially Farouq when he is in Brussels – there are two key moments in the text which, while subtle, indicate an eagerness to disidentify and isolate himself from African diasporic people. In one early scene in the novel, Julius enters a taxi amid a torrential rainstorm. Flustered and exasperated from the rain (plus having impolitely rejected a woman's request to take the taxi ahead of him), he sits in the cab and has trouble remembering his home address. Upon finally recalling the correct destination, he tries to open up a polite conversation with the taxi driver: 'So how are you doing, my brother? The driver stiffened and looked at me in the mirror' (Cole 2011:40). Surprisingly, the cab driver responds with hostility, leaving Julius feeling awkward and confused: 'Not good, not good at all, you know, the way you came into my car without saying hello, that was bad. Hey, I'm African just like you, why you do this? He kept me in his sights in the mirror. I was confused. I said, I'm sorry about it, my mind was elsewhere, don't be offended, ehm, brother, how are you doing? He said nothing, and faced the road' (ibid.). Immediately after this interaction, though, Julius reverts back to his guarded position: 'I wasn't sorry at all. I was in no mood for people who tried to lay claims on me.' (ibid.). This last sentence comes to create an important

motif throughout the novel: Julius resents any cultural system forcing him to act as an obedient subject. As we learn
earlier in the novel (and as outlined in the third section of this
chapter), Julius uses his movement through the city to counteract the 'regimen of perfection and competence' (ibid.:7)
that constitutes his work-life. So, beyond the strictures of his
job, he rejects the expectations of conformity and decorum
dictating his life in the city. Furthermore, he sees no reason
to assume, by default, a connectedness with the taxi driver
based on their shared race and heritage. Although the taxi
driver is 'African just like' Julius, Julius rejects any obligation
or imperative toward identifying with the driver, especially if
that identification affects his feelings of autonomy.

Later in the text, Julius finds a restaurant and sits alone at
the bar. While inside, a man approaches and sits down beside
him: 'You don't recognise me, he said, raising his eyebrows.
My face must have remained foggy because he added: I'm a
guard there, and that was you I saw, right? I nodded, faint
though the memory was. He said, I knew I recognised your
face. We shook hands, and he introduced himself as Kenneth'
(Cole 2011:53). After scrutinising Kenneth, noticing his
physical mannerisms, Julius learns that Kenneth is from
Barbuda. Once again, Julius finds himself in a position where
a shared racial identity presumably brings him into relation with Kenneth: 'Are you Yoruba? Kenneth was, by now,
starting to wear on me, and I began to wish he would go
away. I thought of the cabdriver who had driven me home
from the Folk Art Museum – hey, I'm African just like you.
Kenneth was making a similar claim' (ibid.). In Kenneth's
case, we learn that he has a different expectation of Julius:
'Then it struck me that his eyes were asking a question. A
sexual question. I explained to him that I had to meet a
friend . . . I felt a little sorry for him, and the desperation
in his prattle' (ibid.: 54). Based on Julius's interactions with
both Kenneth and the taxi driver, one of his main sources of

resentment is the feeling of others laying or making a claim upon him. He uses this term 'claim' to describe both scenarios (ibid.:40; 53), deliberately invoking a logic of ownership and power. Such a concept suggests a systematic process of control and discipline, telling Julius precisely how to speak, move and respond to them in a social setting (or, in Kenneth's case, respond to sexual advances). By claiming Julius, Kenneth and the taxi driver have imposed upon Julius a regime of conduct to which he is meant to comply, lest he seem disingenuous, impolite, prudish or intolerant.

In both situations, Kenneth and the taxi driver perform a micro-politics of suspicion. Based on Julius's complexion, they have both decided to profile him, predicting that he will follow expected patterns of behaviour based on his outward appearance. Laying claim upon someone means you can determine the boundaries and limits of their power; and in these situations, Julius feels confined within a cultural system that is forced upon him. This system derives from racial stereotypes and a presumed (social or mental) connection, and they develop it simply based on his appearance. When Kenneth and the taxi driver confront Julius, they arrive with an already-existing suspicion that predicts his actions. Both Kenneth's 'desperation' (Cole 2011:54) and the taxi driver's aggression indicate that they were eager to lay claim upon Julius, but felt disappointed when he thwarted their efforts. Furthermore, rather than demonstrating racism, these moments are, to Julius, nevertheless insidious: they carry out and replicate a racialised logic that presumes an alignment of interests and desires solely on the basis of skin colour.

Although moments of interpersonal stereotyping and profiling such as these are innocuous enough, in their aggregate effect they are easily made more powerful and visible in a broader system of criminalisation. A micro-politics occurs in day-to-day life; but as they become more powerful and reach the wider reaches of a social system, they start to shape the political and ideological assemblage. These moments, then, are a criminalisation at its 'molecular becoming': they are 'pure relations of speed and slowness, pure affects . . . below and above the threshold of perception' (Deleuze and Guattari [1987]2014:327). In other words, we would not notice these instances as having any obvious relationship to criminality and suspicion, because they have not yet been made visible according to systems of power. After all, at first glance, they appear to be merely day-to-day annoyances and indignities. Yet, to Julius, they constitute a 'claim' upon him, suggesting that these moments create affects which animate the systems of surveillance, power, and control that dominate life in a modern city. These smaller, microscopic or 'molecular' moments of suspicion are the moments that often go unnoticed; but, as they compound and circulate in society, they provide a degree of affective support in the service of police power and criminality. These moments interpellate Julius based on his skin colour, much like a police force surveilling the vagabond's wandering and reaction. It is no accident that, particularly in cities like New York City, racial profiling played a major role in their well-known and controversial stop-and-frisk policing that was a longtime norm in the city. These practices also rely on an overbearing police state laying claim upon the Black community, operating according to racist assumptions about their perceived and expected criminal behaviour. The fact that Kenneth first concocted his assumptions about, and sexual expectations of, Julius during his day job as a security guard is by no means incidental.

Like the figure of the vagabond, Julius's identity subjects him to society's surveillance and discipline. Within one chapter, two characters see his skin colour; and although they do not act (at first) angrily toward or scared of him, they have laid 'claim' to him. They have confined him within a limited set of behavioural expectations that they derive solely from his racial identity. Much like the scene in the Brussels café, in which he is conversing with Farouq and Khalil (outlined in the third section), Julius once again thwarts the social expectations of him. Recall in that scene, Julius is keen to avoid conforming to the stereotype of the 'outraged American' (Cole 2011:120). Again, we notice here that the earlier scenes anticipate that Julius is going to avoid any social regime that tries to lay claim to him based on his identity. As a result, Julius again carries out the 'productive alienation' (Woods 2011), or what I have deemed an active dis-identification. These are his micro-political moments of suspicion – suspicion toward social and cultural norms. Julius wanders beyond the pre-ordained pathways that are laid out for him, the dominating structures that determine the spatial, temporal and affective coordinates of his day-to-day life. His efforts to distance himself from those who lay claim to him, or who assume a relation with him merely based on his racial profile, constitute his pedetic force – his rebellion against all coercive regimes of ownership and power that 'claim' any subject. Were they able to claim him, he feels that he would have lost the freedom he gains from walking – the freedom to counteract the 'tightly regulated mental environment of work' (Cole 2011:7) where he is claimed for his labour power. Instead, he shows his freedom in being able to wander where he wants (physically, but also mentally) and in rejecting the claims over his existence. His vagabondage is a source of anguish, hostility and suspicion among those whom he encounters. Yet, he nevertheless affirmatively writes the city and his social power on his own terms, by virtue of his wandering steps and wandering mind.

Brick Lane: *Nazneen's Intensive Knowledge-gathering*

Much like Julius in *Open City* reconstitutes New York City on his own terms, Nazneen, the protagonist and focus of *Brick Lane*, uses her wandering through London's historic

East End to rewrite its structures and patterns of alienation. She arrives from Bangladesh at age eighteen through an arranged marriage with Chanu – an older, academic-minded man, eager to achieve recognition and social capital among the English professional class (including rather pitifully trying to obtain the approval of a local doctor, Dr Azad). The novel begins by shaping the fatalist *ethos* into which she was born and which comes to determine her life's trajectory. After remarkable and nearly tragic circumstances surrounding her birth, Nazneen relays the advice imparted to her by her mother, and proceeds to foreshadow the events of the narrative in a few short sentences:

> What could not be changed must be borne. And since nothing could be changed, everything had to be borne. This principle ruled her life. It was mantra, fettle and challenge. So that when, at the age of thirty-four, after she had given three children and had one taken away, when she had a futile husband and had been fated a young and demanding lover, when for the first time she could not wait for the future to be revealed but had to make it for herself, she was as startled by her agency as an infant who waves a clenched fist and strikes itself upon the eye. (Ali 2003:16)

The fatalist message that Nazneen internalises stems from the systems of domination, tradition, and compliance that structure her existence and from which she frees herself throughout the narrative. Nazneen is encouraged to lead a life of stoic indifference, 'the same indifference with which [life] would treat her' (ibid.:5). Yet, the startling discovery of her own agency, as she also comes to forge her relation to society as such, develops out of her affective-sensory exposure to and embodiment within a wider assemblage, such as 'an infant who waves a clenched fist and strikes itself upon the eye' (ibid.:). In other words, Nazneen's actualisation of subjectivity and agency come from her extensive and intensive movement,

coming into contact with material forces that affect her and
which she in turn affects. In this section, therefore, I will consider Nazneen's vagabondage as, on the one hand, a *gathering*
of affective and relational knowledge and, on the other hand,
a suspicion toward various social regimes throughout *Brick
Lane*. In the section that follows, I will then speak more specifically about Nazneen's active force and desire that coincides
with and activates this search for knowledge.

The fate that befalls Nazneen crystallises in the first chapter when, after her birth (and near-death immediately after)
and childhood are captured in scant detail, the narrative
jumps ahead eighteen years to her marriage and emigration to
London's East End. Her experience in London is initially
described as being the first time in her life 'that she spent alone',
sitting 'day after day in this large box with the future to dust,
and the muffled sound of private lives sealed away above,
below and around her' (Ali 2003:24). Like Julius in *Open
City* seeking a decisive break from the routines of his day job
in his sojourn through New York, Nazneen too sought opportunities to go out beyond the Tower Hamlets and onto Brick
Lane. The idea that such an act is, in itself, an act of rebellion, leading her to being regarded with suspicion, is already
hinted at when Chanu, her 'futile husband', tries to discour-
age her: "Why should you go out?' said Chanu. 'If you go
out, ten people will say, *I saw her walking on the street*. And I
will look like a fool. Personally, I don't mind if you go out but
these people are so ignorant. What can you do?" (ibid.:45).[4]
Already, the lone act of wandering freely beyond the estate is
treated as a potential transgression, exposing Nazneen and
Chanu to gossip, suspicion, and ridicule. The political desire
invested in this act of wandering will be taken up in the next
section. For present purposes, it is clear, though, that walking
is the movement she uses to discover her own agency.

When she takes her first walk out onto Brick Lane, '[t]he
buildings seemed unfamiliar': 'She sensed rather than saw,

because she had taken care not to notice' (Ali 2003:55–6). Absorbing and receiving her surroundings, Nazneen's walking enables her to better apprehend her relation to the people passing by as well as the environment. Her physical limitations (again, like the infant who 'strikes itself upon the eye' [ibid.:16]) are made visible when she twists her ankle on a ledge: 'She bunched the skirts of her sari with one hand and took the steps two at a time until she missed a ledge and came down on her ankle against an unforgiving ridge' (ibid.:54) This injury is at first humiliating and, perhaps, discouraging, but it also reveals to Nazneen the hostile structures of the city, making it more challenging for her to safely navigate the streets in a sari. After later passing through a crowd of people 'brush[ing] past her on the pavement', Nazneen 'hobbling and halting, began *to be aware of herself*' (ibid.:56; emphasis added). The passersby, however, 'were not aware of her. In the next instant she knew it. They could not see her any more than she could see God' (Ali 56). Angelia Poon writes here of Nazneen's response to this situation:

> As she walks the streets feeling cold, hungry, and in pain from twisting her ankle, she also alternates between visibility and enabling invisibility. The fact that nobody notices her pleases her as she indulges in *voyeuristic pleasure* at the lives around her. When she is randomly noticed, approached and spoken to, and when she has to ask for directions, she suddenly becomes visible again. Thus she slips in and out of herself rather than experiencing the self as a consolidated uninterrupted performance. (2009: 432; emphasis added)

Walking through the city without a clear sense of destination or purpose, Nazneen nevertheless uses this movement as a means of gathering epistemic resources; that is, she develops a mental geography of her own maneuverability within the urban landscape. In doing so, she learns to access her desires, agency, and pedetic counterpower that push against the forces of obedience, compliance, and custom. She begins to wonder about what has sparked her mobility: 'What propelled her down all those streets? What hand was at her back?' (Ali 2003:59). Although she is slow to realise it, she is activating and uncovering a hidden sense of self that had previously been consigned to fate. Even in the sentence, 'what hand was at her back?' (ibid.), suggests a reluctance to accept that she is shaping her own fate and moving in her own direction.

As a form of knowledge-formation, Nazneen's forays into the city of London construct the vagabond movement and wandering subjectivity outlined in the first section. She not only receives information about her world, but actively constructs the city on terms that comport with her migrant subjectivity. 'Nazneen's experience,' notes Poon, 'is . . . akin to Michel de Certeau's account of ordinary walkers who nego- tiate the city and make us of spaces with partial knowledge and visibility of the whole picture' (2009:432). Nazneen thus uses her movement to penetrate the city's hostile and alienat- ing structures, laying claim to it on her own terms and from her own embodied location. In relation to the people who brush 'past her on the pavement' (Ali 2003:56), Nazneen's 'walking in the city . . . provides her with first-hand expe- rience of the kinds of neoliberal patterns that are played out . . . across the spaces of the metropolis' (Duff 2014:111). Kim Duff writes (following James Proctor) that '[w]andering, getting lost, and then finding oneself in the city is . . . deeply rooted in the 'migrant tradition' of discovery' (ibid.:112). Poon adds here that 'walking in the city becomes a trope for learning one's place in the world. Nazneen learns in ways which involve risk and openness, as well as unlearning' (2009:430). Nazneen then uses her walking not as a manner of fully assimilating to Englishness nor as a way to retain her 'expected role as a Muslim Bengali mother' (Duff 2014:103), but rather to negotiate and partially affirm the regimes of mobility that constitute her as she passes through different spaces. 'Life', after all, 'made its pattern around and beneath and through her' (Ali 2003:40–1).[5]

Toward the end of the text, another moment of city wandering emerges, when, after several years have passed, and just before Chanu plans to move the family back to Bangladesh, Nazneen searches the city for her daughter, Shahana. Shahana had planned to run away with her friend, Nishi, to eventually hide in Paignton: 'In Paignton, Nishi said, there were no Bangladeshis and they could do what they want' (Ali 2003:466). In the scene that follows, the narrative follows a structure similar to that of someone giving directions, marking important landmarks and recognisable spots. Leaving to find Shahana, Nazneen takes a winding trip: 'Down Bethnal Green Road. Turned at Vallance Road. Jogged down New Road. Stitch in side on Cannon Street' (ibid.:466–7). Arriving at the café on Brick Lane where she expected to see her daughter, Nazneen arrives to discover that Shahana is elsewhere, and runs back out onto the street. At this point in the text, Nazneen's observations of the city are intensified: she notices the forecourt of a pub 'choked with weeds and grass' (ibid.:467); passing by the Berner estate, she sees a 'small child' who 'trundled a red plastic truck along a balcony and back, over and over again', and here recognises 'the face of a refugee child: that traumatised stillness'; and, finally, she arrives at a 'row of police vans', where she is bearing witness to a standoff between police and the Bengali Tigers, a group agitating for justice for the Muslim and Bengladeshi community.

Eventually bypassing the police, and placing herself in further danger, Nazneen nevertheless passes through this restricted and regulated space, claiming it as her own. All of the sensations and movements help her calibrate her position within this city space, seeing its changing facades and characters, but being able to also comprehend her own mobility and sense of attachment to Brick Lane. Moreover, while this scene takes place amid a hostile confrontation between police and two opposing groups (the Bengal Tigers and the Lion Hearts), the narrative voice specifically highlights 'Cable Street' (Ali 2003:467) and 'White Chapel' (ibid.:468), the location of the famous 'Battle of Cable Street' where the British Union of Fascists clashed with police and anti-fascist demonstrators in 1936. Drawing this parallel between a present and past conflict helps draw out the broader political and ideological struggles that continue to converge in and shape this specific setting, and the manner in which immigrants are consistently at the centre of territorial battles.

In these moments, Nazneen's self-realisation develops paradoxical and internally conflicting patterns that thus help her not only forge her identity in relation to the neoliberal society in which she lives – where rushing commuters brush past her on the sidewalk, as if 'on a private, urgent mission' (Ali 2003:56); she also rebels against the stifling domesticity of her home. The perpetual wandering that she performs in her walking enables her to examine the city and write its structure from her situated, migrant standpoint. Yet, as Poon points out, in Nazneen's 'movements along Brick Lane itself' she is 'subject to the informal surveillance of gossip-mongers in a closed immigrant community eager to pounce on the slightest show of female impropriety' (2009:432). One of Nazneen's close friends and confidantes throughout the narrative, Razia Iqbal, conveys the perpetual need to spread rumors about their community: '"Spreading rumors is our national pastime," said Razia. "That's not to say it is a good thing. Most of the time there's not a shred of truth in it"' (Ali 2003:26). It is this regime of rumors and gossip into which Nazneen enters and has to navigate. The informal surveillance of her community – especially that of Mrs Islam, who later comes to dominate Nazneen's and Chanu's life through debt encumbrance – is worth examining further within the context of a micro-politics of suspicion. Nazneen reflects on her feelings toward Mrs Islam early on: 'Nazneen wondered about Mrs Islam. If she knew everybody's business then she must mix with everybody, peasant or not. And still she was respectable' (ibid.:28–9). Nazneen notes that Mrs Islam was 'the first who called on [her], in those first few days when her head was still spinning and the days were all dreams and real life came to her only at night, when she slept' (ibid.:28). As the text proceeds, however, Mrs Islam lays claim to her, leaving Nazneen in a constant state of fear and paranoia, thinking that at any moment Mrs Islam will exact violent recompense for late payments. Already throughout her life, Nazneen had been 'conscious of being watched': 'Everything she did, everything she had done since birth, was recorded' by angels (ibid.:254). Similarly, Mrs Islam weaponises her status as a neighborhood gossip, on the one hand, and an enfeebled old woman, on the other, to further strong-arm and manipulate Nazneen into paying back money beyond the initial principle amount, and submit to higher interest payments.

Nazneen first learns of her debt encumbrance in a rather funny moment of naïveté. Mrs Islam asks Nazneen to place fifty pounds in the sidepocket of her bag, meanwhile reclining onto the couch. Thinking that she is simply helping Mrs Islam locate her own fifty-pound note, the realisation begins to dawn on Nazneen that Mrs Islam is demanding her payment: "Are you trying to rob my grave? Get. Me. My. Money' (Ali 2003:199). Once the reality of the situation crystallizes, Nazneen quickly tells Mrs Islam that she has not had work yet. In reaction to Nazneen's desperate plea for more time, Mrs Islam subtly reveals, through unspoken gestures, a suspiciousness toward her:

Mrs Islam considered for a moment. Her small black bird eyes fixed on Nazneen's burning face. 'I understand. Forgive a sick and anxious old woman. This is an arrangement between friends. Pay when you can.' She made a show of struggling to her feet and Nazneen helped her so that when she was up they stood in a sort of embrace. Mrs Islam kissed her, hard mouth to soft cheek. 'We understand each other. I will come again. My salaam to your husband. (ibid.:199)

The exaggerated physical struggle Mrs Islam exhibits here continues as a pattern throughout the narrative, clearly enabling her to instill constant guilt and sympathy in her indebted subjects. This moment and the subsequent encounters with Mrs Islam carry out a yet another regime of dependence, submission, and obedience to which Nazneen is subjected. Much like the domestic obligations to Chanu, and the fatalistic demands of her mother, Mrs Islam is yet another figure to whom Nazneen must submit herself. Nazneen also, furthermore, gets a stark and tragic lesson in learning that, although Mrs Islam committing usury is itself a heretical act, Nazneen's indebtedness to her in turn puts in her in a position of permanent exposure to blackmail and even more surveillance. Rather than the seemingly harmless 'national pastime' (ibid.:26) of rumours and gossip, Nazneen now arrives at a point in which her day-to-day life, including her romantic affair with Karim, is held under scrutiny. She is, in turn, a criminalised subject, forced into an unbreakable contract of encumbrance and immobility. Despite the irony that Mrs Islam's usury is legally and morally questionable (not to mention strictly prohibited in Islam), it nevertheless places Nazneen's family in a permanent state of financially-enforced compliance. Debt itself operates as a tool for wielding moral control upon social subjects; and, as David Graeber points out, debt was historically a way of subjecting vagabonds and 'masterless men' into indentured servitude (2011:313). Nazneen's domestic work, therefore, in mending clothing is not only an obligation derived from patriarchal traditions (although this is partially true); she is also held under the increasing debt burden, making her every action even more risky.

Nazneen however enacts her rebellious counterpower in a gratifying moment toward the end of the narrative. Knowing that Nazneen is preparing to return to Bangladesh with her family (although ignorant to the fact that Nazneen will in fact stay behind while her husband goes on his own), Mrs Islam arrives with her two sons (described as Son Number One and Son Number Two) to call in her final payments. The two sons act here to give Mrs Islam extra power, a threatening show of physical force. After asking for her final payment of two hundred pounds to settle the debt once and for all, Nazneen insists that she has paid off everything in full, plus any lingering interest above the principle. In response to this, Son Number Two immediately destroys the showcase, causing 'the sound of breaking glass [to shoot] like iced water down Nazneen's spine' (Ali 2003:444). Flinching at first at the sound of broken glass, Nazneen returns to composure. When Mrs Islam repeats her demand for two hundred pounds, Nazneen denies her again: 'Nazneen's blood thickened. Her heart strained to push it round her body. 'No'.' (ibid.:444). Nazneen goes on, insisting that she will not pay anymore 'riba' (the Arabic word for 'usury'). Mrs Islam, blanching at the word, denies the charge: '"Riba," whispered Mrs Islam. "Riba, she says." Her head lolled around as if the word had given her fever. "Do you think, before God, that I would charge interest? Am I a moneylender? A usurer? Is this how I am repaid for helping a friend in need?"' (ibid.). Nazneen, however, returns to Mrs Islam, weaponising the forces of inquisition and religious obligation in the reverse direction.

To expose Mrs Islam, she demands that she swear upon the Qu'ran that she is not a moneylender. Mrs Islam, then, thinking she has one last weapon of blackmail against Nazneen responds, threatening to reveal the affair with Karim to Chanu: 'There are some things a wife does not want a husband to know' (Ali 2003:445). In this moment, we, along with Nazneen, learn that the nature of her affair has been known all along to Mrs Islam; and that her surveilling role within the community gives her a strategic advantage over her indebted subjects. Nazneen, though, makes a risky bet with Mrs Islam: '"My husband," said Nazneen slowly, "knows everything. He'll come soon. Why don't you ask him?"' (ibid.). Although Mrs Islam doubts that Chanu is aware of the affair, considering his manner of upholding patriarchal values, she is unwilling to take such a bet, and realises that she no longer has power over Nazneen. Mrs Islam and her sons eventually leave, and Nazneen finds herself with her newfound freedom: 'Gradually, a thought began to form. God provided a way. Nazneen smiled. God provided a way, and I found it' (Ali 446). It is here where she again gathers her own knowledge and observations about Mrs Islam, using them toward her own counterpower and pedetic force. She escapes the grip of debt and servitude by means of self-discovery and rebellion.

The significance of this scene is crucial when thinking not only about the transgressions that both characters commit, but also the material servitude that Nazneen is held under through debt obligations. Mrs Islam's role within the community is to act as a moral arbiter, surveilling and disciplining other women, particularly immigrants, into compliance and obedience. These moments fit into a much broader pattern of using debt as a means of indentured servitude for immigrants. While indebted subjects still have money they owe with compounding interest, they lose their capacity for mobility, credit, and financial investment; and as long as those obligations are enforced (and, Nazneen's case, violently and illegally so), the subject has to remain obedient, lest the usurer lose their financial returns. The assumed criminality of the propertyless and masterless vagabond necessitates such systems of enforcing obedience; and immigrants, similarly, who have familial ties elsewhere can be forced to remain in conditions of servitude as long as they are indebted to a creditor or lender. Because the vagabond's movement is unpredictable, debt ensures that movement is restricted, so as to prevent them from shirking on and escaping their obligations. Yet, far from denying or attempting to stave off the accusations of vagabondage, Nazneen affirms it. In fact, willingly allowing Mrs Islam to expose her transgression to her husband, Nazneen learns quickly here that this is the only available advantage that Mrs Islam felt she had. Nazneen, however, in a subversion of roles characteristic of the vagabond, uses her own means of account-settling and collecting: she forces Mrs Islam to cash in on the threat she is making. She thus moves into the role of the overseer toward Mrs Islam. Nazneen actively rebels against and interrupts the presumed, alienated power-relation created through financial burdens and informal taxation, rewriting the story and her relation to power that instead leaves her in a position of control. In other words, she *invents* a new affective relation to Mrs Islam. Her knowledge of her own power and Mrs Islam's weakness enables her to construct a new system of intensive movement and affective mobility. Then, as she demands the swearing upon the Qu'ran, she weaponises the precise threat of 'impropriety' (Poon 2009:432) that had been leveled against her. Her victory therefore develops out of gaining advantage through insight, allowing her to rebel against those who wield financial, moral, and religious control. She *collects* in her own way: rather than seising money or property, Nazneen collects *knowledge* and affects that allow her how to use counterpower effectively.

The end of this scene with Mrs Islam contrasts dramatically with the fatalist system to which Nazneen resigned herself at the start of the novel. As she learns more about her own advantage, and her capacity to instill fear and panic in Mrs Islam, she begins to free herself. She can thus wander beyond any expectation of *propriety* (from the same root as 'property') that imposes restrictions on her action and deems her transgressions and trespasses to be criminal. Much like the vagabonds subjected to witch-hunts in the Middle Ages, regimes of *propriety* are a means of containing Nazneen's assumed wickedness – her impious rebellion against patriarchal traditions and religious authority. Instead, however, she seizes the terms of propriety and impropriety, finally enabling her *to move* beyond fate and destiny. Her existence within the demanding urban environment, with its compulsory forces of capital and labour servitude, have engendered a relational, affective sense of her controlled and criminalised subjectivity. As an immigrant, she is already subject to patterns of discrimination, suspicion, and hostility among the English society. The micro-politics of suspicion from her community, and the tyranny of Mrs Islam, stem from their assumed roles in enforcing propriety and power over their fellow immigrants who are expected to retain the patriarchal standards and traditions from their former countries. Yet, Nazneen's wandering has enabled her to create, produce, and positively affirm vagabondage as a force for liberation and recognition; in other words, she enacts a pedetic counterpower that produces a new form of propriety (recall that *proprius*, 'one's own way', is built into the etymology of vagabond) – one that is free, open, and unpredictable. Read kinopoetically, Nazneen writes and invents propriety in her intensive movement. She gathers the affective flows to reconstruct and redistribute the sensible world in a way that makes her not only free, but visible to those who wish to contain and confine her.

Brick Lane: *Becoming-vagabond and the Activation of Rebel Desire*

As stated in the previous section, much of Nazneen's wandering through Brick Lane and East London enable her to become 'aware of herself' (Ali 2003:56). The forces that animate and constitute her subjectivity are generated through the structures of the city itself and the crowds through which she passes. These forces in turn enable her to process her sense of herself as she travels along a line of flight. She produces and enacts desire in developing a connectedness with and to her milieu. We witness her thus not as a fully-actualised vagabond, but a vagabond in becoming – a becoming-vagabond. Through her movement, Nazneen receives affects and intensities that in turn create a relational sense of her own power, freedom, and self, based on her exposures to and encounters within the urban dwelling. Many of the tragedies and hardships that befall her shape and change the intensity of her own power; yet, in other respects, a range of affects activate her desire for defiance and rebellion. In this section, I will highlight a few encounters that, while some may be seemingly insignificant in terms of their position in the overall story, nevertheless compound into constituting and generating Nazneen's self and identity. These pre-figurative moments in turn will help us locate the precise moments that render her vagabond desire visible.

As I outline in Chapter 3, desire can be seen as a productive and creative force, changing and reconstituting the material, affective, and sensible regime in which a person or figure dwells, or through which they wander. In Nazneen's case, walking enables her to *see* an imperceptible world, while in turn activating a new existence – one which is in becoming. As Deleuze and Guattari remind us, 'becoming is to extract particles between which one establishes the relations of movement and rest, speed and slowness that are *closest* to what one is becoming, and through which one becomes. This is the sense in which becoming is the process of desire' (Deleuze and Guattari, 2014:318). In other words, becoming is the active access to the microscopic movements and intensities that one encounters within a social space; these in turn generate affects, power, knowledge, and joy. By participating alongside and immersing ourselves in this world teeming with affects and flows, we in turn enact or produce desire.

Quite early on in the novel, but after she arrives in London, Nazneen's 'voyeuristic pleasure' (Poon 2009:432) directs her gaze at a tattooed woman living in the Tower Hamlet estate:

> The tattoo lady was always there when Nazneen looked out across the dead grass and broken paving stones to the block opposite. . .Morning and afternoon [the tattoo lady] sat with her big thighs spilling over the sides of her chair, tipping forward to drop ash in a bowl, tipping back to slug from her can. She drank now, and tossed the can out of the window. (Ali 2003:17)

The subversion that 'the tattoo lady' is meant to embody within Nazneen's social universe is further accentuated later on when Nazneen takes inventory of the woman's unfeminine and rather unsophisticated mannerisms:

> The tattoo lady waved back at Nazneen. She scratched her arms, her shoulders, the accessible portions of her buttocks. She yawned and lit a cigarette. At least two thirds of the flesh on show was covered in ink. Nazneen had never been close enough (never closer than this, never further) to decipher the designs. Chanu said the tattoo lady was Hell's Angel, which upset Nazneen. She thought the tattoos might be flowers, or birds. They were ugly and they made the tattoo lady more ugly than was necessary, *but the tattoo lady clearly did not care*. Every time Nazneeen saw her she wore the same look of boredom and detachment. *Such a state was sought by the sadhus who walked in rags through the Muslim villages, indifferent to the kindness of strangers, the unkind sun.* (ibid.:18)

I cite the entire passage here because it anticipates and foreshadows Nazneen's development throughout the narrative. From this early moment, we notice that Nazneen's observations allow her to access and activate her desires. Her desires construct the tattoo lady as a subject of curiosity, beauty, and, perhaps, envy. As a result, Nazneen's lifeworld throughout the text continues to produce the sought-after state of indifference, freedom, and subversion prefigured as a virtuality in her reflections on the tattoo lady. The tattoo lady only reappears throughout the text as someone who enters Nazneen's mind at random moments, and otherwise as simply an object of infatuation and curiosity. She imagines, for instance, English words that Chanu says turn into 'other things she could say to the tattoo lady' (ibid.: 37) that could secure a connection. The impact upon Nazneen's affects and desire is nevertheless profound. The tattoo lady's sheer existence exists for Nazneen as a relay of becoming, a figure whose relation to her is nevertheless a 'particle' (Deleuze and Guattari, [1987]2014:318) that generates affects, in turn changing and modulating Nazneen's sense of her own maneuverability (in other words, her power, flow, and potential). They form and culminate in the relations of speed and slowness that ultimately enhance or reduce her power. Thus, in small moments after this, we see more frequent moments of miniature protests on her part: 'All her chores, peasants in [Chanu's] princely kingdom, rebelled in turn. Small insurrections, designed to destroy the state from within' (ibid.:63). More and more, her encounters with other vagabond figures – figures who demonstrate to her the freedom of movement that she grows to admire – start to assemble her own tendencies toward resistance.

In a much later scene, Chanu and Nazneen make an impromptu visit to Dr Azad, a man in whom Chanu has invested affective energy in hoping to leverage gainful employment and status. Arriving unannounced at Dr Azad's home, Mrs Azad opens the door. Nazneen's evaluation of Mrs Azad is reminiscent of that toward the tattoo lady:

A woman in a short purple skirt leaned against the doorpost. Her thighs tested the fabric, and beneath the hemline was a pair of dimpled knees. Her arms folded beneath her

breasts. A cigarette burned between lacquered nails. She
had a fat nose and eyes that were looking for a fight. Her
hair was cropped close like a man's, and it was streaked
with some kind of rust-coloured paint. (Ali 2003:106–7)

This moment reflects Nazneen's initial encounter and her
sensitivity toward Mrs Azad's relational *difference*. Mrs
Azad carries a sense of confidence, a disregard for patriarchal norms and a disdain for decorum: 'Mrs Azad turned on
the television and turned the volume up high. She scowled at
Chanu and her husband when they talked and held up her
hand when she wished to silence them altogether. She drank
a second glass of beer and belched with quiet satisfaction'
(ibid.:109). Mrs Azad's mannerisms in this scene are disarming to Chanu and seemingly embarrassing for Dr Azad. To
Nazneen, however, they are ever more intriguing and a source
for her own marvel. Eventually after a heated exchange
between Chanu and Mrs Azad, in which Mrs Azad makes
her boredom and impatience readily apparent, Mrs Azad
then stands up to leave. Witnessing her departure, Nazneen's
fascination with her grows: 'Mrs Azad struggled out of her
chair. Nazneen thought – and it made her feel giddy – *she's
going to the pub as well*' (ibid.:114). For Mrs Azad to go to
the pub would, to Nazneen, illustrate an act of defiance that
she becomes more and more attached to in her adult life.
As the scene concludes, Nazneen is once again struck by the
confidence Mrs Azad seems to embody: 'Watching her now,
Nazneen felt something like affection for this woman, this
fat-nosed street fighter' (ibid.). Nazneen's affection for her
comes, too, from a sense of solidarity: she shares with her
the burden of being cruelly subjected to unhappy marriages
with unhappy men. The realisation forms for Nazneen that
Dr Azad indulges Chanu with visits, 'not for the food, not to
get away from this purple-clawed woman (although maybe
for these things as well), not to share a love of learning . . .'

(ibid.:114–5). She realises that Dr Azad enjoys, 'as a man of science', coming to their home to simply observe Chanu and see 'unhappiness greater than his own' (ibid.:115). This pitiful realisation only further enhances her understanding of Chanu and their marriage. At the same time, her sensibilities toward propriety, femininity, and marriage start to slowly shift into new terrain. Yet, another apparent source of affection for Nazneen is the confidence with which Mrs Azad moves, apparently unconcerned with patriarchal norms. Much like the tattoo lady, Mrs Azad embodies particularly new relations of speeds and slownesses that become part of her.

In addition to figures like the tattoo lady and Mrs Azad, throughout *Brick Lane*, the perhaps two most prominent figures of vagabond intensities – Karim and Hasina – play a formative role in generating Nazneen's vagabond desire. Both characters attract not only Nazneen's affection and admiration, but activate and permit her becoming. Duff writes that 'Nazneen's initial understanding of herself is in relation to the oppositional "other"' (2014:110); and both Hasina and Karim embody this otherness throughout her life. Hasina is Nazneen's sister, whose early life follows a diametrically opposing trajectory to that of Nazneen: instead of complying with the fatalist imperatives of her mother, she 'listened to no one' (Ali 2003:16) and instead at an early age ran away from home to seek a 'love marriage' (ibid.:50). The narrative is interspersed with letters Hasina sends to Nazneen, each replete with the desperation and difficulty of sweatshop labour and domestic servitude, 'along the way enduring a series of exploitative relationships with men' (Ziegler 2007:147–8). Nazneen nevertheless maintains a relation with her sister that is affectionate and concerned, but also, at times, envious. Yet, as her character grows and changes, her own desires start to resonate with those of Hasina, bringing them into a relational and affective connection though they are still separated geographically for the entirety of the story. Turning her back on the fatalism of her childhood, Nazneen internalises and actualises the vagabond desire partially from the words and affects that Hasina makes visible and available to her. '[T]he story of Hasina's hard life in Dhaka', writes Poon, 'presented in the form of letters written in non-standard English (presumably imitating Bengali), also provides a way of contextualising and relativising Nazneen's experience' (2009:434). Yet, rather than Hasina acting as a 'foil to Nazneen in London' (ibid.) or as a means of Nazneen's 'dialectical engagement' (Duff 2014:111) with society, I would argue that Hasina is another of many connectives or relays in her becoming-vagabond.

Hasina's story is one of many which activate Nazneen's non-atomised subjectivity, a composite of affective forces, or an assemblage that conditions her desires and arranges her mobility within society. Braidotti writes: 'Resonances, harmonies and hues intermingle to paint an altogether different landscape of a self that, not being One, functions as a relay-point for many sets of intensive intersections and encounters with multiple others' (2002:232). From this perspective, Braidotti adds, '"subjectivity" names the process that consists in stringing the reactive and the active instances of power together, under the fictional unity of a grammatical "I"' (2002:75).[6] This theory of becoming thus suggests a range of converging affects ('speeds and slownesses') that shape subject's becoming – not as a unitary, transcendent subject, nor as a dialectical struggle with an other; rather it is a continuous process of developing connections, proximities, and resonances between bodies. This ontology of becoming, of course, derives from Deleuze and Guattari, and helps map out an alternative method for understanding subjectivity that is non-unitary, but always in motion or always in process. For Deleuze and Guattari, writes Jeremy Gilbert, 'becoming is almost never simply a process in itself. Every becoming is a becoming-something: becoming-animal, becoming-child, becoming-woman, and so forth. Becoming always involves a destabilisation of an existent identity and a vector of travel, possibly just a swerve [in other words, an inclination], in the direction of something else' (2008:222). For this reason, it would be a mistake to insist that Nazneen is simply carrying out self-realisation or self-actualisation, and I depart from critics who thus treat *Brick Lane* as a *bildungsroman* representing a universal character type (Valman 2009:3; Perfect 2008:109). Rather, all of her encounters with vagabond intensities, particles, and affects reconstruct her impulse to move beyond atomisation and isolation, and instead enact a becoming-vagabond in and through such connections.

Karim, of course, plays a deeply pivotal role in Nazneen's life, especially in the later parts of the text. Already at this point a mother of two daughters, she has come to develop a keen awareness of her and her children's alienation from Chanu. Furthermore, Chanu's career prospects have severely waned, leaving him instead to seek employment as a taxi driver. Karim's radical political views, along with his sense of confidence act as a source of Nazneen's infatuation and lust for him: 'When Karim could not be still he showed his energy. For a few moments she drifted helplessly on a tide of longing. Her mouth became loose and her eyes unfocused' (Ali 2003:262). The romantic affair with Karim, at first, offers her a respite from the harsh abuses endured with her husband, and the sense of duty with which she is meant to comply. Yet, beyond this, Karim is also another person from whom she accesses her own vagabond intensities. His existence in her life does not remain permanent, as we later discover that he, too, 'reinstates some of the inequities of a traditional marriage [Nazneen] quietly resents' (Poon 2009:431). Nevertheless, his existence affects Nazneen permanently, allowing her to realise and develop her own sense of propriety and power. He is a source of (self-)knowledge, but also a source of energy or speed that mobilises her toward her vagabondage.

A final vagabond encounter arrives toward the very end of the text. Nazneen arrives at a tube station on her way to meet Karim and end their affair. While waiting on the platform, Nazneen is once again taking an inventory of her surroundings – the passersby and sounds that attend to waiting for her train to arrive. At this moment, she is thinking about her conversation with Karim two hours prior: 'Since then, she wanted to knock down walls, banish distance, abolish time, to get to him' (Ali 2003:447). As she is waiting, a woman passes her on the platform: 'A young woman in high-heeled boots and jeans, a denim jacket pegged on her fingers and slung over her shoulder, stalked toward the free bench. Her footsteps rang like declarations" (ibid.:448). Reflecting more on the woman's movement, Nazneen starts to detect a message in the woman's walking: 'Nazneen fell in line behind her. The way the woman walked was fascinating. Nazneen watched her and stepped as she stepped. How much could it say? One step in front of the other. Could it say, *I am this* and *I am not this*? Could a walk tell lies? Could it change you?' (ibid.). After nearly colliding with the woman, and exchanging a polite 'sorry' (ibid.), Nazneen never encounters the woman again. Highlighting this scene tells us, again, the affective orientation and disposition that Nazneen is developing. Nazneen literally follows behind the woman, attempting to follow the rhythm and pattern of her footsteps; to her, the way the woman moves, as if making a declaration, gives her an air of confidence, intrigue, and autonomy. The denim jacket, high-heeled boots, and jeans are indications of a woman who rejects the enforced patriarchal standards of modesty that have dictated Nazneen's entire immigrant life. Much like the tattoo lady and Mrs Azad, the woman on the platform functions as a brief, one-time encounter that nevertheless solidifies her desire and affectation for liberation. The sight of the woman contributes another vagabond 'particle', an imperceptible, but no less significant affect of (im)propriety that adds to Nazneen's subjectivity. Her walking is another active force, assembling Nazneen's maneuverability and wandering rebelliousness. The fascinating quality of the woman's walk is a pedetic, rebellious movement – a rhythmic pattern of defiance that Nazneen wishes to emulate and embody. By walking behind her and following her steps, Nazneen enacts a proximity between herself and the other woman, making them resonate together as wandering vagabonds.

Nazneen's interactions with other vagabond figures and wandering subjects enables her to receive and assemble a sense of self through a continuous becoming, an existence that is not stable but rather always in process. The people who might seem to play the biggest role in her self-liberation, Hasina and Karim, are in fact small parts of a much larger system of affects. Passing through a major city space, where one encounters a large social system of surveillance and cultural contact, imparts new intensities and relational flows that enable Nazneen to discover her position in society and sense of subjectivity. Because of this structure, the people with whom she is most intimate or with whom she relates on a familial level are not the only relay-points through which she creates her becoming-vagabond. Karim and Hasina, but also the tattoo lady, Mrs Azad, and the woman on the tube platform have also been integrated into, and helped activate, Nazneen's becoming-vagabond. These people help make visible and legible her vagabond desire – a desire that Nazneen uses to construct and invent her patterns of movement, and her continuously-changing subjectivity. As such, vagabondage exists only in becoming – not-yet-realised, and as a multiplicity brewing beneath the surface. We can only see it as a 'particle', in these momentary encounters. As an immigrant, and particularly functioning as a vagabond, Nazneen's rejection of propriety, tradition, and obedience have also empowered her to reach beyond her self-contained, isolated, and atomised self. Becoming-vagabond establishes ongoing connections between herself and those whom she encounters, even if those encounters are brief and seemingly unremarkable. Through Nazneen, she and these characters all become more than the sum of their parts. Her existence as a diasporic, immigrant subject is thus never fixed to one particular place, with one particular identity. Rather her subjectivity continues to compound and assemble beyond her home, family, nation, and language, toward those whose wandering and momentary passing calibrate her relation to society. Nazneen, continues to write herself as she writes her surroundings, determining which features to make legible and meaningful to her, and thus inventing, producing, and affirming her selfhood and relational power. As a kinopolitical figure, and as a kinopoetic reading would suggest, Nazneen is inventing the urban space to bend to her desire (not vice versa), to permit her lurch toward becoming-vagabond; and those who wander with her act as relay-points, generating her free, affirmative wandering and rebellion.

Chapter Conclusion

In *Open City* and *Brick Lane*, New York City and London (respectively) function as fast-paced metropolitan spaces that are made legible through the characters' wanderings. The sensations, noises, structures, and people are all written from the vagabond's perspective, thereby inventing a space that has new social relations, hierarchies, and divisions. The restrictions on movement, generated largely through property and other forms of spatial regulation are reactive forces to suppress or contain the vagabond's unpredictable, erratic movement. On the other hand, the vagabond is a figure specific to modernity and industrialisation, emerging out of the expanding patterns of privatisation. Through these novels, the cities' various aspects of financial obligation, regulation, and development dictate the path, speed, and flow of the vagabond's movement. We learn from both characters that wandering and walking are methods for measuring their relation to and power within the city; they can gather information about its various structures, but also overcome the tightly-regulated constraints of professional or domestic life. The urban spaces are therefore made more visible through these wanderings, and the vagabond invents, produces, and redistributes the sensible regime so that imperceptible affects and encounters are made legible. In both novels, the most mundane or innocuous encounters that characters experience nevertheless give meaning to their subjectivities as modern, immigrant subjects. These moments also include the micro-politics of suspicion, whereby they are subject to everyday surveillance, gossip, discrimination, and profiling, from passersby as well as members of their ethnic or immigrant community. Another layer of this is added, since due to their immigrant status, Julius and Nazneen are held to a range of social and cultural expectations by both the local community and those who share their diasporic heritage. It is these cultural forces of propriety and suspicion against which they rebel and from which they wander.

In *Open City*, Julius internalises the glances, sounds, and sensations of New York City, wandering through both its history and its hidden structures of financialisation. Existing as a 'palimpsest' (Cole 2011:59), the city is a canvas on which he rewrites its divisions and hierarchies. His kinopolitical counter-power is to thus produce, create, and reimagine its structures against the rigid confines of his job and the city's own material restrictions on mobility. Careful not to overly anticipate a cosmopolitan or multicultural ideal, the text rather subtly hints that cosmopolitanism may exist as a potential, but never as a reality. Rather, Julius's existence is one that attempts instead to simply rebel against the forces of criminalisation and privatisation. Similarly, he confronts the micro-politics of suspicion, both refusing the discourse of criminality and generalisation, while at the same time challenging the orthodoxies of cultural essentialism and expectations. The text itself relies on vagueness and structural ambiguities to further wander beyond the constraints of narrative reliability. Yet, on the other hand, Julius makes the immigrant's life within the urban setting not only more legible, but also one that is invented and written in his wandering. In *Brick Lane*, Nazneen's walking and escapes through East London are, on the one hand, a form of self-liberation; yet, a deeper function of wandering is, for her, a source of self-realisation and knowledge-gathering. The city's structures produce and are, perhaps paradoxically, produced by the way Nazneen witnesses and observes her surroundings. Her forays down Brick Lane and outside of her estate permanently shift her relationship to her own subjectivity and power; yet, her wanderings bring out and highlight the everyday features that would otherwise go unnoticed. Like Julius, Nazneen writes the city: she creates the meaning out of the passing characters and their movements, affects, and gestures. As a result, her desire integrates and vitalises these affects, acting as relay-points in her becoming-vagabond process. At the same time, she also confronts the forces of power, criminality, and suspicion that restrict her mobility; she in turn uses her observational and creative powers to rebel *against* the regulating patterns of propriety, tradition, custom, debt encumbrance, and domesticity.

Enacting a wandering kinopoetics, both texts make visible the rebellious force against the expansionist ambitions of modernity and urban life depicted in the novels. The vagabond figures invent, produce, and create mobilities that confront and challenge the tightly-regulated spatial arrangements of large metropolitan cities. With these settings, the intensified systems of criminalisation and privatisation play a dominant role in the everyday wanderings and experiences of immigrants. Characters are subject to control and surveillance, and are often taken advantage of for their foreignness and apparent cultural difference. However, by rendering the cityscapes with new lines of identification and alternative modes of coexistence, both Julius and Nazneen use their vagabondage to invent and produce a new mental geography. They are wandering figures whose movement is unpredictable and which cannot be contained within the regimes of surveillance and criminality. Despite all attempts to restrict their mobility (either through profiling, debt encumbrance, or property regulations), these characters demonstrate a capacity to invent their own means of propriety and commit heretical acts. These movements and wandering spatial activities are thus able to make their own affirmative, rebellious counter-power visible and knowable. It is through the vagabond's wandering that we, too, wander into modernity and observe the forces of criminality and surveillance that are everyday occurrences for immigrants, seeing the city as both open and closed.

Notes

1. In many ways, this reference to verisimilitude also reappraises the Realist genre from which the previous chapter departs (see Chapter 3, section headed Magic Realism and the Migrant). Now with an approach toward modernity and industrialisation, the Realist tradition's emphasis on the quotidian and everyday exists as an appropriate genre for wandering kinopoetics.

2. Marx, for his part, analyses this 'bloody legislation' of anti-vagabond laws at length in *Capital* Vol. 1: 'Thus were the agricultural folk first forcibly expropriated from the soil, driven from their homes, turned into vagabonds, and then whipped, branded and tortured by grotesquely terroristic laws into accepting the discipline necessary for the system of wage-labour' ([1867]1990:899).

3. Angela Davis writes: 'We should keep in mind that this was precisely the historical period when the value of labor began to be calculated in terms of time and therefore compensated

in another quantifiable way, by money. The computability of state punishment in terms of time – days, months, years – resonates with the role of labor-time as the basis for computing the value of capitalist commodities. Marxist theorists of punishment have noted that precisely the historical period during which the commodity form arose is the era during which penitentiary sentences emerged as the primary form of punishment' (2003:44).

4. In the original text, Chanu's mocking and imaginary question ('I saw her walking on the street') is written within double quotation marks. To avoid confusion, and since I am citing the framing narrative as well, I have chosen to italicise the inside quote within Chanu's statement.

5. This reference to the city's patterns emerging 'through her' also functions in a metafictional way to convey the novel's internal focalisation, wherein the narrative perspective brings these patterns alive in its 'vision with' (Genette 1988:65) Nazneen.

6. These 'reactive and active instances of power' (a reference to Friedrich Nietzsche) are consistent with the 'relations of speeds and slownesses' referenced throughout this chapter and previous chapters.

CHAPTER 5

STUTTERING KINOPOETICS

Stuttering Language and Migrant Literature

Arrival in a country as a new resident often comes packaged with the need to learn a new language. The difficulties, embarrassments, alienation, and frustration that this can cause is a common experience among immigrants.[1] Yet, immigrants and newcomers often forge their own ways of utilising a second language creatively and playfully. In *Familiar Stranger*, Hall remembers that '[l]anguage-teaching in [his] school consisted of 'ironing out' the broader vernacular traces among the students' speech, a practice [his] parents consistently reenforced' (2017:75). In an attempt to formalise and standardise language-learning, such educational practices were attempting to obliterate any remnants of foreignness that might linger in someone's way of speaking. 'Nevertheless,' he adds, 'all of us spoke a moderated Jamaican patois and used it informally among ourselves' (ibid.). These methods of speaking resulted in 'a vigorous, richly creative, humorous, lively, supple mode of expression which is capable of capturing – as standard English, in any of its received local variants, is not – the emotional inflections, humour and nuance of local life' (ibid.). Deploying these creative modes of expression generate, according to Hall (channelling Kobena Mercer), 'diasporic discursive strategies' – a 'complex "double language"' (ibid. 74) that is well-documented throughout diasporic history (Gates 1988; Brathwaite 1984). Hall is pointing out here a well-understood device utilised in the immigrant and diasporic cultural tradition: the exposure to, use, and rejection of, national languages. Immigrants find that their cultural and social position in the arrival country is one in which they are denied or, even, insulted for their struggles with a new language – especially a language as complex and prone to slippage as English. Having an obvious foreign accent, coupled with difficulties with grammar, syntax, verbiage, and idiomatic phrases, immediately marks someone as an outsider within their new place of residence.

Much like the previous chapter, whereby walking and wandering constitute daily practices of modernity, in this chapter speaking and communicating are of equal importance. Instead of focusing on the vagabond or the nomad, this chapter's emphasis on language will focalise the barbarian as the third, and final, kinopolitical figure. Rather than a figure interpellated within a regime of criminality (the vagabond) or destructiveness (the nomad), the barbarian is perceived within an ideology of inferiority and invasion, derived from the perceived foreignness and contamination of speech. Generally speaking, we find our bearings and orient ourselves in society according to how well we can speak, read and write. Furthermore, of course, language is quite obviously connected with one's cultural identity and subjectivity. As a result of having been exposed to a new language or (as is often the case) having a new language imposed on one's self, immigrants will often have to renegotiate their experience of the world through new languages, but also strategically alter their use of the dominant language (Papastergiadis 1999:127). In some ways, these uses of language are 'strategies of survival and adaptation' (ibid.:128); yet in other ways, '[l]anguage systems emerged in which necessary truths could be expressed and collective aspirations take shape and be spoken' (Hall 2017:75). In other words, for immigrants, their practices within a particular language were strategic mechanisms for thriving and living within a new social setting. Their approach to language creates a liberating and empowering system of meaning. The migrant's new place in a language thus enables them to forge, create, and affirm a new cultural possibility and a new means of collective power.

Writers within the migrant tradition are keenly aware of language's cultural force. As I detail in Chapter 2, there is a long tradition of migration texts that shape and create a poetics of migration. Here we understand poetics in the more conventional sense: that is, it reflects the formal composition of poems, with much attention paid to language and sound. In these cases, poets experiment with code-switching, changing metaphors, and utilising innovative rhythmic conventions – all to convey the complexity of migration, and the myriad linguistic codes and signifiers the migrant navigates. As I will detail below, this consideration of language coincides with the figure of 'the barbarian' whose social motion is largely centrifugal, but who operates as a figure of inferiority and enslavement, based on their foreign speech-patterns.

One's identification with languages is also a theme in migrant literature. To take just one example, in Wang Ping's 2018 poem, 'The Things We Carry On the Sea', she deploys nearly a dozen languages in order to demonstrate the fact that language is an item or tool used to survive as a refugee:

We're orphans of the wars forced upon us
We're refugees of the sea rising from industrial wastes
And we carry our mother tongues
爱(ai), حب (hubb), ליבע (libe), amor, love
平安 (ping'an), سلام (salaam), shalom, paz, peace
希望 (xi'wang), أمل ('amal), hofenung, esperanza, hope, hope, hope
As we drift . . . in our rubber boats . . . from shore . . . to shore . . . to shore. . .

Describing the centrifugal forces of exile and dispossession, the speaker regards 'our mother tongues' as traits akin to life vests or supplies to bring on the 'sea rising'. The flourish of languages that follow, which translate to 'love', 'peace' and 'hope', are deployed as tools for survival; and given the sheer breadth of languages, we are thus aware that these words are utilised for a plurality of migrant subjects, whose voices no doubt can be heard drifting in the 'rubber boats'. The ending line, 'from shore . . . to shore . . . to shore. . .', conveys, on the one hand, a sense of drifting off, as if there is the voice of a traveller farther from the listener in space and distance; yet, on the other, it also reflects a geographical inventory – lands and people one encounters as one travels from shore to shore. This powerful moment provides a broader commentary on migrants and their relationship to language: it is something carried with them as a source of comfort and familiarity, but also something providing the capacity for survival.

As another dimension of kinopoetics, language provides an important consideration and system of meaning within migrant literatures. Yet, in order to properly account for a migrant poetics, I insist that a poetics has to be based on and in movement; it does not just represent movement and migrancy, but it makes (in the sense of *poiesis*) movement at the intensive and affective level. Entering into the discourse on language and form, Deleuze and Guattari have some useful insights for this discussion. In a way that is compatible with Foucault's analysis of discourse – as something invested with and supported through regimes of productive power – for Deleuze and Guattari, language, too, engenders relational, affective power and potential. For Deleuze, '[t]here is a constitutive corporeality of language as forces come from and act on bodies. Thus, language issues forth from the body and exerts pressure on it: it expresses and embodies active forces, bears witness to reactive forces'

(Lecercle 2002:167). This conception of language is consistent within 'Anglo-Saxon pragmatics' and, in particular, shares assumptions with the performative speech-act theories of J. L. Austin. Such a theory carries with it the notion that, 'in our ordinary uses of language, we do not simply convey information, but exert force, we do things with words' (ibid.:165). Such a theory has been taken up most prominently by Judith Butler who has designated performative speech-acts as constitutive regimes of gender identity-formation (Butler 1990) as well as hate speech (Butler 1997).

From such a theory, performative speech-acts, such as a judge laying down a verdict 'that transforms the accused into a convict' entails the relation of 'actions-passions affecting bodies' (Deleuze and Guattari [1987]2014:95). As I have already outlined, the capacity to affect bodies is a function of relational power, the shifts and speeds of which determine one's capacity for freedom and joy, or coercively restrict them into a reactive mode of resentment and disaffection. Moreover, in terms of a political ontology, affect determines the subject's sense of connectedness and autonomy within any given space or regime. Through linguistics and language, we find that speech can just as easily produce speeds and slownesses of affectivity depending on the given assemblage (that is, internal and external arrangements of materiality). For this reason, according to Deleuze and Guattari, '[p]ragmatics is a politics of language', as it constitutes 'incorporeal transformations' capable of 'effectuating immanent acts' (ibid.:96) – that is making manifest certain internal, affective capacities and connections. Language retains a capacity to reorient and recompose the social attributes of a subject by issuing forth affects; it retains a performative capacity that induces an intensive movement at the level of subjectivity.

What concerns this project, however, is how language can produce intensive movement and affects through variations in form or style.[2] For Deleuze and Guattari, however, one way to assure such variation is through 'stammering': 'It's easy to stammer, but making language itself stammer is a different affair; it involves placing all linguistic, and even non-linguistic, elements in variation, both variables of expression and variables of content' (2014:114). What this stammering produces then is a 'mad production of speeds and intervals' (ibid.). For Deleuze, in particular, stuttering and stammering language is the currency of poets, showing what variations they are capable of creating within language. Rather than viewing stammering and stuttering as cognitive deficiencies or speech impediments, they are regarded as a force of creative and experimental power. Jean-Jacques Lecercle explains:

> Stuttering for Deleuze is, therefore an equivalent of poetic language. . . The hero of stuttering, the philosophical characters needed to support the concept, is the exiled poet, who subverts *langue* and aims at the noble form of silence, the silence of the ineffable, as opposed to the mute inglorious silence of stupidity. (2002:234).

This 'silence of the ineffable' describes the poet's force of deterritorialisation, whereby language's signifying capacity breaks down beyond representation. It becomes irreducible and, perhaps even, incomprehensible.[3] The poet brings 'language to this limit' (Deleuze 1997:112) and instead performs variations in sound and syntax.

In a collection of essays devoted to literary analysis, Deleuze writes that a 'great writer' can make

> the language take flight, they send it racing along a witch's line, ceaselessly placing it in a state of disequilibrium, making it bifurcate and vary in each of its terms, following an incessant modulation. This exceeds the possibilities of speech and attains the power of the language, or even of language in its entirety. This means that a great

writer is always like a foreigner in the language in which he expresses himself, even if this is his native tongue. . . He is a foreigner in his own language: he does not mix another language with his own language, he carves out a nonpreexistent foreign language within his own language. He makes the language itself scream, stutter, stammer, or murmur (1997:109–110)

In other words, this stuttering and stammering that a poet is able to perform assures that language de-stabilises 'a system of equilibrium' (ibid.:110), or, rather, the clarity and precision of communication through direct language. This force occurs at the moment when language starts to break down and lose representational fixity. Again, stuttering is partially what Deleuze and Guattari insist is built into Kafka's capacity to minorise language, broadly inventing a new mode of enunciation from within (1986:16–17), and stretching language to its signifying limits through new sounds, metaphors, and syntactical patterns. Combined, then, with pragmatics and the performative structure, stammering thus wills into existence a system of de-stabilisations, vibrations, and disequilibriums that exceed the boundaries of representation. Utilising rhythm, repetition, alliteration, or onomatopoeic sounds, poets can assure that the unsignified is nevertheless experienced in its affective force. Although the structures and sounds used do not comply with the dominant models of language and representation, they are nevertheless expressing in poetry a sensible world that can be read. As a result, 'the silence of the ineffable' (Lecercle 2002:234) becomes nevertheless knowable at the level of affects and intensities, reconstructing the regime of thinkability.

As mentioned above, a useful currency among migrant writers and poets is to playfully experiment with language, especially that which is dominant in the arrival country. Such experimentations enable writers to carve a space within language within which a collective, diasporic identity can identify, or where 'collective aspirations take shape' (Hall 2017:75). Being able to access these singular cultural dynamics can ensure belonging for those who reject the stifling forces of language and grammar, changing, in turn, the regime of what is permissible speech. It expands the boundaries of understanding one's subjectivity. The task then for kinopoetics is to show how this discursive diasporic strategy that Hall locates connects with the stuttering and stammering of language that Deleuze and Guattari describe, thus ensuring that experimentation also produces intensive transformations and affects. Where these two systems of meaning connect is in what I am calling a 'stuttering kinopoetics', the final type of kinopoetics. Here the experimentation with English in the hands of the migrant writer produces an intensive movement, reshaping the regime of what is knowable and thinkable. In their challenge to and de-stabilisation of dominant linguistic forms and grammatical patterns, migrant poets are in turn able to assert a power within the language – a singular force and joy that empowers their sense of belonging. Their stuttering affirms their positive capacity to transform, restructure, and invent language. Linguistic tricks, stutters, and stammers *move* language to a new assemblage of sound, style, convention, and function, thereby transforming the borders and boundaries of the dominant language. As a result, communication is expanded (although not indefinitely) beyond a pre-established regime, making the migrant existence within this language thinkable and knowable. Furthermore, by challenging the hierarchies of standard English grammar, stuttering kinopoetics enacts a 're-distribution of the sensible', making legible forms of language and style that are otherwise excluded (Rancière 2004:89). The systems of power that attempt to police these boundaries of acceptable uses of language also preclude the migrant from affirming their place within a language, further subjecting them to an outsider status. Through a stuttering kinopoetics, the

migrant figure of the barbarian asserts a poetics by intensively invading a language and re-appropriating it to their
own ends.

   In this chapter, the appraisal of a stuttering kinopoetics
will be sought through the poem 'Listen Mr Oxford Don'
(1967) by John Agard and 'New Craas Massakah' (1983)
by Linton Kwesi Johnson. Although these two poems differ
in theme and focus, they share a keen interest in distancing
their poetic utterances from the dominant Englishness of the
time. In Agard's poem, this function of his poetics is more
immediately realised in the poem's content, being as it is a
direct challenge to the restrictive grammatical conventions
of English that are imposed upon immigrants. Thus in both
his form and content, he not only rejects the dominant, ruling linguistic system; he moves, stretches, pushes, and breaks
open the language itself in order to transform and invent a
new linguistic function. The stuttering and stammering of
language, wherein the speaker in the poem insists upon new,
non-preexisting spellings, sounds, and structures, thus produces and invents a de-stabilising force through its variation,
oscillation, and movement. In Johnson's poem, we are taken
to a scene commemorating 'the 1981 death by fire of thirteen
young Afro-Brixtons attending a sixteenth birthday party
in New Cross, near Brixton' (Ramazani 2015:173). This
tragic event poses plenty of significance, not least because
the circumstances of the fire 'led many to suspect a racially
motivated arson attack' (ibid.). In Johnson's reflection on the
poem, he attempts to, on the one hand, 'make sense of the
senseless' (ibid.), while, on the other hand, produce a 'stark
contrast to white Englishness' (ibid.:174). The outcome is
a poem of stylistic inventiveness, bringing the targeted and
restive immigrant community into relation with one another.
The poem ensures a collective expression of outrage and
anger, and stylistically reflects the dancing patterns of the
partygoers and the rage in the riotous aftermath of the fire.

In this case, Johnson brings us to the edge of signification and representation when one lacks sufficient language to conjure up such a horrific tragedy. His rhythmic style acts as a catharsis for the immigrant community. The migrant speaking voice thus invents, transforms, and creates a language with which the community can identify but which actively pushes against the stifling structures of the dominant language.[4] Such a strategy functions even broader as a rejection of authority and a revolt against cultural, imperial power. The pedetic force of a stuttering kinopoetics has a double-punch: firstly, it challenges the assumption that new uses of language are inferior and unworthy of study, since they do not conform to imperial standards of 'proper language'; and, secondly, it more broadly questions the discourse around mastery that lays upon immigrants an expectation of linguistic competence when they enter a new country.

In both poems, I will interpret them stanza-by-stanza, attempting to detail the variations, shifts, vibrations, stammers, and stutters that emerge in the language. How these moments in the poems are performative will also be an object of study: how they not only *represent* something but bring an assemblage or intensity into existence through affective movement. This kinopoetics will supply the final dimension to the creative, inventive capacity of the migrant subject, demonstrating power and force in their utterances and speech-acts. This study of language will thus also coincide with a more traditional meaning of 'poetics', which more often entails an emphasis on linguistic style and form. Yet, what I will add to this discourse is an attentiveness and sensitivity toward language's capacity to *move* and enact affective forces. So, a stuttering kinopoetics does not just represent disequilibriums and instabilities; it creates them. Before proceeding onto the close readings of these poems, I shall now analyse in more detail the migrant figure that carries out this kinopoetics: the barbarian.

Barbaric Dispossession

The barbarian is the next (and final) kinopolitical figure that fits within a counter-history of the migrant. The history of the term 'barbarian' is both fraught and complicated, but it also helps to understand what the barbarian refers to historically. There are two historic groups to which the barbarian retains a connection: the slave and the refugee. 'Only when there is barbarism and slavery', writes Nail, 'can there be the escaped slave who seeks asylum. It is therefore no surprise that we find for the first time in ancient history, among the nested figures of the barbarian (*nitakur, shasu, arad*), the emergence of the figure of the refugee and the practice of asylum' (2015:135). The barbarian figure exists with the emergence of the centralised states of 'Mesopotamia, Egypt, Greece and Rome,' where 'large-scale slavery emerges, but also the right to asylum' (ibid.:135–6). Throughout these various ancient civilisations, the barbarian figure came to designate a disenfranchised subject who needs to be captured, caught, or enslaved. These forces of expulsion and kinopower that capture and depoliticise barbarian culminate in what Nail calls 'centrifugal force':

> This outward and expansive force is made possible by the storage and release of social kinetic force. The great releases of war, public works, taxation, and transportation are all made possible by a central administration that expands outward. Social stratification follows the movement of concentric circles in the form of a social and political hierarchy based on increasingly 'superior' inner circles of the city plan: template, courtyard, inner city, outer city, countryside, and so on. (ibid.: 50)

In other words, the continuous expansion of political power and accumulation required processes of differentiation and hierarchisation. These processes in turn produced a permanently relegated and de-politicised figure, expelled from the franchise and interpellated as inferior (ibid.:52). Political kinopower attempts to construct concentric points of power relative to the political center; and the wider outward it expands, the more it needs to designate those beyond its yoke as inferior and unworthy of political representation. As a result, the barbarian becomes 'the ancient migrant figure defined by the motion of political expulsion'; and, barbarism, 'above all, designates a . . . natural *incapacity for proper speech* and reason that disallows political life' (ibid.: emphasis added). So, as regimes of political power sought their continuous outward expansion, they began to identify the barbarian figure with inferiority, naturalising a hierarchy that justified the barbarian's enslavement and expulsion from political participation. Characteristics of foreignness and speech patterns were identifying traits that allowed the central dominant regime to de-politicise this migrant figure.

The barbarian has figured prominently as an object of interpretation within the domain of critical theory and, in particular, within the Black Marxist and postcolonial tradition. Cedric Robinson, in his book *Black Marxism*, famously and convincingly shows how the barbarian came to be an important figure for European social formation: 'Prior to the eleventh or twelfth centuries, the use of the collective sense of the term 'barbarian' was primarily a function of exclusion rather than a reflection of any significant consolidation among these people' (1983:10). Robinson adds that 'with respect to the emerging European civilisations whose beginnings coincide with the arrival of these same barbarians, slave labour as a critical basis of production would continue without any significant interruption into the twentieth century' (ibid.:11). This thesis forms the basis for Robinson's well-known concept of 'racial capitalism', suggesting the ideological hierarchies and racialised logics upon which capitalism relies for its processes of continuous accumulation and expansion.[5] Crucially, though, Robinson uncovers an ideological link that ties together different historic ages in which slave labour and exploitation have been utilised, since they all in some form relied upon the presumed inferiority of their enslaved subjects. Moreover, such a designation enabled a growing bourgeoisie to consolidate their power and define themselves in opposition to those whom they expel and de-politicise. Throughout history, then, even if the word barbarian falls out of favour, the racialised logic to which the barbarian adhered largely persisted in all regimes whereby enslaved labour formed the basis of production. In a similar vein, in Ania Loomba's historical analysis of colonial power, she locates the relationship to racial stereotyping in colonialism to a much earlier history: '[R]acial stereotyping is not the product of modern colonialism alone, but goes back to the Greek and Roman periods which provide some abiding templates for subsequent European images of 'barbarians' and outsiders' (1998:105). Loomba reminds readers of the long-standing pattern of identifying foreignness with inferiority and stereotypes of aggression, greed, and sexual promiscuity (ibid.:106–7) – all of which provide useful racialised discourse for colonial expansion. Such signifiers and stereotypes persisted from the ancient civilisations well up into the present, although the names for the figures shifted. Broadly, though, both Robinson and Loomba agree that the barbarian stands as the figure of foreignness and inferiority upon which these historic processes of expulsion and dispossession rely. The barbarian figure casts a long shadow over centuries of racialisation, colonisation, and dispossession which have shaped the global system of power.

To return to the historic figure of the barbarian there is another aspect to consider: the connection to language. Loomba and Robinson are correct to identify the political character of the barbarian; but the history of this figure should always include the linguistic dimension. 'The Greek word βάρβαρος, *barbaros*', writes Nail, 'originates from the onomatopoeic sound of the babbling of the foreigner who does not speak Greek. Thus, the determination of the 'nature' of the barbarian is already relative to a geographic and political centre, in this case the Greek polis' (2015:53). Those who held the levers of centralised power in the Greek *polis* used this determination of political inferiority to deprive the barbarian figure of political participation and activity. Their linguistic capacities, according to the political authorities, made it so that they were incapable of proper reasoning necessary for democratic representation (ibid.). Connecting foreign speech patterns with a lack of reasoning skills persists in many domains of politics today, especially within right-wing and reactionary government policies that restrict the franchise to those competent enough in the national language. In the ancient world, these foreign 'babbling' or 'stuttering' linguistic traits marked the barbarians' difference from, and inferiority to, the dominant citizenry; and it is under this basis that barbarism is, even today, treated conceptually in a dialectical opposition to 'civilisation'. Furthermore, these observations of foreignness in speech patterns fail to consider the liberatory force that creative stutterings enable, as I outlined in the first section. Instead, the linguistic markings of a foreigner – in the way they speak or pronounce words – often affects how the immigrant subject is perceived in terms of cognitive, rational, or deliberative capacities.

Another facet of the barbarian involves the relation to two historic figures, the slave and refugee. These figures are related in that their de-politicisation has left them in a position of needing to seek refuge and escape the yoke of political violence or coercive and forced labour. Crucially, though, the barbarian's assumed inferiority in relation to the Greek *polis* explains their status as 'naturally' incapable of anything other than enslavement, according to, for example, Aristotle (Nail 2015:52). To put this another way, the term barbarian contains two interrelated meanings: first, a foreignness based on their *incomprehensible*, babbling speech patterns; and, second, one who is a 'slave by nature' (ibid.:135). In both of these definitions, there is an interconnected system of displacement, both internal and external. The internal one subjects a person to forced labour that was required in order to continuously expand public works projects. Their labour is appropriated by and integrated into the state's concentrated power. The external displacement pulls in prisoner slaves who were often taken by military force and who, in turn, are conscripted into military service; that is, a centrifugal force 'was deployed to the periphery to capture barbarians', who were 'then sent out to gather even more slaves or to conquer more territory for the ruler' (ibid.:57–8). In either case, as a migrant figure, the barbarian's (counter-)history is one developed through their presumed political inferiority – an inferiority that leads to their capture and enslavement, and that becomes audible in their stammering.

There is a further connection to enslavement and stammering language that Nail does not acknowledge, and it is one connected to the barbarian's expression of mobility and movement: the slave song and dance. This perspective takes me back to Stuart Hall. In the same context in which he explains the use of *creolised* Jamaican English as an immigrant, Hall describes his intellectual awakening from learning about a slave song and dance tradition. Because of the detail it displays, I shall quote his reflections in full:

> Later in my intellectual life there was one aspect of [slavery] in particular to which I found myself returning. At special times of the year the slaveholders permitted the enslaved occasions when they were allowed to dance, sing, dress up and celebrate – for all the world as if they were free. Slaves embraced these pantomime moments to act out, or rehearse, the dream of freedom to which they remained tenaciously wedded. The celebrations acquired something of what Bakhtin identified as the carnivalesque anticipation, in masquerade, of the day

when the world would be turned upside down and slaves set free from bondage. Threaded through these festivals of artfully concealed mimicry were the manifest ridicule and contempt with which the enslaved – out of earshot, but *'speaking' through distorted codes of masquerade* – regarded those above them. They signified through indirection what they actually thought of the customs, antics, dress, manners, habits and pretentions of their masters and mistresses. (Hall 2017:73; emphasis added)

Although the enslaved people were likely aware that these permitted occasions were used by slaveholders as a means of humiliation and amusement, they nevertheless embraced the opportunity to indirectly, yet effectively, mock their masters. This opportunity granted slaves a chance for resistance and power, where they could 'speak' in 'distorted codes' that masked their true contempt for their abusers, but also granted the collective a chance to express their aspirations for freedom. Hall identifies with these practices in shaping how he sees the immigrants' relation to *creolised* language that I outline in the beginning of this chapter – where artful uses of language brought people together in their collective yearnings for emancipation. In the case of slaves, they 'were customarily forbidden to speak their own languages for fear that this would facilitate collective forms of resistance' (ibid.). Still in a position of political inferiority in relation to their European masters, however, Hall adds: '[E]nslaved Africans were also required to understand English enough to obey orders and to service their masters and mistresses' (ibid.:75). The opportunity to sing and dance, distorting their tones and gestures in creative, playful ways were but small moments of resistance and force to which their sense of collectivity could adhere. These were glimpses and moments that offered a challenge to political hierarchy, redistributing the sensible order of inclusion and exclusion.

In slave narratives and slave fiction, there are references to and depictions of slave songs and dance, presenting these similar opportunities of resistance. In Toni Morrison's classic novel, *Beloved*, we have references to the ways in which songs and dances are used among enslaved people. The novel is a Magic Realist text depicting the traumas of enslavement as they are embodied and remembered in the life of an escaped slave, Sethe Suggs.[6] Paul D, a former slave who had previously been held at the same plantation (called 'Sweet Home') that held Sethe and her family, arrives at Sethe's house. This house, 124, is where she has been living since her escape and has been hiding since her daughter, Beloved's, death. Paul D arrives to first banish Beloved's ghost that makes the house 'spiteful' (Morrison 1987:1); and he then later forms a romantic relationship with Sethe. Initially, his role in the house takes on a caregiving role in order to minimise the tensions arising from within a space that had been previously haunted. Later, however, out of jealous rage, Denver and a revived Beloved force him to leave the house permanently, allowing them to keep Sethe's affections for themselves.

Throughout the novel, we have Paul D reflecting and reminiscing upon his enslavement. Paul D thinks about how music played a role in guiding his movement and enabling him to endure the unbearable torture. These were songs 'where yearning fashioned every note' (Morrison 1987:48). He reflects: 'Some old pieces of song he'd learned on the prison farm or in the War afterward... The songs he knew from Georgia were flat-headed nails for pounding and pounding and pounding' (ibid.). In other words, songs provided a rhythmic sound that he could affectively associate with the cruelty of forced labour. During his time at Sweet Home, songs coincided with the 'pounding' sound of manual labour; they were 'loud songs' (ibid.:48) with 'too much power' (ibid.). They fit the life that he was having to live under his captivity, but they did not fit the world that he lives in now – one of refuge. Songs, then, for Paul D matched the circumstances of abuse and toil to which he was subjected as a slave, and offered for him a brief respite from his surroundings. The music helps him externalise his rage upon the abuse happening to and around him, while internally he can escape and preserve his sense of self. In this context, the slave song adds a means for escape, using language, sound and rhythmic patterns to avoid losing what is left of himself.

In addition to songs, many of the characters in *Beloved*, who were either forced into slavery or had narrowly escaped it, also use dance as a means of radical self-creation. This form of artistic expression is mostly clearly illustrated in the character Baby Suggs, the mother-in-law of Sethe Suggs, whose son purchased her freedom, and whose sermons and spiritual practices arguably liberate an entire community of formerly enslaved people. She arrives at what is described in the novel as The Clearing, 'where Baby Suggs danced at sunlight' (Morrison 1987:101), and gathers strangers into a ritual of self-acceptance and empowerment:

> It started that way: laughing children, dancing men, cry-ing women and then it got mixed up. Women stopped cry-ing and danced; men sat down and cried; children danced, women laughed, children cried until, exhausted and riven, all and each lay about The Clearing damp and gasping for breath. In the silence that followed, Baby Suggs, holy, offered up to them her big heart. . . She told them the only grace they could have was the grace they could imagine. That if they could not see it, they would not have it.
>
> 'Here,' she said, 'in this here place, we flesh; flesh that weeps, laughs; flesh that dances on bare feet in grass. Love it. Love it hard.' (ibid.: 103)

Such a scene offers up to us a powerful instance of collective joy and love. It also, furthermore, presents a multi-layered force of resistance against the coercive power of enslavement, where the people are not allowed to 'love' their own 'flesh'. In their trance-like dances, too, the people in The Clearing dispel the bodily coercion and capture of enslavement, and instead express a freedom, a counter-force against the political regimes that enforce and determine their inferior status. In a manner compatible with what Hall describes as dancing 'for all the world as if they were free', Baby Suggs and her followers at The Clearing, too, carry out a performance of their own power and freedom, over and against the dominant powers of subjugation and abuse. Through dance and through song, therefore, the slave characters in *Beloved* produce rhythmic patterns in their feet and in their voices, further structuring a new, creative language of power that challenges both the disciplined labour to which their feet and arms must move, and the enforced speech (in other words, either silence or speaking the master's language) that derives from their enslaved status. Characters like Paul D and Baby Suggs destabilise the capturing and silencing effects of their dispossession and depoliticisation – regimes which treat them as inferior barbarians, incapable of reasoning and therefore only worthy of forced labour. Instead, they use song and dance to produce their own assemblage of affective, relational power.

This discussion of song and dance leads me to what Nail describes as the barbarian's pedetic force: 'the refuge' (2015:135) and 'the revolt' (ibid.:136). The first one of these, 'refuge (asylum)', however, 'is a kinetic strategy for diffusing the pressure of revolt . . . and is thus ultimately in the service of political power. The slave flees one master in favour of another in the refuge (the temple master, or god)' (ibid.). For Nail, the slave revolt presents the real radical form of counter-power:

> The slave revolt, unlike the refuge, posed a real threat to political kinopower in the ancient world. While not the only form of counterpower, it was by far the most frequent and statistically significant, since most of the lower classes were slaves or non-citizens. While the nomad could simply retreat to the mountains and deserts, the barbarians were relentlessly pursued and captured by a farther-reaching centrifugal

force. The fact that the barbarian migrant is captured and
enslaved by a centrally directed political force thus changes
the coordinates of kinopolitical domination from one of ater-
ritorial abandonment to apolitical disenfranchisement. . .
[T]he apolitical barbarian is disenfranchised by a centrifugal
force that captures it, so the barbarian tries to reflee (as a
refugee) or return home (revolt). . . Accordingly, the origins
of revolt are in barbarian counterpower (2015:136–7)

It is in the revolt or escape from capture that the barbarian migrant figures pose the biggest threat to the political
kinopower and centrifugal force. Escaping their captors and
thus returning home, they find themselves beyond the reach
of the dominant centre of politics that would have them kept
as labourers and prisoners, and in whose ideology they are
seen as inferior. Finding their own homes, they 'live among
flows that are too hard to capture' (ibid.:137) and also carry
out a 'social disturbance that spreads throughout society'
(ibid.:139). As a form of political kinopower, therefore, the
barbarian slave revolt disturbs and circumvents the reach of
political capture and dispossession. While the political centre
expands outward using centrifugal force, the revolt, in turn,
acts as a bulwark against those forces. The centre thus loses
its source of free labour.

The barbarian slave revolt, as Nail characterises it, is a
physical escape from the boundaries and structures of political kinopower. It is an extensive movement that seeks refuge
in areas outside of political reach. What I would like to suggest, though, is that the stuttering vocal patterns that *also*
characterise the barbarian are a revolt of a different sort, an
escape from the grip or yoke of comprehension and representation (Derrida 2002:362). Using shifting tones, rhythms,
vibrations and onomatopoeic sounds, the barbarian can also
produce their own language that exceeds the reach of the
dominant cultural power. In the following, I will therefore
expand this idea that the stuttering kinopoetics enacted in

the poems below perform their own form of revolt: a revolt that oscillates, zig-zags, and vibrates in a manner that is unable to be captured by the models of proper grammar and linguistic convention. The speakers in these poems thus use a language that matches a barbarian counterpower, revolting against the systematic domination of imperial language, and instead enables them to distance themselves even further from the political center. Yet, far from these techniques rendering the speakers inferior and incapable of reasoning, stuttering language provides for them a means of counterpower and liberation. Like their movement, which is 'the result of a multiplicity of non-centric micro-movements and collisions at varying velocities within certain constraints,' (Nail 2015:142), the language also relies on a multiplicity of discrete and repetitive sounds, rhythms, and vibrations. It produces, after all, '[l]anguage systems . . . in which necessary truths could be expressed and collective aspirations take shape and be spoken' (Hall 2017:75). The stuttering language, song, and dance are all combined into the stuttering poetics in direct and indirect ways, producing sounds and rhythms that are defiant, joyful and creative. Such an approach then presents the kinopoetics that can perform an affective revolt – a vibrating, sonorous outcry – against political kinopower. With these strategies, the barbarian dances, sings, stutters and stammers their way to liberation.

'Listen Mr Oxford Don': Stuttering the Queen's English

Agard's 'Listen Mr Oxford Don' is included in his 1980 collection, titled *Mangoes and Bullets*. The period in which it is released constitutes a pivotal moment for British racial politics and the national relationship to language education. 'The fraught language politics of the period,' writes Rachael Gilmour, 'particularly around issues of race and class, established language as a privileged locus of resistance,

and individual and collective self-determination' (2014:345).
Gilmour explains:

> In black British politics, such a focus on language had
> been emergent since the founding of the Black Education
> Movement in the 1960s. By the 1970s and 1980s, and
> in contexts of deepening crisis in British race relations,
> wider struggles over race and representation were played
> out through strategic deployments and interpretations of
> creole languages. . . Arguments about assimilation, authen-
> ticity, and cultural legitimacy, meanwhile, were often routed
> through language. (ibid.)

In this particular context, language and education were
fraught cultural battlefields through which discursive struggles over race and power were fought. Some contemporary
British politicians and conservative pedagogues were keen
to reject the legitimacy of vernacular language forms. They
saw them as 'lacking in expressive precision, abstraction, and
complexity' (ibid.), on the one hand, and as promoting 'social
divisiveness, aggression and even criminality' (Honey qtd in
Gilmour 2014:346), on the other. These attitudes solidified
creolised languages as a threat to the dominant regime of English language education. Because of this conservative social
and political campaign to de-value vernacular language forms
– forms perceived as stylistically and grammatically inferior –
'black British poetry emerges as an important mode of contestation in the 1970s and 1980s' (Gilmour 2014:346), giving
an opportunity to revolt against the dominant prescriptions of
language. Agard and Johnson's poems, being solidly in this tradition, stand as valuable studies within this tradition.

   This wave of poetic experimentation provides a meaningful
backdrop to the poem. For many other poets, especially those
from the Caribbean, poetry 'works to challenge monolithic
notions of British culture, language, and national belonging' (Gilmour 2014:345). As mentioned above, with respect

to Stuart Hall, these active experimentations with language helped shape a collective engagement with and aspiration toward new possibilities of identity-formation and expression. 'Important to many of the poets' of the late 1970s and 1980s is 'experimentation with vernacular and creole language forms; and a concomitant emphasis on orality, voice, and sound, as reflected in emerging forms like dub poetry' (ibid.). These linguistic forms and techniques shape a unique and, at the same time, collective experience that continuously confronts the systems of language competence and aptitude within immigration enforcement systems. They assert, claim, or, even, demand legitimacy within an otherwise stifling and racist context. Gilmour writes on the poets' capacity to pose challenges to this social regime:

> The use of creoles served as one potential such marker of communal identity and engagement, and at the same time served purposes of legitimation, in a prevailing climate of language activism pitted against linguistic racism. Poets' deployment of creole forms also asserted them as languages of Britain, appropriate to the expression of new experiences of British exclusion and belonging; challenging the sovereignty of British English synchronically, in maintaining transnational connections to the Caribbean, and diachronically, in language that in its very existence memorialises histories of empire. (2014:346)

It is therefore these historical and systemic challenges that provide the context for Agard's poem. Agard 'playfully represents his use of West Indian creole as political rebellion by linguistic means' (Ramazani 2001:14). His linguistic experimentation, particularly within the context of rhythm, syntax, rhyme and grammar, stutter and stammer away from the capture of the hegemonic system; yet, they also demand his legitimacy in a system that would rather treat the speaker's language as inferior and unworthy of recognition.

The poem thus begins with lines that, in both form and content, distinguish the speaker as an immigrant in opposition to the 'Oxford don':

> Me not no Oxford don
> me a simple immigrant
> from Clapham Common
> I didn't graduate
> I immigrate (Agard 1967)

The first three words, 'Me not no', at first glance convey a confusion about grammar and proper logical consistency. Generally, such turns of phrase are meant to mark the speaker as a foreigner whose exposure to language is minimal at best. Using the accusative form 'Me' signals the racist trope of 'jungle talk' that one associates with non-Western cultures or 'primitive' societies. Following with 'not no' has a double negative logic, but is also characteristic of vernacular languages more broadly – emphatically rejecting the accusation of being an 'Oxford don', or humbly asking for their listener's patience. In terms of rhythmic patterns, the first line follows an iambic trimeter (although this meter does not carry through the whole stanza), and the non-resonant m- and n-sounds in 'Me', 'not', 'no', and 'don', alongside the d-sounds at the end of 'Oxford' and beginning of 'don', all produce a rhythmic, almost dancelike pattern. These repeated sounds also can convey a hesitation or linguistic defect, as the speaker either has an impediment or is simply confused. However, read kinopoetically, they are producing a stuttering in the words, making the words stammer from within by deliberately and circuitously avoiding the standards of English grammar. 'Me', 'not', and 'no', followed in that order do not communicate the immediate meaning as fluidly and directly as 'I'm not'; but the creative stammer invented in this pattern suggests a challenge against an 'Oxford don' who would likely demand proper verbiage and more precise structure. Embodying a 'simple immigrant' (again preceded by the simple 'me') shows once again ironic humility of the speaker, begging for the mercy of their listeners, based on the obvious stammering of the language. 'Clapham Common', refers to the deep air raid shelters where several Caribbean immigrants of the Windrush Generation temporarily resided after World War II. Yet, the repeated c-sound, again, creates a rhythmic pattern (also demonstrated in the word 'Clap' at the beginning of 'Clapham') that stages onomatopoeic clicking sounds, back to back. These repetitions create another stutter that is clearly deliberate, but also parallels the repeated alliterations in the first line. In both cases, the stammer does not mean a linguistic defect, but a creative experimentation with sound that stretches and modifies the normal structural patterns of English, moving the language to step and dance through sound and rhythm.

The final two lines of the stanza, 'I didn't graduate/I immigrate' have a double irony. They first depart from the grammatical slippage of the first two lines, indicating that the speaker does after all recognise the proper use of nominative pronouns. Yet, the tenses change between these two lines, one being a past that did not happen (graduating) with a past that did (immigrate). Yet, the final line, 'I immigrate' has us thinking it is an improper use of the past tense. However, rather than seeing this as an error in tense, we can see it instead as the speaker showing that they 'immigrate' continuously and permanently. Immigration is part of their continuous present, something they do rather than did or did not do. Their movement is ongoing, never commencing (as one does when they graduate), and this continuous repetition is sonically conveyed in the rhyming '–ate' (graduate and immigrate) sound that ties together this couplet. So, not only does the present-tense in 'immigrate' signal a continuous present; the sound, too, takes a past that 'didn't' happen (because the speaker did not graduate) that collapses into a present (the speaker immigrates), making the sound carry itself onward in a flowing and circulating continuation of sound and stuttering.

The interlocutor, this imagined 'Mr Oxford don' whom the speaker sees as a dominating and oppressive force, from whom one perhaps seeks approval for their linguistic capacities, is now warned of the speaker's continuous movement and refuge:

> But listen Mr Oxford don
> I'm a man on de run
> and a man on de run
> is a dangerous one (Agard 1967)

The repeated lines 'man on de run' and 'dangerous one' all signal a slant rhyme to the 'Oxford don'; on all four lines, the ending consonant sound, interspersed with hard d-sounds ('Oxford', 'don', and 'de') all produce movement sounds and dancing rhythms that parallel the trajectory of the 'man on de run'. A 'man on de run' similarly indicates a figure whose escape is worrisome and unsettling – traits characteristic of the barbarian migrant whose propensity for revolt and apparent inferiority is cause for political kinopower's expansion. In the case of language, the two middle lines indicate a refrain that connects and makes clear the 'dangerous' manner of the speaker. Anyone who is on the run is likely to steal, escape from the grips of servitude, or stage a collective revolt against their owners. In this case, the speaker is not only on the run in a physical or extensive sense; they run, too, from the grip and power of the Oxford don imposing on them a linguistic system of grammar. The words themselves take flight, running into and then out of the boundaries of proper English; the words take momentary solace in the proper standards of English, only to escape them again by replacing 'the' with 'de'. Such a back-and-forth movement, in and out of the domain or national home of English grammar, carries through the entire poem.

The next two stanzas present the speaker's emphatic challenge to 'de Queen's English' and his attempts to disarm the fearful attitudes of conservative English listeners:

> I ent have no gun
> I ent have no knife
> But mugging de Queen's English
> Is story of my life
>
> I don't need no axe
> to split/ up yu syntax
> I don't need no hammer
> to mash/ up yu grammar (Agard 1967)

The coupling of 'I ent have no gun/I ent have no knife' suggests once more a double negative logic through 'ent' ('ain't') and 'no', leaving listeners unsure about whether to trust the speaker, or figuring their creolising language to be lacking in clarity and precision. Again, though, the repeated motif 'I ent have no. . .' is a song-like repetition, memorable and easy-to-follow, creating a chorus-like refrain as one would in a pop song.[7] 'Mugging de Queen's English', however, appropriates the language of 'mugging' built into English social imaginary and anxiety are around race that Hall et al. document (Hall, Critcher and Jefferson [1978] 2013:321–389; see also Gilmore 2014:349). The speaker is not guilty of wielding deadly weapons, as many within British society assumed immigrants to be doing; but rather his only crime and assault is against 'de Queen's English'; and this activity is 'story' of their 'life'. The meter of the couplet, 'But mugging de Queen's English/ Is story of my life' keeps a consistent iambic pentameter that adds more 'feet' to the previous two lines of trochaic trimeter ('I ent have no gun/I ent have no knife'). The stamping sounds of the extra metric stresses also parallel the 'mugging' that is committed against the Queen's English, that require none of

the weaponry of a 'gun' or 'knife' but which does, nevertheless, 'mug' the Queen's English. 'Mug', too, in British slang has
another meaning, referring to someone who is easily fooled
or easy to take advantage of; that the speaker is 'mugging'
the Queen's English suggests that he is reducing or minimising
its high social capital. The removal of 'the' or its replacement
with 'de' change the claim to ownership and exclusiveness that
is associated with proper grammatical convention – conventions that are surely authorised in the British cultural empire,
but now belong to no one. In both cases, it obliterates the
definitude of both the story and the Queen's English, making
the language neither the property of the Queen, nor something
that has claim to the speaker's 'life'.

In a metapoetic gesture, then, the speaker seizes language
on his own terms, resisting the Queen's claim to ownership
and instead claiming it (and their mugging of it) for their
own story. Without weapons, neither a gun, a knife, 'axe', or
'hammer', the speaker can nevertheless 'split/up yu syntax'.
The violent imagery of both 'mugging', 'split[ting] up', and
'mash[ing] up' have each, for the first time in the poem, the
traits of a violent revolt against a master language. Mugging,
smashing, or mashing a language from within generates a
rage-filled challenge to and confrontation with grammar and
syntax imposed upon immigrants and subjects more generally; in turn, going against these conventions de-stabilises
any group's power to secure hierarchies of domination
and inferiority. At the same time, and at the formal level, the
logics, spelling, and punctuation each collectively stammer
and stutter the words and make visible the ineffable joy felt
in inventing new uses of language and speech. Not needing
a hammer, knife, gun or axe, the speaker is empowered
nevertheless to use writing as a weapon against linguistic
convention and the ideology of language mastery.

Attentive again to the fact that the Oxford don likely
upholds the same panic-stricken attitude toward immigrants

and their creolised language, the speaker presents a sardonic
warning to his listener. The next two stanzas, thus, reveal
his dangerous tendencies that come not only from being 'on
de run' as we read above, but also for the supposed assaults
committed against language:

> I warning you Mr Oxford don
> I'm a wanted man
> And a wanted man
> Is a dangerous one
>
> Dem accuse me of assault
> On de Oxford dictionary/
> Imagine a concise peaceful man like me/
> Dem want me to serve time
> For inciting rhyme to riot
> But I tekking it quiet
> Down here in Clapham Common (Agard 1967)

Once again, we have 'a dangerous man', not just one 'on de
run', but one 'wanted'. Both being 'on the run' and 'being
wanted' imply a fugitive. The word 'fugitive' and 'refugee' share
an etymological root (Latin word *fugere*), and in both cases
they are escaping from conditions of either state and political
capture, or state and political violence. The former implies a
criminality, but has also been used to apply to fugitive slaves
who have, through escape, revolted against their masters. The
Oxford don here appears more and more to coincide with a
dominating or coercive master over the speaker, indicating
that the speaker knows himself to not only be 'wanted' in the
sense of a law, but also 'wanted' as a form of enslaved property. Similar to the second stanza in the poem, here again there
are repetitive sounds at the end of each line, landing on the
letter 'n'. The motif 'I'm a wanted. . .' and 'And a wanted. . .'
acts as a continuous reminder of the speaker's characteristics,
and their pedetic force being both a fugitive on the run and a

fugitive from the law. Instead of begging the Oxford don to 'listen' the speaker is warning him: act with more caution and be sure to look upon the assaults on language with anxiety and fear. The speaker knows himself to be accused 'of assault/ On de Oxford dictionary': such is the crime that has sent him 'on the run' as a 'wanted man'.

The speaker is a 'concise peaceful man' but is nevertheless compelled to 'serve time'. 'Concise' and 'peaceful' are not typically words that go together – the former rarely describes someone's demeanour, and the latter seems out of place in describing linguistic aptitude. One is hardly ever a 'peaceful' speaker, and we are not inclined to describe someone's composure as 'concise'. Nevertheless, the speaker is aware that his linguistic 'assaults' on the Oxford dictionary – a dictionary meant to index a complete record of the English language – affectively resonate with his physical demeanour and disposition. His manner of speaking, whether 'concise' or 'long-winded', are attached to how he is perceived on a spectrum between 'peaceful' and 'violent'. So, in his case, it is important to align both his linguistic capacities with his apparent behavioural tendencies, insisting that he is 'peaceful' in his actions and 'concise' in his speech. Furthermore, these terms confirm how the speaker sees the performativity of his own utterances: speech patterns and grammatical (mis)uses create social attributes for the speaker and effects upon the listener, much in the same way that one's physical and affective movements can create specific outcomes in a social situation. Not being peaceful nor concise are both qualities that make listeners ill at ease; and the speaker is ironically gesturing to this social attitude, both of which are rooted in racist perceptions of immigrants. He is meant to 'serve time' for 'inciting rhyme to riot/But I tekking it quiet', inserting his poetic power over rhyme and words. Rhyme riots in a chaotic, disorderly way – it breaks through normative structures in the form of slant rhymes and near rhymes. Specifically, as Gilmour outlines,

[c]reolisation is not incidental, but material, to the poem's functioning at the levels of rhythm and rhyme. The end-rhymes of 'graduate'/'immigrate', 'riot'/'quiet' depend on the basilectal lack of grammatical marking (instead of standard English 'immigrated' and 'quietly'), demonstrating not just how rhyme may be provoked to linguistic 'riot', but how linguistic 'riot' may be crucial to rhyme'. They also reveal the phonological and morphological flexibility of a creole continuum (2014:348).

Causing the rhyme to riot parallels the message in the title, confronting the Mr Oxford Don to listen to the 'language of the unheard', to use Martin Luther King Jr's famous (1967) definition of a riot. The rhyme has to stutter and stammer; it has to dance, march, or run, and may sometimes cause damage (by 'assault[ing] the Oxford dictionary' or 'mugging de Queen's English'). These are necessary expressions of barbarian revolt and escape from the forces of enslavement; and they escape, in this case, the constraints of language that confine the speaker to the requirements of mastery and competence. These requirements contribute to the illicit normative privileging of standard language and thus reducing the creative potential, speed, mobility and affectivity of immigrants. Deliberately making language stutter, however, the speaker demands their escape and the joyful invention of a new collectivity and relational power.

Contrasting with the refrain from stanza four ('I warning you Mr Oxford don/I'm a wanted man'), the speaker now shifts to easing his listener's fears, and then demanding freedom from a 'jail sentence' on the basis of 'self-defence':

I'm not a violent man Mr Oxford don
I only armed wit mih human breath
but human breath
is a dangerous weapon

So mek dem send one big word after me
I ent serving no jail sentence
I slashing suffix in self-defence
I bashing future wit present tense
And if necessary

I making de Queen's English accessory/to my offence
(Agard 1967)

Not being a 'violent man' but nevertheless armed 'wit mih
human breath' highlights the premium the speaker places
on vocal sounds and their ability to performatively produce
new social attributes for both himself as well as the Oxford
don. Gilmour notes how combining 'wit' and 'breath' on the
same lines signals that the 'th'-sound in 'breath' is meant to
be more prominent: 'Agard uses the acrolectal or Standard
English pronunciation of 'breath', with its final fricative;
switching from the meso- or basilectal 'wit', which precedes
it in in the same line' (2014:348; emphasis in the original).
There are plenty of occasions in which the speaker switches
back and forth between Standard English and creole phonology. Rapidly moving from 'wit' to 'breath' in the same line
is one such change. 'This code-switching', Gilmour adds,
'flaunts a creole phonological flexibility that is exploitable
for poetic effect' (ibid.). I would take Gilmour's thesis a step
further. These phonemes (such as the change between 't' and
'th') are flexible and useful tricks to bend sound and push
out flows of air-waves.

As one stutters, we linger over phonetic sounds and con-
sonants, grasping for the word we are trying to articulate. As
a poetic quality, it is a deliberate vibration and repetition of
sounds, much like the onomatopoeic sounds the barbarians
were thought to be making in their foreign speech. It asserts
a foreignness whereby their language marks them as inferior
to the dominant group. Yet, in this case, the speaker claims

foregnness in a way that is celebratory, affirmative, and positive. Using breath to then shift to an aspirated phonological sound (from 't' to 'th') is a 'dangerous weapon', even if the speaker is not a 'violent man'. After all, the breath is escaping the speaker's mouth, rapidly, in order to produce the necessary fricative consonant for the word 'breath' to mark its difference from 'wit'. It passes through the teeth, causing a vibration of the jowls and lips, and pushes out air molecules, saliva, and lingering dust particles in front of the speaker's mouth. Moving from a 't' sound to a 'th' sound, then, supplies the power of breath to produce, invent, and create aspirated movement at the physical and sonic level. It causes a rupture, producing affects and intensive movements, whereby creole phonology and linguistic difference is made visible and thinkable. The move from standard English phonology to creole phonology causes breath to escape in a chaotic motion that is unpredictable and even inconsistent. Such disorderly use of language threatens and challenges conventional English morphology and phonology as it, at the same time, creates new rhythms and sonic patterns. Urging his listener to 'mek dem send one big word after me', he is enticing or taunting the Oxford don; and he issues this pronouncement in anapaestic trimeter, rendered with three back-to-back sequences of two short accents followed by a long stress. Such a meter enables a degree of internal complexity in the line, and in this one opens up room for ambiguity. The speaker could either be asking for a message to be sent after him, or asking that they attempt to capture him within a regime of criminalisation. In either case, the meter resembles a kind of preacherly flourish, made in protest or as a testimony at a criminal trial.

This provocation then bleeds into the final lines of the stanza. From here the speaker offers a statement of resistance and defiance: 'I ent serving no jail sentence/I slashing suffix in self-defence/I bashing future wit present tense' (Agard 1967). Because his act was taken in 'self-defense', as a means of protecting himself from cruelty, enslavement, or control, the speaker will serve no jail sentence. He will not allow the enslavement, interpellation, or enforcement of grammar that would rather have him stifled, stigmatised, ostracised, or rejected because of his syntax or pronunciation. A play on the word 'sentence' is quite obvious here. The speaker is suggesting that the typical, proper, and grammatical structure of sentence resembles the intensive confines of a jail. As such, this structure confines his speech to specified, pre-ordained parameters. Furthermore, there is also a figurative jail sentence that conservative English society would force him into, out of their hostility toward his language. He does not 'serve' that kind of sentence, as he is not enslaved by master's language or the master's sentence, nor would he serve criminal time as punishment for any supposed crimes. 'Slashing suffix in self-defence' and 'bashing future wit present tense', the speaker cuts words short as a form of protection, and shifts the temporalities of future with present tense (referring back to the first stanza: 'I didn't graduate/I immigrate'). 'Tense', 'self-defence', and 'sentence' all combine in a rhyme scheme that indicates a stuttering repetition – a pattern of consistence and rhythm – but also brings these ideas into relation with one another: the use of tense as a self-defence against the sentence. The speaker finally ends on a veiled threat: 'if necessary/I making de Queen's English accessory/to my offence' (Agard 1967). The speaker can take the Queen's English and render it equally culpable for his 'offence', making it an accomplice or co-conspirator, enabling his misdeed. The play on the word 'accessory' also suggests an ornament that he can wear and display. He can use the Queen's English as a form of decoration to provide him the power of 'offence', or for the sake of offending his listeners. Here it is a defiant ending to suggest that the speaker will use the Queen's English however he chooses, and it will be deployed to the listener's offence and consternation. If he has to, as a last resort against the jail sentence, the speaker will take the Queen's English as his partner in crime. The Queen's English now comes under the control of the speaker, used on his own terms and for his own access to power.

The poem 'Listen Mr Oxford Don' stands as a useful, metapoetic reflection on the stuttering kinopoetics of migrant poetry. Breaking from, while at the same time commenting on, the structures of grammar, syntax, and pronunciation, the speaker invents a place within the language that is both joyful, positive, and affirmative. The speaker's invocation of 'Me' and 'I', moreover, structures the internal focalisation from which we gather his relation to the 'Oxford Don.' His defiance against the perceived violence or, even, enslavement imposed by grammatical convention and the conservative attitudes of an 'Oxford Don' shows him capable of rendering a new intensity in the language, making his migrancy more visible and thinkable. As a result, the clever and deliberate use of creolised English opposes and confounds the perception of it being inferior to the 'Queen's English', or somehow lacking in complexity. Instead of accepting these racialised notions of language and linguistic ability, the speaker challenges the entire basis of linguistic mastery and competency. Asserting migrancy as a barbarian figure, this poet uses not only song and dance to mock his captors, masters, and rulers; he also incites riots, violence, and 'mugging' to revolt against the regime that systematically excludes him. He flees to a new realm of language, feeling at home in a collectivity of language that is unique, positive, and worthy of recognition, rather than how it is perceived: a sign of inferiority or cognitive deficiency. Much like, too, a stutter is seen as a sign of a speech impediment or aphasia, it is instead in this poem – and, as we will see, in the poem in the next section – a creative way to produce new vibrations, patterns, and intensities. Having then analysed 'Mr Oxford Don' for its metapoetic reflections on language and the stuttering of 'mastery' as such, I will now turn to a poem that more directly engages song and dance.

'New Craas Massakah': Stuttering, Dancing and Rioting

In a January 2021 article for *Tribune Magazine*, Adam Almeida writes to commemorate the 40th Anniversary of the New Cross Fire. This tragedy, Almeida argues, offers important insights about Britain's troubled history with race, and relates to the present era's encounters with austerity and institutional racism. He writes:

> The New Cross Fire represents a politicising moment of a previous generation when black Britons refused to be marginalised in their own neighbourhoods and took to the streets to make their voices heard and their story known in the halls of power. Our generation's reckoning with the institutional racism of Britain has come multi-fold, with the Grenfell Fire marking a defining event in the public consciousness. The significance of both events represents the deep inequalities that occur throughout the United Kingdom and are concentrated in London. (2021)

In 1981, a deadly firebombing attack at 16-year-old Yvonne Ruddock's birthday party killed 13 teenagers, leading to outrage and mourning from the predominantly Black British community in south London at the time. This moment, writes Almeida, 'represented one of the starkest indictments of Britain's indifference to the safety, security and humanity of black children and families to take place in the metropole' (2021), prompting the slogan '13 dead, nothing said' to be a rallying cry of the local community. After all, for this predominantly immigrant community – composed of those from the Windrush Generation of the post-war era – not only did the event itself seem to reflect the virulent racism of English society; its aftermath, reporting, and ensuing riots spoke to the long-standing grievances of the black British community, many of which persist into the present.

'By the 1970s and '80s', writes Ramazani, 'after British politicians and neofascists had fomented racist attitudes, and also after black Britons inspired by decolonisation, the civil rights movement, and Black Power had mobilised resistance, poets of African descent in England began to reimagine the colonial metropolis still more assertively' (Ramazani 2015:172).[8] Linton Kwesi Johnson, known for his pioneering dub poetry, migrated from Jamaica to London at a young age. Similarly radicalised by the growing discontent among the black community and inspired by the broader, international struggles for liberation, Johnson 'joined a London-based wing of the Black Panthers' (ibid.). Channelling, then, these global radical currents alongside the alienation and resentment of the immigrants who deal with further processes of internal displacement and dispossession, Johnson draws 'on reggae, mento, ska, and other African Caribbean oral music and on the militancy and musicality of the US Black arts movement's poetry' (ibid.). All of these forces culminate in an aesthetic preoccupation with reggae-infused rhythm and the creole Jamaican orality (also discussed in the previous section). Such aesthetic preoccupations stand largely as an act of resistance against the racialising structures of British society, many of which manifest in the tragedy of the New Cross Fire.

The same year as the fire, Johnson composed 'New Craas Massakah' to commemorate the tragedy. Not only is Johnson paying tribute to the young victims whose lives were cut short by this terrifying arson attack; he also identifies with the partygoers with his own subjective experience with discontent, migration, movement, and exclusion. Just as the young dancers look for a place of comfort and warmth at the party, so too he sought a place of comfort and warmth in his new London home. He uses rhythmic patterns to

emulate the sound of dancing at the party and the community's ensuing rage and protest. Ramazani writes:

> In this poem, London is no longer a place where peoples of
> African descent expect to be warmly welcomed: they know
> they may be brutally attacked. But the event itself is no
> less traumatic for that knowledge, and the poem's refrain
> repeatedly replays the transformation of a dance party –
> captured in loosely anapestic cadences and sensual descrip-
> tion – into fiery death, as if to make sense of the senseless
> (2015:173).

The speaker starts, then, by illustrating the sensations of
the party-goers, with their dancing steps and joyful music.
He produces the opening sequence of events, noting how
the sounds and rhythms precede and anticipate the tragedy
to come:

first di comin
an di goin
in an out af di pawty

di dubbin
an di rubbin
and di rackin to di riddim

di dancin
and di scankin
an di pawty really swingin (Johnson [1983] 2002:54)

The song version of 'New Craas Massakah' takes these lines
in an intense syncopated pattern, with the snare drum beat
falling on the 'coming', 'going', 'out', and '-ty' (from 'pawty')
of the first three lines.[9] Even without the backing musical
instruments, though, there is a natural rising and falling four-
beat rhythm to the way these words are stressed and follow a
repetitive meter. The natural phonetic clicks from the words

'coming' and 'going' create their own stresses, emulating the sounds of people filing into a party, almost as if they are marching, and then eventually to the dancing that begins in the following lines. The speaker here affectively and intensively attaches his subjectivity to these dancers, being, too, someone who entered into a new home expecting to be welcomed or to find camaraderie. The party, in other words, represents an analogical space for English society as a whole – a place where one expects to feel at home, but is instead on the receiving end of racism and violence. The use of 'di' to stand in for 'they' and 'the' ('di comin/di going/di party') creates an unaspirated vibration in the speaker's throat as opposed to the aspirated consonant in the 'th' sound. This phonetic technique enacts a dancelike rhythm at the level of form that matches the dancing in the content; the 'd' sound after all emulates the sound of feet tapping and stepping. The speaker is describing not only the carefree arrival and departure ('comin' and 'goin'), but the rich variety of dancing ('rubbin', 'rackin', 'scankin'); and all of these movements match the joyous, musical atmosphere of the party ('riddim' and 'swingin'). Here again, much like Agard's poem, Johnson produces a complex syntactic and oral pattern through non-standard English vernacular. Like the dance-moves he is describing, the words he uses are a defiant form of collective expression; these become an articulation of joy that brings together a community of those who find solidarity and connectedness within an otherwise hostile environment. Johnson employs a Jamaican creole that expresses in form a relation to his fellow immigrants; and his migrant subjectivity affectively resonates with the young people at the party: 'Because the partygoers are at first doing what the poet is doing – 'di dubbin/an di rubbin/an di rackin to di riddim' – the poem intimately enmeshes the speaker in the African Caribbean London he describes' (Ramazani 2015:174). The poem itself produces both dance-like sensations and rhythms that move along with the moves of the dancers. Trying to seek a brief respite from their hostile British society, they forge a connectedness at the bodily and intensive level; and the poem similarly engenders this connection at the level of language.

The poem itself dances from one focus to the next. It leaps out from the previous rhythm, almost as one would leap away from a fire, shifting to shorter syllables and a harsher meter that then describe the violence and horror of the arson attack:

> den di crash
> an di bang
> an di flames staat fit rang
>
> di heat
> an di smoke
> an di people staat fi choke
>
> di screamin
> and di cryin
> and di diein in di fyah. . . (Johnson 2002:54)

'The poem switches', writes Ramazani, 'from syncopated rhythms and gerundive feminine rhymes (dubbin/rubbin, dancing/scankin/swingin) to abrupt, bottled, monosyllabic masculine rhymes (bang/rang, smoke/choke)' (2015:173). The stark contrasting sounds, sensations, and affects between the first lines and this second cluster illustrate the suddenness of having their entire night torn apart by violence. 'Choke' is a key word here, where the people choke upon the inhaling smoke; but also the figurative meaning of choke, whereby the sound of something is quickly and deliberately subdued or cut short (such as the phrase 'choking back anger'). Choking the words with shorter syllables also coincides with the reader being drawn into the 'flames', 'heat', and 'smoke'. We not only read about, but experience affectively, what choking does to one's words. Suddenly we are unable to speak or produce more sounds as our lungs fill with smoke. As the syllable constellation in the previous line is cut short – and with it its rhythm and meter – so, too, is the dancing and music. The onomatopoeic sounds of 'crash', 'bang', 'rang', make the poem itself crash, bang, and ring, producing the sensuous experience of being among the chaos; it changes to a situation that one grows to fear and run from, much like the way that the barbarian's speech patterns instilled fear in the Greek *polis*. The creole English combined with the suddenly shifting rhythmic pattern produces itself a system of destruction through its poetic form; it stutters and stammers in that it ruptures how English is conventionally used, but also suddenly ruptures the feeling of freedom and joy that characterised the party and dance of the opening lines.

The heartbreaking lines that follow, where the partygoers are 'screamin/cryin/diein in di fyah' poses a horrifically contrasting image to the first set of lines and stanzas. After all, 'screamin', 'cryin', and 'diein' return to the two-syllable patterns we found in the lines, 'dubbin/rubbin/dancin/scankin'; the words parallel how the partygoers were moving along to the rhythm and into the party, but instead both the rhythm and party are cast into 'fyah'. This syllabic structure offers a reminder of the joy and exuberance these youthful partygoers experienced only moments before, and how quickly it can be stolen from them at the hands of racist violence. This moment, again, analogously reflects occasions of racist violence, terror, and murder experienced among immigrants; and the speaker draws himself into relation with these young people. Once again the four-beat rhythm returns, where the downbeat hits directly on the words 'screaming', 'cryin', and 'diein', building a sense of fear, but also declaring rage in a march-like sequence. The spelling of 'diein' deliberately confounds the standard spelling of 'dying'; but it also entails two meanings. It is both 'dying' as a present continuous sense, just like the screaming and crying. Yet it also suggests 'die in', signalling the clear horror of imagining that people actually die in the fire and, with it, their youth, happiness, joy, and collective power. Ending with 'fyah' as opposed to 'fire' creates here a one-syllable alternative, keeping with the rhythm of the poem, but also again evoking a sudden ending and loss that chokes and extinguishes their lives instantaneously. The constraints on expression here constitute another stuttering; instead of the constraints on speech created from a cognitive deficiency or linguistic ineptitude, they reflect the experience of racial violence and terror – terror that snuffs out the joy of song and dance.

Further carrying on this point of ending the song and dance, after the line 'diein in di fyah', the rhythm of the poem seems to fall away. In the song version, the backing instruments are at rest, and Johnson's voice carries on as if delivering a speech. This change demonstrates a change in tone, as the speaker now reflects upon the aftermath of the fire and the ensuing rage of the community. The music of the party has ended and, therefore, so does the poem's musicality. Nevertheless, the vernacular constellation of creole Jamaican is maintained, and with it moments of defiant force and rage in speaking on behalf of the community. Responding to the confusion, the speakers says 'everybady woz still shack/wen we get di cowl facks' (Johnson 2002:55), learning about the heavy truths, 'die innocent life dem whe lass/bout di physically scard/di mentally mard/an dem relatives who tek it so aad' (ibid.). While there is hardly a recognisable meter or rhythm to these lines, one can detect rhymes that describe the 'shock' from the 'facts' of the brutal 'attack' – these three words only rhyming within the creolised accent, even if they do not in standard English. The ending words '-ack' also represents the disgust and rage of those who likely scream this sound upon hearing 'bout di fyah owevah New Crass' (ibid.). The shock and horror itself flows through the sparse rhymes in these free verses, almost pulsating outward as news travels throughout a community, and a sense of collective anger begins to build. The speaker channels the confusion and shock, invoking here the typical, sometimes banal and anodyne reactions to such tragedies. People wonder 'fi know she dem kine a ting deh/ could happn to wi/inna disya Great Britn' (ibid.), and they realise 'it coulda be mi/it coulda be yu' (ibid.). These lines read as if they are the everday conversations that people have with one another as they come to terms with an awful tragedy.

The speaker, too, brings his migrancy and racial sub-jectivity to bear on these conversations, identifying and bringing himself into relation with the people there, and channeling their grievances through his utterances. Replac-ing standard language with his non-standard creole, the speaker describes the young teenagers as 'pickney', apply-ing a typical West Indian term for children. This creates, through this category, a way for the largely immigrant community to forge bonds through a shared language. The speaker uses patois to remind us of his migrancy and his investment in this collective pain. The stuttering and stam-mering of non-standard spelling, phrases, words words helps to illuminate the ruptures caused by that 'terrah by nite' (Johnson 2002:55). In this last phrase, there is also a pun: it is meant to sound like 'terrible night', but ends up looking like 'terra by night' – a territory or plane, in other words, that appears to be in a dark place and time. This shared memory is evoked in his rhymes and sounds that represent pain, anger, and violence.

After twenty-seven lines of free verse, the poem gradually returns to a rhythmic pattern again, turning now to confront the ruling society's indifference to, and ignorance of, this community's suffering. Speaking lines that follow a repeated motif, the speaker reminds us of what ensued after the fire:

but wait
yu noh remembah
how di whole a black Britn did rack wid grief

how di whole a black Britn tun a melancally blue
nat di passible blue af di murdarah's eyes
but like di smoke af gloom on dat cowl sundey mawnin

but stap
yu noh remembah
how di whole black Britn did rack wid rage
how di whole black Britn tun a fiery red
nat di callous red af di killah's eyes
but red wid rage like di flames af di fyah (Johnson
2002:55–56)

Describing how the 'whole black Britn did rack wid grief'
and '. . .did rack wid rage' employs, again, the term verb
'rack' as another onomatopoeia. The term here holds two
meanings appropriate to the poem's form and content. On
the one hand, to be 'racked' with grief or guilt is to experience a normal emotional response to tragedy. Yet, saying 'did
rack' turns 'rack' into a verb form: '(w)rack'. To 'wrack' with
grief and rage is to also destroy with grief and rage, using
them as weapons or expressions of anger. By doing so, the
'whole black Britn' turned their experience of rage and grief
outward, seeking to destroy the indifference and apathy that
the British society at large has toward them. Similarly, the
speaker uses the sound of 'rack' to stammer the poem itself
– its form and structure – creating a mixed sound of chaos,
rage and sadness to reveal itself at the level of language.
The '-ack' sound at the end of 'rack' combines a resonant,
almost screaming 'a' sound with the crashing, thunderous
'–ck', repeating it twice as something 'Britn did'. Similarly,
describing the 'murdurah's eyes' as 'passible blue' contains
a pun on both 'possible' and 'passible.' When uttered aloud,
using Jamaican patois, it would be easily heard as 'possible', speculating on what they imagine the racist killer's eyes
must look like. Yet, 'passable', too, follows a racialised logic,
wherein someone's skin pigmentation (or, in this cause, iris

pigmentation) could legitimately pass as a specific race. The speaker is thus leaning on this double-logic of racialisation that constructs differences in pigmentation as having political significance.

Immersing himself in their pain, the speaker uses the rage and anger of experiencing this community's struggle and thus reflects his own migrant subjectivity in these words. He expresses the intensity and affective relation that his movement and migrancy create alongside the black British community and the West Indian diaspora. His feeling of anger is a product of his own arrival; and his poetic stuttering and stammering with rhythmic shifts, inconsistent (but nevertheless observable) rhyme schemes, and Jamaican patois revolt against the structures of a system that would rather leave him and his immigrant community excluded. Moreover, the 'rage' he refers to parallels the 'riots' in Agard's poem. In this case, as mentioned at the beginning of this section, there was in fact a notable outcry from the black British community at the callous disregard for this event. The ensuing response from the community was a justified expression of anger and sadness. Toward the end of the poem, after a refrain that resembles the rhythm of the poem's opening lines and returns us to the party (Johnson 2002:56), the speaker begins in free verse to chastise 'di police an di press' who 'try dem despahret bes/fi put a stap to wi ques fi di trute' (ibid. 57). The police and media's apparent hesitation, indecisiveness, and negligence showed in how they appeared to forestall further investigations. As a result, the public was kept unaware of the apparent threat that such an attack signifies for the non-white residents of London: 'instead a raisin di alaam/mek di public know wha gwaan/plenty paypah print pure lie' (ibid.). This poem, much like Agard's, stands as its own form of protest, utilising musical patterns and sounds to claim both the joy and exuberence of dance, and it stands next to the collective grief and pain. As he says, employing a collective we: 'wi refuse fi surrendah/to

dem ugly innuendoh' – innuendo that was evidently used by
the police to 'canfuse an canceal' with 'prapahganda' (ibid.).
This refusal to surrender is, again, an intensive demonstration
of a barbarian revolt. Much like the slave who escapes his
captor and refuses to surrender to servitude, the speaker and
the community to whom he attaches himself run from and
reject the police's narrative of the events. These institutions'
efforts to determine the limits of acceptable stories, language,
and discourse were roundly challenged, in no small part
thanks to the rage-filled outcries of the community. They will
not allow their own minds and memories be captured by the
police's efforts to conceal the true nature of the tragedy or to
avoid the truth of the entrenched racism from which it arose.

In line with this pronouncement, the poem itself stands
as a form of protest. It uses the Jamaican creole and patois,
combined with Johnson's pioneering dub poetry style, to
claim a position in the social imaginary that would otherwise
neglect the struggles of immigrants and ignore their cries of
anger and rage. It performs its own unwillingness to surrender to the indifference and neglect that extends from British
society at large. While the press and the police may be trying
to offer bromides and half-truths about the New Cross Fire,
the poem itself instead places that event – with all of its sensations, sounds, and intensities – into its form and language,
ensuring that they do not choke or burn out with the victims.
In its act of protest, the poem itself sings and dances, as its
own rhythmic patterns move alongside the movement of the
dancing partygoers, and its own sounds emulate song-like
refrains. The poem, in this case, does not focalise one immigrant and their movement, but several immigrants and a range
of movements. Yet, the speaker attaches his own subjectivity
with the community, making his movement the creative and
productive system of meaning in the poem. The movements
on the dance floor, followed by the tragic movement through
fire, and the affective movement of the community in their

outrage and anger all produce a stammering and stuttering at the level of language. It follows a non-standard structure, experimenting with both sound, rhyme, and rhythm in order to invent, produce, and affirm migrancy's centrality in this event. It also highlights intensive movements, turning 'di jallity into a ugly trajedy' (ibid.:58). The New Cross Fire, after all, cannot be understood without the dispossession and exclusion of the black immigrant community; not only was the attack itself carried out as a viciously racist attack, but the response by the society was also symptomatic of an exclusionary regime. This apparent negligence explains the efficacy of the rallying cry, '13 Dead, Nothing Said' (Almeida 2021). Such a statement renders visible the need for recognition within a national system in which immigrants are largely erased. The poem, then, supplies another cry to this chorus of voices who speak on behalf of this collective. Revolting against and escaping the grip of propaganda and negligence, the poem itself stutters and stammers, moving against the political forces of racial violence, making migrant existence visible and thinkable.

Chapter Conclusion

Stuttering kinopoetics connects migrancy, movement, and knowledge together by means of experimental language. The creative ability to fashion grammatical structures, new spellings, odd pronunciations, and shifting rhythms are all ways for the migrant to actively produce and constitute the regime of meaning. Stuttering acts as a form of counterpower against the regimes of mastery, competence, and standardisation that enter into not only language education, but also inform the basis for migrant settlement. One's ability to comply with and conform to a national language determines whether one can procure visas and employment. Instead, the migrant figure joyfully, creatively, and inventively produces variations and ruptures within language as a means of forging collective bonds with other immigrants. In doing so, the migrant redistributes the sensible regime of what counts as a language and what one considers to be an appropriate way of speaking. As these poems show, non-standard languages – in particular, Jamaican creole English – are equally complex, musical, expressive, and moldable; these vernacular systems of speech help to articulate the singularity of migrancy that claims its own position within a social milieu. So, these maneuvers with language also challenge the tendency to perceive experimental language with suspicion, assuming that the person speaking lacks intelligence or reasoning capacities. As the poems' speakers prove, their language suggests an even deeper form of perception and power. It expresses the ineffable and inexpressible, deterritorialising and breaking open the strictures of grammar and, with it, those associated with powerful institutions (such as media and universities). So, as the speaker in Agard challenges the 'Oxford don' (Agard 1967) and Johnson's speaker confronts 'di police an di press' (Johnson 2002:57), they in turn actively, creatively, and affirmatively produce their own power through language, independently of what these forces deem appropriate or acceptable.

The migrant figure who embodies this stuttering kinopoetics is the barbarian. The barbarian has historically created the conditions for expansion by means of 'centrifugal force'; and as political forces attempt to expand their reach outward, they worked to designate populations as inferior and thus unworthy of political recognition, or as suitable chattel for forced labour. Yet, the barbarian enacts a pedetic force of revolt and escape, enabling them to apply collective pressure against these political forces by causing a 'social disturbances that spreads throughout society' (Nail 2015:139). Stuttering kinopoetics is a force of counterpower that adds an extra dimension to the barbarian's intensive and affective capacity: it calls upon the sound of the slave song and the movement of dance, both of which were utilised as forms of resistance that could not be contained or stifled by political forces. So, in the poems that enact a stuttering kinopoetics, song and dance arise from the non-standard patterns, vibrations, and shifts within language that are used to sometimes mock, ridicule, challenge, or confront the systems of national power that work to silence them or assume them unworthy of political consideration. Whether or not the people to whom these poems are directed embrace the vernacular traces or hear the subtle rhythms in language, the speakers nevertheless assert a power that makes migrancy visible and knowable. Language's stuttering and stammering movement, then, generates another poetics that instantiates migrancy through intensive and affective movement.

Notes

1. I write here from personal experience.
2. 'Because a style is not an individual psychological creation but an assemblage of enunciation,' they write, 'it unavoidably produces a language within a language' (Deleuze and Guattari [1987]2014:113–4). This 'language within a language' parallels the minor *use* of language, demonstrating the capacity of the subject to creatively forge new 'functions of language' (Deleuze and Guattari 2014:121).
3. One might think of this stuttering variation as a poetics of 'opacity', as Glissant describes it: 'The opaque is not the obscure . . . It is that which cannot be reduced' (1997:191).
4. Although I will not be relying on Edouard Glissant heavily in this section, there is a useful connection to Glissant's concept of creolisation, especially since both authors arise from the Caribbean context. Glissant famously describes creolisation as 'a poetics that is latent, open, multilingual in intention, directly in contact with everything possible' (1997:32).
5. See also Chapter 1 (section headed Kinopolitics: Expansion by Expulsion) and Chapter 2 (section headed Sedentarism

and Sovereignty: The Master Texts Behind the Nation) for a discussion of 'primitive accumulation'.

6. Perhaps in the future, one can imagine a kinopoetic reading of *Beloved* that combines stuttering poetics and destructive poetics (see Chapter 3).

7. One thinks for example of The Rolling Stones's 'Can't get no satisfaction', also following a double negative logic.

8. I mostly rely on Ramazani for this section, as there is surprisingly precious little scholarly work available on this poem. A search in the MLA bibliography in fact returns zero results if one is to search the title of the poem.

9. The song version of the poem can be found at https://sonichits. com/video/Kwesi_Johnson_Linton/New_Craas_Massahkah.

CONCLUSION

The Migrant Text as a Kinetic Cultural Object

Kinopoetics exists as a movement-oriented method and theory for analysing migrant literature. To bring this project to its conclusion, and further position it within the broader scope of the field, I shall now use a similar perspective to underscore the circulating processes that give migrant literature a social life of its own. To begin this exercise, I will turn to Subha Xavier who, in her 2016 book, *The Migrant Text*, writes that '[n]o theory of the migrant text can exclude the market considerations that have made this type of literature especially viable today' (70). I would like to take up Xavier's injunction and examine these wider social and economic dynamics. I will consider the possibility that migrant literature *flows* as a kinetic cultural object, compelled into motion by forces of commodification and globalised market capitalism. Xavier continues, noting that, after all, migrant literature

> is a literature of otherness that falls prey to the fear of the market. It is a literature often written by immigrants themselves, one that deals in an exoticism that is exploited for the sake of the literary marketplace. These works are then packaged, distributed, and sold and when successful, reprinted, repackaged, and sold again (ibid.).

Writing about the Anglophone context, and in a similar vein, Sarah Brouillette writes: '"Books" are not just books; the word stands in for an assemblage of separate entities, and variety in content leads to complexity of ordering and distribution, and in turn to special technologies for stock control and consumer profiling' (2007:49). This approach toward the distribution and production of postcolonial migrant literatures concedes that these literatures have produced a cultural effect on Anglo-American readers. In particular, one finds that there is a unique market interest in diversifying the representation of authors and ethnic groups within a publisher's catalogue: 'The more literature associable with specific national or ethnic identities enters the market, the more the market, despite increasing concentration and globalisation, can make the claims to inclusivity and universality that justify its particular form of dominance' (ibid.:58). What emerges, then, is a market incentive for migrant authors to fulfill a cultural need and expectation – on the one hand, to be self-exoticising and, on the other hand, to demonstrate narrative and linguistic complexity alongside an attentiveness to nation, identity, and power.

Without overstating the triumphs of consumer capitalism, it is nevertheless the case that postcolonial migrant literatures have grown in popularity since the 1990s. This shift is largely thanks to a growing form of cultural capital that attends publishing books written by authors beyond the Anglo-American metropoles. Such a trend in turn carves a market niche that migrant authors fulfill, however reluctantly. A question remains, though, about whether we can locate or theorise migrant literature's constitutive role as an object of knowledge-production. Throughout this book, I have attempted to convey, through kinopoetics, a methodology that can draw out the affective features (that is, poetics) within and from a migrant text, redistributing the sensible in a way that makes migrancy legible. But thinking broadly, and according to the wider network of forces (such as publishing, marketing, writing, distributing, selling, reading, teaching, reviewing, adapting), the migrant text acts as an object in itself, moving throughout a social system and acting as an entity invested with counterpower. As it stands now, migrant literature is regarded (problematically) as an extension of the author's cultural relation and national identity: 'The author's name and attached personae have become key focal points for the marketing of literary texts, such that one could argue that the current industry brands literature more by author- ship than by other aspects of our ways of approaching a given work's meaning' (Brouillette 2007:65–66). As mentioned above, this tendency dovetails with a rather complicated rela- tionship to cultural representation, demanding that migrant authors act as cultural ambassadors to a discerning reader- ship. Arguably, too, the paradigm within which this market system operates is one that 'privilege[s] work that can be identified with a specific geographical struggle or political history' (ibid.:71). Yet, throughout this book, I have argued that a perspective based on and in movement can work to overcome such static, state-based paradigms, and shift there- fore toward recognising the constellation of forces and flows of movement that shape migrant subjectivity.

As texts working within these same commodifying forces, migrant literature (that is, its material manifestation in the form of a printed, bound book) has mobile qualities, both intensive and extensive, that I shall attempt to locate. Taking on Marx's well-known analysis of value-form in *Capital*, Nail extracts important dimensions to this theory of value, namely that 'Marx's theory of value is a fundamentally kinetic theory of value in which matter-in-motion forms the being of value . . . Matter-in-motion is primary to and constitutive of the being of value itself' (2020:129). Any commodity enter- ing into production is invested with value; for Marx, value as such contains both use-value and exchange-value. Both types of value exist within a commodity, but the exchange value in particular is the one determined according to an assemblage of social relations.¹ Value as such increases and decreases – that is, becomes valourised or devalourised – in accordance with the associated labour power needed to produce that commodity ('socially-necessary labor time' [Marx 1867/1990: 129–30]). Furthermore, exchange-value becomes a system of representation through which the commodity can be recognised within a wider market system: 'Value . . . transforms every product of labour into a social hieroglyphic' (Marx 1990:167). Value-form is the objective form the commodity assumes when it enters into a relation, measured alongside other commodities through exchange. Much like languages, affects, narrative forms, and subjectivities that I analysed throughout *Poetics of the Migrant*, value is another material quality that develops through motion and movement. It moves between various systems of expansion and contraction, starting from the moment of accumulation, moving to the labour production, the exchange, and finally the extraction of surplus.

Thus, I would like to assess the book as a commodity whose value can be read kinopoetically. In *Capital* Vol.1, Marx writes that the commodity 'reveals its thoughts in a language with which it alone is familiar, the language of commodities' (Marx 1990:143). 'Commodities', adds Nail, 'like all sensuous material things, have both active and subjective dimensions and passive objective dimensions. Their 'thoughts' here should be broadly defined as their intensive qualities or affections and their 'language' as their extensive qualities and effects' (2020:138). This manner of treating a commodity with a degree of agency is consistent with Marx's understanding of how a commodity's value operates (2020:137).² Like characters or forms within a literary text, moreover, we can understand how these systems of value work toward shaping the visible and sensible world. As a kinetic object, a commodity is capable of recognising (that is, expressing its value alongside) other commodities in an exchange relation; and, at the same time, it expresses this value-form through appearances (or, sensations). These forces mirror each other and become aspects of value as it increases or decreases according to the material circumstances. These are the ways in which commodities both think and act in the world, but also how they are related to one another.

How, then, does a migrant text think and act? As I noted above, books coincide with a broad range of market forces; yet, the cultural significance of migrant literature is still broadly construed according to the author's relationship to national identity. Instead, though, if we concede that books are agents or non-human actors acting in the world, then it follows that they can also redistribute the sensible world, much like the narratives and migrant figures within those texts. The systems of distribution and publishing that a book undergoes already entails patterns of movement (quite literally using transportation networks that begin from the printing-press to the point of sale; not to mention book tours). In addition, the contracted writer's labour (along with editors, indexers, translators and cover artists) and the subsequent process of marketing all invest the book with an expectation of a valourised exchange-value (that is, surplus-value). Accordingly, all of these processes derive from laws of motion that either require the flow of money and capital, or the literal movement of paper, packaging, and binding materials from one place to another. The mediating language behind this entire process is value, insofar as it articulates the agency or power of the commodity itself (and such power appears, for Marx, in the form of 'fetishism' [Marx 1990:163]); value-form's coherence relies upon the social relations into which it enters. The book's price and investment (such as a guarantee through writing advances), for example, express its quantitative movement. This movement is its language that enables it to be sold and consumed – in other words, its extensive force. This is its value that can be traced, located, and measured according to rate, mass, and magnitude. Its intensive quality on the other hand might act more abstractly, but is no less a material (affective) force. Alongside other texts within the Anglophone tradition, for example, a migrant text might shift the canonised expectations of language, identity, narrative form and subjectivity. Throughout this project, I have attempted to show many ways in which this can be done kinopoetically. Additionally, the book can, in turn, be taught, reviewed, translated, critically-analysed, awarded, or adapted into a film; and, furthermore, the text can simply be read, enjoyed and consumed freely, generating affective relations with readers and audiences. These dynamics constitute a book's intensive force – its thought that produces qualitative movement within a social regime. Much like the migrant figure, a book's extensive and intensive movement are not necessarily separate, but operate in a metabolic relationship. We might think of value as a poetics, a system of meaning, that makes the text-commodity's extensive and intensive movement. The text itself is the use-value, while its value-form moves in accordance with social relations.

This analysis of the text, and particularly its intensive movements, coincides with the post-critical paradigm mentioned in the Introduction, broadly associated with Rita Felski. Taking cues from Bruno Latour, Felski rather provocatively argues that an '[i]nterpretation becomes a coproduction between actors that brings new things to light rather than an endless rumination on a text's hidden meanings or representational failures' (2015:174). Felski here wants to correct the manner in which reading merely is a matter of 'plumbing depths or tracing surfaces', and rather move toward treating it as 'creating something new in which the reader's role is as decisive as the text' (ibid.:173–4). The point here is to examine the text as its own non-human actor, a body moving across a network of material relations; once we 'allow ourselves to be marked, struck, impressed by what we read', reading becomes a 'form of making rather than unmaking' (ibid.:12). From here, we can read the whole writer-to-reader process, and the network of mediating forces therein, as a kinetic movement; the book acts upon a system, and the system acts back upon the book – creating a circulation of motion that eventually leads to it being read. When thought of in this way, the migrant text need not be confined to the geographical, national, or cultural status of its author; and we can overcome the need to exoticise the author or force their text to conform to a canonised expectation. After all, the book is not merely a fixed entity whose meaning has to satisfy cultural standards of literary difference, hybridity, or experimentation (although, as I have shown, they often do). Instead, the text's movement is primary, producing effects and affects; and its motion throughout the system acts as an agential, intervening force. It is itself a kinetic cultural object.

As a cultural object, the migrant text moves intensively and extensively, complying with forces of marketisation, but also productively engaged by everyone from writers, editors, publishers, readers, reviewers and students. It contains its own kinetic qualities, then, that move – as the migrant does – according to material and political forces. In the next section, I will analyse more specifically the transformative relation that a migrant text has, given its affective and intensive qualities. As a non-human body moving throughout a social milieu, I would like to suggest that a migrant text is able to create the conditions for solidarity.

Affective Relations and Solidarity

In Chapter 1, I examined how literature and poetics can contribute to individual and collective knowledge by way of an 'affect-sensation' continuum. On the one hand, a text generates intensive movements, changing the relations of speeds and slownesses that constitute a subject's political power, freedom, knowledge, and maneuverability; and on the other hand, it redistributes the sensible, reconstituting and reimagining the social assemblage such that movement and migrancy are made legible. The political efficacy of this form of cultural knowledge is not merely that it can make us empathise with characters; rather, an even deeper proximity of collective power emerges in the form of solidarity. Through many of the novels I examine in previous chapters, characters are shown as capable of reaching beyond their atomised selves, forging lines of connection, relation, and intensity. We can think of Tilo in *The Mistress of Spices*, whose powers to access other characters' inner worlds and thoughts commits her to a shared struggle, particularly with other women who feel stifled by responsibility and obligation. Her responsibility to the community leads her toward sacrificing her vocation as a mistress of spices for the sake of a wider social and emotional connection. Similarly, Julius in *Open City*, uses his wandering desire to draw the crowd of New York City commuters into relation with himself, overcoming the regulated spatial structures of urban life that deliberately alienate people from one another. Their walking and steps coincide with his walking and his steps, bringing them into proximity, both physically and, perhaps, spiritually. Or, and finally, the speaker in Linton Kwesi Johnson's 'New Craas Massakah' identifies with the party-goers in the poem who, in a tragic instant, are horrifically and brutally massacred. His migrant subjectivity and voice enters the room, bringing him into relation with the partygoers, and uses his relationality to perform their dances and their movements through speech and language. In all cases, characters reach beyond themselves, recognising the shared struggles of class, race and gender that connect them, finding lines of collectivity that compound their relational power.

By virtue of their epistemic and affective qualities, these texts have the capacity to tie intensive relations together, allowing the connection to be more than merely a one-to-one, unmediated communication between book and reader. Affect is the mediating force of relationality and intensity that reaches between these two bodies, making them resonate together. With these affects, therefore the migrant subject and the reader add up to more than the sum of their parts. This combination develops a configuration of solidarity, a way of generating the necessary connections for building mass political struggle and liberation. Similarly, such solidarity establishes open-ended systems of belonging and affiliation, one based on a continuous, unchanging processes of movement, togetherness, affirmation, creativity and invention. The 'becoming-vagabond' that Nazneen enacts in *Brick Lane* offers a useful model here: the more she comes across 'relay-points' that connect her to vagabond desire, the stronger her affirmations of her selfhood and sense of belonging with the people she encounters. From these texts, a becoming-migrant may perhaps exist as 'new ways of seeing and hearing' and 'new ways of feeling' (Deleuze 1995:165). But, beyond this, we are given new arrangements of desire and knowledge amid the 'struggle of political hegemonies' (Gramsci 2003:333).[3] Seeing, hearing and feeling in new ways brings us beyond ourselves, orienting us to struggles which cannot be achieved alone, but which rather always implicate the collective.

Reactionary and nationalist political leaders are well aware of the efficacy of language's affective power, reshaping the range of what is thinkable and knowable in a social regime. As I outlined in the introduction (through the use of a political pamphlet), right-wing groups often employ a combination of paranoia-inducing language, combined with dog-whistles and other subtle rhetorical cues, that help generate racial and nationalist resentment. One outcome of these political tactics is a reassertion of cross-racial and cross-cultural antagonism conditioned within a social structure of atomisation, alienation, and fragmentation, thereby weakening genuine solidarity. Yet, the configurations of migrancy made visible and legible within migrant literatures, when read kinopoetically, help activate a politics and ethics of collective power, beyond the boundaries of power, dispossession, and national identity. Solidarity, such that it is generated through affects, expands and strengthens through the creation of joy, creativity and affirmation – active intensities that can transform the regimes of kinopower. Art, literature, song, films, and dance produce intensities, thereby charging the entire social and political assemblage with the energy and power to keep us going. The pedetic force of the migrant is thus best animated by and through flows of affects that we, as a human collective, give and receive.

The Uses of Kinopoetics

The typology of kinopoetics that this book has introduced – destructive kinopoetics, wandering kinopoetics, and stuttering kinopoetics – corresponds to different systems of kinopower. With these kinopoetics arose a (re-)appraisal of the figures of the migrant: the nomad, the vagabond, and the barbarian. As a result, different stylistic, generic, and narrative concerns emerged which, I feel, best embody the literary poetics of these migrant figures; and the approach required a set of terms and concepts that then enliven the political constellations and relations of migrant movement. This theoretical framework was largely adapted and adopted from kinopolitics, affect theory, narrative theory, spatial theory and pragmatic linguistics. In this final section, I would like to imagine how subsequent scholars and students may be able to make productive use of kinopoetics.

According to Nail, there remains an additional figure of the migrant who has not figured prominently in this thesis: the proletariat. This figure's pedetic force is, according to Nail, 'defined by its creation of social pressure' (Nail 2015:171). Thus, adds Nail, 'proletarian resistance takes a different form from previous migratory forms of counterpower. Against the economic silent compulsion to move, the proletariat refuses to move' (ibid.). While this migrant figure is certainly a meaningful and important figure of class struggle and counterpower, this last defining feature – going on strike, or 'refus[al] to move' – makes it challenging to imagine what this figure's poetics would be, and how, in fact, this would offer a qualitatively new, movement-oriented poetics that has not been rendered previously.[4] For his part, Nail registers an account of proletarian action in the figure of the migrant worker who, through 'strikes' and worker co-operation, produces social pressure in holding the forces of capital and surplus hostage. This form of resistance, when speaking in terms of literature, would require an expanded corpus of texts beyond the scope of this project. Several novelists (Dickens, Gaskell, Steinbeck, Melville, Dreiser) are known quite well for their depiction of proletarian struggle and class consciousness. Beyond this, migrant texts that illustrate working class life, but functionally act through movement and refusal while also focalising cross-national migration, are certainly available and worthy of consideration.[5] Having gestured toward this figure as a potential, I leave this as a challenge to subsequent critics and scholars to revise kinopoetics and add an analysis of the proletarian migrant.

Other such figures, too, are worthy of their own study as literary figures: 'tourists, diplomats, business travellers, explorers, and state functionaries' (Nail 2015:5–6). These specific figures differ from the nomad, the barbarian, the vagabond, and the proletariat, as they uphold a relative degree of mobility, both in the literal sense of the term (that is, physically mobile), but also in the figurative sense (or, economically privileged and affluent). As a result, their social relations stand in stark contrast to the figures analysed in this project, whose movements are produced through the forces of kinopower (in other words, through expansion by expulsion). Yet, so long as the relative social positions and privilege of the tourist, diplomat and business traveller are kept in mind – that is, without collapsing the differences in political power among all moving, migratory figures – I see here plenty of opportunity to expand kinopoetics to an even wider constellation of poetics, texts and figures. One could imagine how these specific mobile figures carry with them unique subjectivities that, in turn, change and shape the system of poetics, and the discursive regimes that make their specific movements thinkable and knowable. As such, the articulations of mobility, political power, and identity will still remain fundamental concerns, as will their affective, relational potential. In either case, a kinopoetics derived from these figures and their unique movements can and ought to redistribute the sensible, making their singular relationships to power legible. Finally, on a few occasions throughout this project, readers may have noticed texts mentioned which can be engaged from more than one kinopoetics. For example, in Chapter 4, I briefly mention Toni Morrison's *Beloved* – a text that both works within the generic tradition of Magic Realism, but also thematically and stylistically depicts slave movement, language and subjectivity. In this way, that novel produces both a destructive kinopoetics and a stuttering kinopoetics. By now it should be clear that migrancy is never an isolated or self-contained process, as there are multiple regimes of social motion which overlap and coincide in creating the conditions of kinopower. There is no reason to assume that kinopoetics would be any exception. As humans continue to be forced into situations of mobility and dispossession, the complexities of migration will demand new forms, concepts, discourses, and systems of meaning – a new poetics – to develop alongside this condition.

It is from here, then, that I invite readers and scholars to creatively (and productively) combine, rework, and reconsider kinopoetics for wider expansive purposes – perhaps even beyond migrant literatures, perhaps even beyond literature. As such, the capacity and breadth of available texts that can make movement and migrancy legible and knowable seems, to me, endless. Moreover, the stakes to do so could not be higher, as our relationship to and solidarity with migrant struggle is continuously under threat. As we reckon with the global crisis of migration and displacement and imagine a future of justice for moving people, we can modify the famous slogan: 'no one is illegal'. Through kinopoetics, a critical analysis of migrant literatures can also assure that no one is illegible.

Notes

1. '[T]he commodity never has [exchange-value] when looked at in isolation, but only when it is in a value-relation or an exchange relation with a second commodity of a different kind' (Marx [1867]1990:152).
2. This is also comparable to the traditions of vital new materialism (Bennett 2010:21).
3. Anzaldúa notes that the 'ability of a story to transform the storyteller and the listener into something or someone else is shamanistic' ([1987]2012:88), meaning that it reaches within our immanent relations to build a new proximity.
4. See Chapter 2, section headed Poetics of Migration: A Typology.
5. I have previously written about the connection between Shailja Patel's *Migritude* in relation to concepts of refusal and parallels to Herman Melville's 'Bartleby, the Scrivener'. See Potter 2021, '"Don't Get Too Comfortable": Regimes of Motility in Shailja Patel's *Migritude*.' Pp. 176–188 in *Cultural Mobilities Between Africa and the Caribbean*.

REFERENCES

Abbas, Tahir. 2004. 'After 9/11: British South Asian Muslims, Islamophobia, Multiculturalism and the State.' *The American Journal of Islamic Social Studies* 21(3):26–38.

Agamben, Giorgio. [1995] 1998. *Homo Sacer: Sovereign Power and Bare Life*. Translated by Daniel Heller-Roazen. Stanford: Stanford University Press.

—. 2005. *State of Exception*. Translated by Kevin Attell. Chicago: Chicago University Press.

Agard, John. 1967. *Listen Mr Oxford Don*. Genius.com. <https://genius.com/John-agard-listen-mr-oxford-don-annotated>.

Ahmad, Dohra. 2019. 'Introduction.' Pp. xv–xxix in *The Penguin Book of Migration Literature*. New York: Penguin.

Ahmed, Sara. 2014. *The Cultural Politics of Emotion*. 2nd ed. Edinburgh: Edinburgh University Press.

Alexandru, Maria-Sabina Draga. 2012. 'Urban and Rural Narratives of Female Relocation in Chitra Banerjee Divakaruni's Novels *Queen of Dreams* and *The Mistress of Spices*.' *American, British, and Canadian Studies* 77–86.

Ali, Monica. 2003. *Brick Lane*. London: Doubleday.

Almeida, Adam. 2021. '*13 Dead, Nothing Said*': The New Cross Fire at 40. *Tribune Magazine*. <https://tribunemag.co.uk/2021/01/13-dead-nothing-said-the-new-cross-fire-at-40>.

Anderson, Benedict. [1983] 2006. *Imagined Communities: Reflections on the Origin and Spread of Nationalism*. Rev. ed. London: Verso.

Anderson, Kevin B. 2020. *Dialectics of Revolution: Hegel, Marx, and its Critics Through a Lens of Race, Class, Gender, and Colonialism*. Daraja Press.

Anzaldúa, Gloria. [1987] 2012. *Borderlands/La Frontera: The New Mestiza*. 4th ed. Aunt Lute.

Appadurai, Arjun. 1996. *Modernity at Large: Cultural Dimensions of Globalisation*. Minneapolis: University of Minnesota Press.

Aristotle. [c. 335BCE] 1996. *Poetics*. Translated by Malcom Heath. London: Penguin.

Arnold, Matthew. [1875] 2010. 'The Function of Criticism at the Present Time.' Pp. 695–714 in *The Norton Anthology of Theory and Criticism*, edited by William E. Cain, Laurie A. Fink, Barbara E. Johnson, Vincent Leitch, John McGowan, T. Denean Sharpley Whiting, Jeffrey J. Williams. 2nd ed. New York: Norton & Company.

Ashcroft, Bill, Gareth Griffiths and Helen Tiffin. 2007. 'Hybridity.' Pp. 108–111 in *Post-Colonial Studies: The Key Concepts*, edited by Bill Ashcroft, Gareth Griffiths and Helen Tiffin. 2nd ed. London: Routledge.

Attridge, Derek. 2004. *The Singularity of Literature*. London: Routledge.

Bailey, Gordon and Noga Gayle. 2003. *Ideology: Structuring Identites in Contemporary Life*. Broadview: University of Toronto Press.

Bal, Mieke. 2021. *Narratology in Practice*. Toronto: University of Toronto Press.

Barnard, Don. 2014. *Walcott's* Omeros: *A Reader's Guide*. Boulder and London: First Forum Press.

Barry, Peter. 2009. *Beginning Theory: An Introduction to Literary and Cultural Theory*. 3rd ed. New York: Palgrave.

Barthes, Roland. [1967] 1997. 'The Death of the Author.' Pp. 120–123 in *Twentieth Century Literary Theory*, edited by K. M. Newton. 2nd ed. New York: St Martin's Press.

Bauman, Zygmunt. 1996. 'From Pilgrim to Tourist – or a Short History of Identity.' Pp. 18–36 in *Questions of Cultural Identity*, edited by Paul Du Gay and Stuart Hall. Los Angeles: Sage.

—. 2005. *Globalisation: The Human Consequences*. Oxford: Polity Press.

Bennett, Jane. 2010. *Vibrant Matter: A Political Ecology of Things*. Durham: Duke University Press.

Bennett, Louise. 1947. 'Back to Africa.' Pp. 155–116 in *Selected Poems*, edited by Mervyn Morris. Kingston: Sangster's.

Berman, Marshall. 1982. *All that Is Solid Melts Into Air: The Experience of Modernity*. New York: Penguin.

Bhabha, Homi. 1994. *The Location of Culture*. London: Routledge.

Bieber, Florian. 2022. 'Global Nationalism in Times of the COVID-19 Pandemic.' *Nationalities Papers*. 50(1):13–25.

Bignall, Simone. 2021. 'Cesaire and Senghor alongside Deleuze: Postimperial Multiplicity, Virtual Assemblages and the Cosmopolitan Ethics of Négritude'. Pp. 245–70 in *Minor Ethics: Deleuzian Variations*, edited by C. Ford, S. McCullagh and K. Houle. Toronto: McGill-Queens University Press.

Bogue, Ronald. 2012. 'Deleuze and Literature.' Pp. 286–306 in *The Cambridge Companion to Deleuze*, edited by Daniel W. Smith and Henry Somers-Hall. Cambridge: Cambridge University Press.

Braidotti, Rosi. 2002. *Metamorphoses: Towards a Materialist Theory of Becoming*. Malden: Polity.

—. 2011. *Nomadic Theory: The Portable Rosi Braidotti*. New York: Columbia University Press.

Brathwaite, Kamau. 1984. *History of the Voice: The Development of the Nation Language in Anglophone Caribbean Poetry*. London: New Beacon Books.

Brooks, Peter. 1981. 'Introduction.' Pp. vii–xix in *Introduction to Poetics*, Tzvetan Todorov. Minneapolis: University of Minnesota Press.

Brouillette, Sarah. 2007. *Postcolonial Writers in the Global Literary Marketplace*. New York: Palgrave Macmillan.

Buchanan, Ian. 2021. *Assemblage Theory and Method*. London: Bloomsbury.

Butler, Judith. 1990. *Gender Trouble: Feminism and the Subversion of Identity*. London: Routledge.

—. 1997. *Excitable Speech: A Politics of the Performative*. London: Routledge.

—. 2009. *Frames of War: When is Life Grievable?* London: Verso.

Çağlar, Ayşe and Nina Glick Schiller. 2018. *Migrants and City-Making: Dispossession, Displacement, and Urban Regeneration*. Durham: Duke University Press.

Camara, Babacar. 2005. 'The Falsity of Hegel's Theses on Africa.' *Journal of Black Studies*. 31(1):82–96.

Césaire, Aimé. 1972. *Discourse on Colonialism*. Translated by Joan Pinkham. New York: Monthly Review Press.

Chakrabarty, Dipesh. 2000. *Provincialising Europe: Postcolonial Thought and Historical Difference*. Princeton: Princeton University Press.

Chambers, Claire. 2019. *Making Sense of Contemporary British Muslim Novels*. Basingstoke: Palgrave.

Chibber, Vivek. 2013. *Postcolonial Theory and the Specter of Capital*. New York: Verso.

Chrisman, Laura. 2021. '"A Crude, Empty, Fragile Shell?' – Postcolonial Consciousness in an Era of Global Capitalism.' Pp. 30–42 in *Ideology in Postcolonial Texts and Contexts*, edited by Katja Sarkowsky and Mark U. Stein. Leiden: Brill.

Christ, Birte and Stephanie Mueller. 2017. 'Toward a Legal Poetics.' *Amerikastudien*. 62(2):149–168.

Clough, Patricia T. 2008. 'The Affective Turn.' *Theory, Culture & Society* 25(1):1–22.

Cohen, G. A. 2000. *Karl Marx's Theory of History: A Defence*. Expanded ed. Princeton: Princeton University Press.

Cole, Teju. 2011. *Open City*. London: Faber and Faber.

Collins, Francis L. 2017. 'Desire as a theory for migration studies: temporality, assemblage and becoming in the narratives of migrants.' *Journal of Ethnic and Migration Studies*: 1–17.

Cresswell, Tim. 2006. *On the Move: Mobility in the Modern Western World*. London: Routledge.

D'Andra, Anthony, Luigina Ciolfi and Breda Grey. 2011. 'Methodological Challenges and Innovations in Mobilities Research'. *Mobilities*. 6(2):149–160.

Damon, Maria and Ira Livingston. 2009. 'Introduction.' Pp. 1–20 in *Poetry and Cultural Studies: A Reader*, edited by Maria Damon and Ira Livingston. Urbana: University of Illinois.

Davis, Angela. 2003. *Are Prisons Obsolete?* Toronto: Open Media.

de Certeau, Michel. 1984. *The Practice of Everyday Life*. Translated by Steven F. Rendall. London: University of California Press.

Dean, Jodi. 2020. *Neofeudalism: The End of Capitalism? LA Review of Books.* <https://lareviewofbooks.org/article/neofeudalism-the-end-of-capitalism/>.

Deleuze, Gilles. 1988. *Spinoza: Practical Philosophy.* London: City Lights.

—. 1994. *Difference and Repetition.* Translated by Paul Patton. New York: Columbia University Press.

—. 1995. *Negotiations.* Translated by Martin Joughin. New York: Columbia University Press.

—. 1997. *Essays Clinical and Critical.* Translated by Daniel W. Smith and Michael A. Greco. Minneapolis: University of Minnesota Press.

Deleuze, Gilles and Félix Guattari. 1986. *Kafka: Toward a Minor Literature.* Translated by Dana Polan. Minneapolis: University of Minneapolis Press.

—. 1994. *What is Philosophy?* New York: Columbia University Press.

—. [1983] 2013. *Anti-Oedipus: Capitalism and Schizophrenia.* London: Bloomsbury.

—. [1987] 2014. *A Thousand Plateaus. Capitalism and Schizophrenia.* Translated by Brian Massumi. London: Bloomsbury.

Deleuze, Gilles and Claire Parnet. 1977. *Dialogues II.* Translated by Hugh Tomlinson and Barbara Habberjam. New York: Columbia University Press.

Deleuze, Gilles and Elias Sanbar. 1998. 'The Indians of Palestine.' *Discourse* 20(3):25–9.

Derrida, Jacques. 1997. *Of Grammatology.* Translated by Gayatri Chakravorty Spivak. Corrected ed. Baltimore: Johns Hopkins University Press.

—. 2002. 'Lecture on Hospitality.' *Acts of Religion.* London: Routledge.

Divakaruni, Chitra Banerjee. 1997. *The Mistress of Spices.* London: Black Swan.

Duff, Kim. 2014. *Contemporary British Literature and Urban Space After Thatcher.* London: Palgrave.

Engels, Friedrich. 1845. *The Condition of the Working Class in England. Marxists.org.* <https://www.marxists.org/archive/marx/works/1845/condition-working-class/>.

—. 1847. 'The Principles of Communism.' *Marxists.org*, edited by Paul Sweezy.

Fanon, Frantz. [1952] 1986. *Black Skin, White Masks*. Translated by Charles Lam Markmann. London: Pluto Press.

Faris, Wendy. 2004. *Ordinary Enchantments: Magical Realism and the Re-mystification of Narrative*. London: Eurospan.

—. 1995. 'Scheherazade's Children: Magical Realism and Postmodern Fiction.' Pp. 163–190 in *Magical Realism: Theory, History, Community*. Durham: Duke University Press.

Federici, Silvia. 2014. *Caliban and the Witch: Women, The Body and Primitive Accumulation*. 2nd ed. New York: Autonomedia.

Felski, Rita. 2008. *Uses of Literature*. Oxford: Blackwell.

—. 2015. *The Limits of Critique*. Chicago: University of Chicago Press.

Fields, Barbara Jeanne. 1990. 'Slavery, Race and Ideology in the United States of America.' *New Left Review* 181:95–118.

Filipczak, Iwona. 2016. 'Marginalisation of South Asians Based on the Race and Skin Color in Bharati Mukherjee's *Jasmine* and Chitra B. Divakaruni's *The Mistress of Spices*.' *Respectus Philologicus* 29(34):46–56.

Fongang, Delphine. 2017. 'Cosmopolitan Dilemna: Diasporic Subjectivity and Postcolonial Liminality in Teju Cole's *Open City*.' *Research in African Literatures* 48(4):138–154.

Foucault, Michel. 1977. *Discipline and Punish: The Birth of the Prison*. Translated by Alan Sheridan. New York: Random House.

—. 2007. *Security, Territory, Population: Lectures at the Collège de France 1977–1978*, edited by Michel Senellart. Translated by Graham Burchell. New York: Palgrave.

Frank, Søren. 2008. *Migration and Literature: Günter Grass, Milan Kundera, Salman Rushdie, and Jan Kjærstad*. New York: Palgrave Macmillan.

Freud, Sigmund. [1919] 2010. 'The "Uncanny".' Pp. 824–841 in *The Norton Anthology of Theory and Criticism*, edited by William E. Cain, Laurie A. Fink, Barbara E. Johnson, Vincent Leitch, John McGowan, T. Denean Sharpley Whiting, Jeffrey J. Williams. 2nd ed. New York: Norton & Company.

Gamble, Christopher N, Joshua S. Hanan and Thomas Nail. (2019). 'What is New Materialism?' *Angelaki* 24(6):111–134.

Gates, Henry Louis. 1988. *The Signifying Monkey: A Theory of Afro-American Literary Criticism*. Oxford: Oxford University Press.

Genette, Gérard. 1988. *Narrative Discourse Revisited*. Translated by Jane Lewin. Ithaca: Cornell University Press.

—. [1967] 1997. 'Structuralism and Literary Critcism'. *Twentieth Century Literary Theory: A Reader*, edited by K. M. Newton. 2nd edition. New York: St Martin's Press.

Giddens, Anthony. 1985. *The Nation-State and Violence*. Cambridge: Polity Press.

Gilbert, Jeremy. 2008. *Anticapitalism and Culture: Radical Theory and Popular Politics*. Oxford: Berg.

Gilmore, Ruth Wilson. 2007. *Golden gulag: Prisons, surplus, crisis, and opposition in globalising California*. Berkeley: University of California Press.

Gilmour, Rachael. 2014. 'Doing voices: Reading language as craft in black British poetry.' *The Journal of Commonwealth Literature* 49(3):343–357.

Glick Schiller, Nina and Noel B. Salazar. 2013. 'Regimes of Mobility Across the Globe.' *Journal of Ethnic and Migration Studies* 39(2):183–200.

Glissant, Edouard. 1997. *Poetics of Relation*. Translated by Betsy Wing. Ann Arbor: University of Michigan Press.

Graeber, David. 2011. *Debt: The First 5000 Years*. Brooklyn: Melville House.

Gramsci, Antonio. 1999. *A Gramsci Reader: Selected Writings 1916–1935*, edited by David Forgacs. London: Lawrence and Wishart.

—. 2003. *Selections from the Prison Notebooks*, edited by Quintin Hoare and Geoffrey Nowell Smith. London: Lawrence and Wishart.

Greenblatt, Stephen. 1997. 'What is the History of Literature?' *Critical Inquiry* 23(3):460–481.

Hall, Stuart. 2015. 'Cultural Identity and Diaspora.' Pp. 392–403 in *Colonial Discourse and Post-Colonial Theory: A Reader*, edited by Patrick Williams and Patrick Chrisman. London: Routledge.

—. 2017. *Familiar Stranger: A Life Between Two Islands.* Durham: Duke University Press.

Stuart Hall, Charles Critcher, Tony Jefferson, John Clarke and Brian Roberts. [1978] 2013. *Policing the Crisis: Mugging, the State and Law and Order.* 2nd ed. London: Palgrave.

Hallward, Peter. 2001. *Absolutely Postcolonial: Writing Between the Singular and the Specific.* Manchester: Manchester University Press.

Hamid, Mohsin. 2017. *Exit West.* London: Penguin.

Hardt, Michael and Antonio Negri. 2000. *Empire.* Cambridge: Harvard University Press.

Haritaworn, Jin, Adi Kuntsman and Silvia Posocco. 2014. *Queer Necropolitics.* New York: Routledge.

Harvey, David. 2003. *The New Imperialism.* Oxford: Oxford University Press.

—. 2007. 'Neoliberalism and the City.' *Studies in Social Justice.* 1(1):1–13.

Heath, Malcom. 1996. 'Introduction.' Aristotle. *Poetics.* London: Penguin: vii-lxvi.

Hegarty, Paul. 2010. 'Giorgio Agamben.' Pp. 14–28 in *From Agamben to Žižek: Contemporary Critical Theorists*, edited by Jon Simons. Edinburgh: Edinburgh University Press.

Hegel, Georg W. F. [1837] 1988. *Introduction to the Philosophy of History.* Translated by Leo Rauch. New York: Hackett.

—. [1807] 2010. 'Phenomenology of Spirit.' Pp. 541–547 in *The Norton Anthology of Theory and Criticism*, edited by William E. Cain, Laurie A. Fink, Barbara E. Johnson, Vincent Leitch, John McGowan, T. Denean Sharpley Whiting, Jeffrey J. Williams. 2nd ed. London: Norton & Company.

Heller, Charles, Lorenzo Pezzani and Maurice Stierl. 2019. 'Toward a Politics of Freedom of Movement.' Pp. 51–76 in *Open Borders: In Defense of Free Movement*, edited by Reece Jones. Athens: University of Georgia Press.

Hobsbawm, Eric. 1975. *The Age of Capital: 1848–1875.* London: Abacus.

Horace. [10BCE] 2010. 'Ars Poetica.' Pp. 122–132 in *The Norton Anthology of Theory and Criticism*, edited by William E. Cain,

Laurie A. Fink, Barbara E. Johnson, Vincent Leitch, John McGowan, T. Denean Sharpley Whiting, Jeffrey J. Williams. Translated by D. A. Russel. 2nd ed. New York: Norton & Company.

Huddart, David. 2011. 'Homi K. Bhabha.' Pp. 60–76 in *From Agamben to Žižek: Contemporary Critical Theorists*, edited by Jon Simons. Edinburgh: Edinburgh University Press.

Hutcheon, Linda. 1988. *A Poetics of Postmodernism*. London: Routledge.

Jameson, Fredric. 1983. *The Political Unconscious: Narrative as a Socially-Symbolic Act*. London: Routledge.

Johnson, Linton Kwesi. [1983] 2002. 'New Crass Massakah.' Pp. 54–59 in *Mi Revalueshanary Fren: Selected Poems*. London: Penguin.

Jones, Reece. 2019. 'Introduction.' Pp. 1–22 in *Open Borders: In Defense of Free Movement*. Athens: University of Georgia Press.

Kaiser, Birgit. 2012. 'Poésie en éntendue: Deleuze, Glissant, and a Post-colonial Aesthetics of the Earth.' Pp. 131–144 in *Revisiting Normativity with Deleuze*, edited by Rosi Braidotti and Patricia Pisters. London: Continuum.

Kant, Immanuel. [1790] 2007. *Critique of Judgment*. Edited by Nicholas Walker. Translated by James Creed Meredith. Oxford: Oxford University Press.

Kearny, Richard. 2014. 'Preface.' *The Poetics of Space* by Gaston Bachelard. New York: Penguin Random House.

King, Martin Luther. 1967. 'The Other America.' *Civil Rights Movement Archive*. <https://www.crmvet.org/docs/otheram.htm>.

Kramnick, Jonathan. 2018. *Paper Minds: Literature and the Ecology of Consciousness*. Chicago: Chicago University Press.

Krishnan, Madhu. 2015. 'Postcoloniality, spatiality and cosmopolitanism in the *Open City*.' *Textual Practice* 29(4):675–695.

Kumar, Amitava. 1998. 'Louder than bombs.' *Transition*: 80–101.

Lagji, Amanda. 2018. 'Waiting in motion: mapping postcolonial fiction, new mobilities, and migration through Mohsin Hamid's *Exit West*.' *Mobilities* 14(2):218–232.

Lecercle, Jean-Jacques. 2002. *Deleuze and Language*. New York: Palgrave.

Lefebvre, Henri. 2014. *Critique of Everyday Life*. Translated by John Moore. London: Verso.

Lehan, Richard. 1998. *The City in Literature: An Intellectual and Cultural History*. London: University of California Press.

Loomba, Ania. 1998. *Colonialism/Postcolonialism*. London: Routledge.

Malkki, Liisa. 1992. 'National Geographic: The Rooting of Peoples and the Territorialisation of Identity among Scholars and Refugees.' *Cultural Anthropology* 7(1):24–44.

Marcus, Morton. 1997. *The Spice of Life* <http://www.metroactive.com/papers/metro/05.08.97/books-9719.html>.

Márquez, Gabriel García. 2019. 'Something Else on Literature and Reality.' Pp. 231–235 in *The Scandal of the Century and Other Writings* by Gabriel García Márquez. Translated by Anne McLean. New York: Alfred A. Knopf.

Marx, Karl. 1859. 'Preface.' *A Contribution to the Critique of Political Economy*. Translated by S. W. Ryazanskaya. Online version. Marxists.org. https://www.marxists.org/archive/marx/works/download/Marx_Contribution_to_the _Critique_of_Political_Economy.pdf.

—. [1847] 1955. *The Poverty of Philosophy*. Translation: Institute of Marxism-Leninism. Progress Publishers. Online Version. Marxists.org. https://www.marxists.org/archive/marx/works/1847/poverty-philosophy/.

—. [1852] 1978. 'The Eighteenth Brumaire of Louis Bonaparte.' Pp. 594–617 in *The Marx-Engels Reader*, edited by Robert C. Tucker. 2nd ed. London: Princeton University Press.

—. [1857] 1978. 'The Grundrisse.' *The Marx-Engels Reader*, edited by Robert C. Tucker. Translated by Martin Nicolaus. 2nd ed. Princeton: Princeton University Press.

—. [1867] 1990. *Capital*. Translated by Ben Fowkes. Vol. 1. London: Penguin.

Massumi, Brian. 2015. *Politics of Affect*. Cambridge: Polity.

Mbembe, Achille. 2003. 'Necropolitics.' *Public Culture* 15(1):11–40.

McLeod, John. 2004. *Postcolonial London: Rewriting the Metropolis*. London: Routledge.

Meese, Elizabeth A. [1985] 1997. 'Sexual Politics and Critical Judgment.' Pp. 220–5 in *Twentieth Century Literary Theory:*

A Reader, edited by K. M. Newton, 2nd ed. New York: St Martin's Press.

Merriman, Peter and Lynne Pearce. 2017. 'Mobility and the Humanities.' *Mobilities.* 4(12):493–508.

Mezzadra, Sandro and Brett Neilson. 2013. *Border as Method, Or, The Multiplication of Labor.* London: Duke University Press.

Monegato, Emanuele. 2010. 'On Migritude: A Conversation with Shailja Patel.' *Migritude* by Shailja Patel. New York: Kaya Press.

Mongia, Radhika V. 2007) 'Historicising State Sovereignty: Inequality and the Form of Equivalence.' *Comparative Studies in Society and History* 49(2):384–411.

Morris, Mervyn. 2005. 'Introduction.' Pp. ix-xxvii in *Selected Poems* by Louise Bennett. Kingston: Sangster's.

Morrison, Toni. 1987. *Beloved.* London: Vintage.

Morton, Stephen. 2011. 'Gayatri Chakravorty Spivak.' Pp. 210–226 in *From Agamben to Žižek: Contemporary Critical Theorists,* edited by Jon Simons. Edinburgh: Edinburgh University Press.

Moslund, Sten Pultz. 2010. *Migration Literature and Hybridity: The Different Speeds of Transcultural Change.* London: Palgrave Macmillan.

Mumford, Lewis. 1956. 'The Natural History of Urbanisation.'

Nail, Thomas. 2015. *The Figure of the Migrant.* Stanford: Stanford Universtiy Press.

—. 2016. *Theory of the Border.* Oxford: Oxford University Press.

—. 2019. *Being and Motion.* Oxford: Oxford University Press.

—. 2020. *Marx in Motion: A New Materialist Marxism.* Oxford: Oxford University Press.

Naydan, Liliana M. 2019. 'Digital Screens and National Divides in Mohsin Hamid's *Exit West.*' *Studies in the Novel* 51(3): 433–451.

Nietzsche, Friedrich. 1874. 'On the Use and Abuse of History.' *Untimely Meditations.* London.

Papadopoulos, Dimitris and Vassilis Tsianos. 2007. 'The Autonomy of Migration: The Animals of Undocumented Mobility.' Pp. 223–235 in *Deleuzian Encounters: Studies in Contemporary Social Issues,* edited by Anna Hickey-Moody and Peta Malins. New York: Palgrave.

Papastergiadis, Nikos. 1999. *The Turbulence of Migration.* Cambridge: Polity Press.

Patel, Shailja. 2010. *Migritude.* New York: Kaya Press.

—. 2014. 'A Conversation with Poet Shailja Patel.' April 11 in *Art Works Podcast* National Endowment for the Arts, produced by Jo Reed, podcast 29:28, https://www.arts.gov/stories/podcast/shailja-patel.

Perfect, Michael. 2008. 'the multicultural bildungsroman: Stereotypes in Monica Ali's *Brick Lane.*' *The journal of commonwealth literature* 43:109–120.

—. 2019. '"Black holes in the fabric of the nation": Refugees in Mohsin Hamid's *Exit West.*' *Journal for Cultural Research* 23(2):187–201.

Ping, Wang. 2018. *Things We Carried on the Sea.* https://poets.org/poem/things-we-carry-sea.

Poon, Angelia. 2009. 'To know what's what: Forms of migrant knowing in Monica Ali's *Brick Lane.*' *Journal of Postcolonial Writing* 45(4):426–437.

Potter, Kevin. 2019. 'Centrifugal Force and the Mouth of a Shark: Toward a Movement-Oriented Poetics.' *ARIEL: A Review of International English Literature* 50(4):51–78.

—. 2021. '"Don't Get Too Comfortable": Regimes of Motility in Shailja Patel's *Migritude.*' Pp. 176–188 in *Cultural Mobilities Between Africa and the Caribbean* edited by Birgit Englert, Sigrid Thomsen and Barbara Gföllner. London: Routledge.

Preshad, Vijay. 2010. 'Preface.' Pp. i–v in *Migritude* by Shailja Patel. New York: Kaya Press.

Qadir, Neelofer. 2018. '*Migritude*'s Decolonial Lessons.' *Eastern African Literary and Cultural Studies* 4(3–4): 221–243.

Quayson, Ato. 2013. 'Postcolonialism and the Diasporic Imaginary.' Pp. 139–159 in *A Companion to Diaspora and Transnationalism*, edited by Ato Quayson and Girish Daswani. London: Wiley Blackwell.

Quayson, Ato and Girish Daswani. 2013. 'Introduction – Diaspora and Transnationalism: Scapes, Scales and Scopes.' Pp. 1–26 in *Companion to Diaspora and Transnationalism*, edited by Ato Quayson and Girish Daswani. London: Wiley Blackwell.

Rajan, Gita. 2002. 'Chitra Divakaruni's *The Mistress of Spices*: Deploying Mystical Realism.' 2(2):215–36.

Ramanujan, A. K. 1995. 'Waterfalls in a Bank.' Pp. 189–190 in *Collected Poems*. Oxford: Oxford University Press.

Ramazani, Jahan. 2001. *The Hybrid Muse: Postcolonial Poetry in English*. Chicago: University of Chicago Press.

—. 2015. *A Transnational Poetics*. Chicago: Chicago University Press.

Rancière, Jacques. 2004. *The Politics of Aesthetics: Distribution of the Sensible*. Translated by Gabriel Rockhill. London: Bloomsbury.

Reed, B. M. 2012. 'Poetics, Western.' Pp. 1058–1064 in *The Princeton Encyclopedia of Poetry and Poetics*, edited by Claire Cavanagh, Stephen Cushman, Ronald Greene, Jahan Ramazani, Paul Rouzer. 4th ed. Princeton: Princeton University Press.

Robbins, Bruce. 2009. 'Comparative Cosmopolitanism.' Pp. 309–328 in *The Princeton Sourcebook in Comparative Literature*, edited by David Damrosch, Natalie Melas and Buthelezi Mbongiseni. Princeton: Princeton University Press.

Robinson, Cedric J. 1983. *Black Marxism: The Making of the Black Radical Tradition*. London: University of North Carolina Press.

Ruddick, Susan. 2010. 'The Politics of Affect.' *Theory, Culture & Society* 27(4):21–45.

Rushdie, Salman. 1981. *Midnight's Children*. London: Vintage.

—. 1992. *Imaginary Homelands: Essays and Criticism 1981–1991*. London: Granta.

Sadaf, Shazia. 2020. '"We are all migrants through time": History and geography in Mohsin Hamid's *Exit West*.' *Journal of Postcolonial Writing*. 56(5):636–647.

Sager, Alex. 2020. *Against Borders: Why the World Needs Free Movement of People*. London: Rowman & Littlefield.

Said, Edward. 1978. *Orientalism*. London: Penguin.

—. 1993. *Culture and Imperialism*. New York: Vintage.

Sassen, Saskia. 2008. *Territory, Authority, Rights: From Medieval to Global Assemblages*. Updated ed. Princeton: Princeton University Press.

—. 2001. *The Global City: New York, London, Tokyo*. Princeton: Princeton University Press.

Schenstead-Harris, Leif. 2017. 'Between "home" and migritude: Louise Bennett, Kamau Brathwaite and the poet as migrant.' *Crossings: Journal of Migration and Culture* 8(2):131–149.

Scott, James C. 1998. *Seeing Like a State: How Certain Schemes to Improve the Human Condition Have Failed*. New Haven: Yale University Press.

Seigworth, Gregory J. 2010. 'From Affection to Soul.' Pp. 159–169 in *The Affect Theory Reader*, edited by Gregory J. Seigworth and Melissa Gregg. Durham: Duke University Press.

Seigworth, Gregory J. and Melissa Gregg. 2010. 'An Inventory of Shimmers.' Pp. 1–25 in *The Affect Theory Reader*, edited by Gregory J. Seigworth and Melissa Gregg. Durham: Duke University Press.

Seyhan, Azade. 2001. *Writing Outside the Nation*. Princeton: Princeton University Press.

Sharma, Nandita. 2019. 'Dispossessing Citizenship.' Pp. 77–88 in *Open Borders: In Defense of Free Movement*, edited by Reese Jones. Athens: University of Georgia Press.

Shklovsky, Viktor. [1919] 2015. 'Art, as Device.' *Poetics Today* 36(3):151–174.

Showalter, Elaine. [1979] 1997. 'Toward a Feminist Poetics.' Pp. 216–220 in *Twentieth Century Literary Theory: A Reader*, edited by K. M. Newton. New York: St Martin's Press.

Sidney, Sir Philip. [1595] 2010. 'The Defence of Poesy.' Pp. 254–282 in *The Norton Anthology of Theory and Criticism*, edited by William E. Cain, Laurie A. Fink, Barbara E. Johnson, Vincent Leitch, John McGowan, T. Denean Sharpley Whiting, Jeffrey J. Williams. New York: Norton & Company.

Skopeliti, Clea. 2020. 'Reform UK: Brexit party to rebrand as anti-lockdown voice'. The *Guardian*, November 2. https://www.theguardian.com/politics/2020/nov/02/reform-uk-brexit-party-to-rebrand-as-anti-lockdown-voice.

Slemon, Stephen. 1995. 'Magic Realism as Postcolonial Discourse.' Pp. 407–426 in *Magical Realism: Theory, History, Community*, edited by Lois Parkinson Zamora and Wendy Faris. Durham: Duke University Press.

Smith, Neil. 2002. 'New Globalism, New Urbanism: Gentrification as Global Urban Strategy.' *Antipode* 34(3):427–450.

Spivak, Gayatri. [1988] 1994. 'Can the Subaltern Speak.' Pp. 66–111 in *Colonial Discourse and Post-Colonial Theory: A Reader*, edited by Laura Chrisman and Patrick Williams. New York: Columbia Universtiy Press.

—. 2003. *Death of a Discipline*. New York: Columbia University Press.

—. 2012. *An Aesthetic Education in the Era of Globalisation*. Cambridge: Harvard University Press.

Stevens, Jacqueline. 2019. 'Habeas Corpus and the New Abolitionists.' Pp. 110–126 in *Open Borders: In Defense of Free Movement*, edited by Reece Jones. Athens: University of Georgia Press.

Tihanov, Galin. 2012. 'Russian Formalism.' Pp. 1239–1242 in *The Princeton Encyclopedia of Poetry and Poetics*, edited by Claire Cavanagh, Stephen Cushman, Ronald Greene, Jahan Ramazani, Paul Rouzer. 4th ed. Princeton: Princeton University Press.

Todorov, Tzvetan. [1939] 1981. *Introduction to Poetics*. Minneapolis: University of Minnesota Press.

United Kingdom Independence Party. 2019. 'What We Stand For.' *UKIP*. <UKIP.org>.

Valman, Nadia. 2009. 'The East End Bilgungsroman from Israel Zangwill to Monica Ali.' *Wasafari* 24(1):3–8.

Varvogli, Aliki. 2017. 'Urban Mobility and Race: Dinaw Mengestu's *The Beautiful Things That Heaven Bears* and Teju Cole's *Open City*.' *Studies in African Fiction* 44(2):235–257.

Vermeulen, Pieter. 2013. 'Flights of Memory: Teju Cole's *Open City* and the Limits of Aesthetic Cosmopolitanism.' *Journal of Modern Literature* 37(1):40–57.

Walcott, Derek. 1990. *Omeros*. New York: Farrar, Strauss and Giroux.

Walia, Harsha. 2021. *Border and Rule: Global Migration, Capitalism, and the Rise of Racist Nationalism*. Chicago: Haymarket.

Warwick, Alexandra. 2008. 'The Historical Context of Victorian Literature.' Pp. 27–44 in *The Victorian Literature Handbook*. London: Continuum.

Watt, Ian. 1957. *The Rise of the Novel: Studies in Defoe, Richardson and Fielding.* Los Angeles: University of California Press.

Weizman, Eyal. 2006. 'The Art of War.' *Frieze*, 99, May.

Wilder, Gary. 2015. *Freedom Time: Negritude, Decolonisation and the Future of the World.* Durham: Duke University Press.

Williams, Patrick. 2004. 'Edward Said.' Pp. 269–285 in *Contemporary Critical Theorists: From Lacan to Said*, edited by Jon Simons. Edinburgh: Edinburgh University Press.

Wittgenstein, Ludwig. 1967. *Zettel.* Edited by Elizabeth Anscombe and G. H. von Wright. Oxford: Blackwell.

Woods, James. 2011. 'The Arrival of Enigmas.' *The New Yorker.* February. Accessed July 2021. https://www.newyorker.com/magazine/2011/02/28/the-arrival-of-enigmas.

Wondreys, Jakub, and Cas Mudde. 2022. 'Victims of the Pandemic? European Far-Right Parties and COVID-19.' *Nationalities Papers.* 50.(1):86–103.

Wordsworth, William. [1802] 2009. 'Preface to Lyrical Ballads.' Pp. 21–24 in *Poetry and Cultural Studies*, edited by Maria Damon and Ira Livingston. Urbana: University of Illinois Press.

Xavier, Subha. 2016. *The Migrant Text: Making and Marketing in a Global French Literature.* London: McGill-Queen's University Press.

Young, Iris Marion. 1990. *Justice and the Politics of Difference.* Princeton: Princeton University Press.

Yuval-Davis, Nira. 2018. 'Racism and Everyday Bordering'. Pp. 137–144 in *Frontiers of Global Sociology: Research Perspectives for the 21st Century*, edited by Markus S. Schulz. Berlin: ISA Research.

Zamora, Lois Parkinson and Wendy Faris. 1995. 'Introduction.' Pp. 1–11 in *Magical Realism: Theory, History, Community*, edited by Lois Parkinson Zamora and Wendy Faris. Durham: Duke Universtiy Press.

Zedner, Lucia. 2019. 'The Hostile Border: Crimmigration, Counter-Terrorism, Or Crossing the Line on Rights.' *New Criminal Law Review.* 22(3):318–346.

Ziegler, Garrett. 2007. 'East of the City: *Brick Lane*, Capitalism, and the Global Metropolis.' *Race/Ethnicity: Multidisciplinary Global Contexts* 1(1):145–167.

Zillman, Lawrence and Clive Scott. 2012. 'Terza Rima.' P. 1423
    in *The Princeton Encyclopedia of Poetry and Poetics*, edited
    by Claire Cavanagh, Stephen Cushman, Ronald Greene, Jahan
    Ramazani, Paul Rouzer. 4th ed. Princeton: Princeton Univer-
    sity Press.
Žižek, Slavoj. 1997. 'Multiculturalism, or, the Cultural Logic of
    Multinational Capitalism.' *New Left Review* 225:28–51.

INDEX

References to notes are indicated by n.